# INNER SHAMAN

## JOURNEY THROUGH DARKNESS INTO LIGHT

# INNER SHAMAN

## JOURNEY THROUGH DARKNESS INTO LIGHT

### Margaret M Schneider PhD

Mind Rivers Publishing

ISBN: 0-9665691-4-8
Printed in the United States of America


1 2 3 4 5 6 7 8 9 10 11 12


Credits:
Cover Illustration by Trish Evers
Cover Design by Gerald Moscato
Text Design by Chris Carlsen
Editing by Cornelia Navari

# TABLE OF CONTENTS

# ACKNOWLEDGMENT

I would like to acknowledge my deepest respect and appreciation of all indigenous shamanic cultures that have preserved and maintained the essence of the shamanic consciousness throughout the centuries. Although I have drawn upon some of the essential elements of this consciousness in the writing of this book, I have done so with the spirit of sharing, rather than taking or borrowing. It has been my intent to honor the spirit of Oneness, which emanates from this consciousness, thereby bearing testimony to the Sacred Truth that *We Are All Related.*

We are Aquarian shamans. We came into this Earth Walk ready to reconnect humankind and Nature. We were born with abilities barely dreamed of by the shamans of old. We are here to reawaken the shamanic consciousness of humankind. This consciousness lies deep within us all, sleeping fitfully in the midst of a nightmare of disconnection. It has already awakened in many of us. It will continue to awaken in many more. Each person who awakens his own shamanic consciousness awakens those of others—without a sound, without a fuss. That is still another wisdom of shamanism.

— Amber Wolfe
*In the Shadow of the Shaman, 1991*

# INTRODUCTION

I FIRST MET THE SHAMAN on a beautiful, sunshiny day during the summer of 1989. I had gone for my morning walk and found myself attracted to a small pond on a construction site about a mile from my home. I walked over and stood by the pond and was enchanted by the sun glistening on the clear, dark blue water. As I stood there I closed my eyes and immediately felt myself drifting into meditation—a dreamlike state wherein all things are possible. Quite unexpectedly, the image of an American Indian, dressed in buckskin with long black hair pulled back behind his head, soon came to me. He identified himself as "Sky Hawk" and told me that he was my spirit guide. He said that he had come to teach me the way of the Shaman, and that I was to become his apprentice. With out a word, he handed me a small leather pouch, and I understood that it contained all of the things that I would need on my journey into the world of the Shaman. I timidly accepted the pouch and thanked him, feeling a little incredulous and quite skeptical about what had just happened. Then, as quickly as he had appeared, he was gone.

I stood there dazed and puzzled. I had only some vague idea that a "shaman" had something to do with being a "medicine man," but that was about it. "What is a shaman?" I thought. "What is this all about? Why had I been chosen for this unusual calling?" A Clinical Social Worker by profession, I had often thought of myself as a healer of sorts, but this puzzled me. It was all quite confusing, but I trusted that somehow in time I would understand the significance of this experience. For now, I would just go about my everyday life pleased with knowing that I had a Native American for a spirit guide, and trusting that I would know what I needed to do when the time came.

For the next several years, Sky Hawk made many appearances in my regular meditations. We became wonderful friends, but he never seemed to be giving me any substantive instruction—at least what I expected that a Master Shaman would give to his apprentice. As I recall, he would come to me in my meditations. We would mount a winged, white horse and fly off together (to what I know now, but didn't know then, was the Upper World of the Shamanic Journey), but that didn't seem like an apprenticeship to me at the time. During these journeys into what appeared to be imaginary realms, we would visit teachers and guides who offered direction and guidance, but, not understanding what exactly it was that a shaman did, I didn't view this as anything related to shamanism. I thought these were nice experiences, but wondered when my "apprenticeship" would begin, or if there ever was to be one.

In the fall of 1991, two years after my first meeting with Sky Hawk, I had a memorable experience, which made me begin to feel like there really was something to this apprenticeship I had been promised. It happened while my husband and I were visiting Sedona, Arizona for the very first time. While meditating in a spot overlooking Long Canyon amidst the incredible beauty of the red rock terrain, I once again was visited by The Shaman, only this time I didn't recognize him. His dark-skinned, muscular body was clothed only in a loincloth, and he had the skin of a wolf on his head. I was quite puzzled, not knowing the significance of the way he was dressed, but I was happy to see him nonetheless. His dark eyes fixed deeply on mine, and without speaking, he purified me with the smoke of burning sage and anointed me with some type of oil. I had a sense that I was being prepared for an initiation of some sort, (perhaps related to my apprenticeship?) but I was still at a loss as to its meaning. It all seemed very real and had a profound effect on me; I was moved to tears.

Later that week, my husband and I returned to this same spot; Sky Hawk appeared to me in my meditation once again. Sitting around a fire, Sky Hawk and I smoked a pipe together and he told me that the pipe was mine to keep. I was then given three eagle feathers with the clear message that one was for *Love,* one was for *Light* and one was for *Illumination.* Then Sky Hawk performed another ritual in which my chest was cut open to form a vertical incision about five or six inches in length. Sky Hawk then told me in a very clear, voice, "Now you are a shaman." Letting go of my confusion as to whether this meant that I was a "full-fledged shaman" or still an apprentice, I simply accepted the fact that I had progressed to another level in my journey to become a shaman. A celebration with drumming and dancing around the fire followed. I felt very strongly that something powerful and deeply mystical, magical and profound was happening to me; I was once again moved to tears.

After returning home from Arizona, I began to take this shaman concept a little more seriously and I began to think that maybe there was more to it than merely a meditative fantasy. A small voice from deep inside kept prompting me to not take it lightly, telling me that it would be best if I went along with it all, even if it seemed silly. So, still unaware at the time of what exactly was going on, I decided that I needed to take this apprenticeship into my own hands and to learn all that I could about the shaman and shamanism. My trip to Sedona—my first visit to the Southwest—had given me a taste of Native American culture and spiritual practices and it had instilled in me a desire to learn more. Interestingly enough, upon my return from this trip, there was a brochure advertising the 1992 Jean Houston Mystery School waiting for me in a pile of mail. The topic for the year was "Rediscovering America," dealing in part with Native American spirituality. It seemed the perfect opportunity to learn more about Native American spiritual traditions, and so I decided to attend the program that took place one weekend a month (for nine months) over the course of a one-year period. During the following months, both at Mystery School weekends and on my own at home, I set out to learn more about the shaman's world. At Mystery School I learned about Power Animals, the Shamanic State of Consciousness, the Upper, Middle and Lower worlds of the Shamanic Journey and how to perform Shamanic Soul Retrievals. I learned that the shamanic state of consciousness was often induced by repetitive sounds such as drumming or rattling, and so I bought an authentic Native American rattle. At home, while shaking my rattle, I would venture into another reality, into the world of the shaman. During these times, with Sky Hawk and my power animals always present, I would journey into the Lower, Middle and Upper worlds of the shaman. It was here, during these magical journeys, that my inner teacher, Sky Hawk, led me on numerous adventures in the world of Spirit.

My next significant encounter with my friend, The Shaman, came in May of 1992, during another visit to Sedona. While mediating at the Airport Mesa, I was told that I must die and be reborn as the Bear. I was given a vision of Sky Hawk, with his dark eyes peering out at me, once again, from underneath the wolf skin. In the vision, he rubbed my naked body from head to toe with what I was told was "bear oil." I was then placed into a shallow hole in the ground lying on a bearskin and was completely covered with leaves. As I lay there, I counted three sunsets and three sunrises. I had been left in the ground for three days and three nights, with nothing to eat or drink. I understood this to be symbolic of my death. After the three days had passed, Sky Hawk returned, took me to the river, and washed me and dressed me in white ceremonial clothing. I was then given a new name, an Indian name, *Thunder Song.* I was told that thunder was the voice of the Great Spirit and that I must "sing his song," that I must "proclaim his message." I had a deep knowing that I had just gone through a sort of symbolic death and resurrection, that I had been born anew, with a new identity, and a new name. I had "died and been born again as the Bear," and my new name was *Thunder Song*.

Later that day, while hiking through Boynton Canyon, a place held sacred by some Indian tribes, my husband and I were caught in a magnificent thunderstorm. As we stood huddled under a tree with the thunder resounding through the canyon, my husband was concerned about the lightening, but I felt no fear, only elation. The thunder was like a song to my ears. It seemed to be awakening and activating an energy deep inside, calling to me to BE *Thunder Song*, so that I might come one day to sing my song of thunder. It was as if Mother Earth was somehow validating my experience and celebrating the new name I had been given earlier that day. I still didn't fully understand the meaning of all of this, yet I felt so blessed and joyful. As I stood in that canyon, being drenched by the pouring rain with thunder booming and lightening crashing all around me, I was, once again, moved to tears.

This experience proved to have a profound and lasting impact on my life. The notion of being called by Great Spirit to "sing his song" stayed with me over the weeks and months to come. Although, I was still unsure of exactly how I was to do this, I took it seriously and remained open, waiting for further instructions. While meditating one cold morning in January of 1993, my instructions came. I heard the voice of Sky Hawk saying clearly, "It is now time to get your act together and take it on the road, and you will prepare yourself to do this by getting a Ph.D." This apprenticeship was beginning to get really serious! I was now being asked to take a major step, one that would drastically change my life. It didn't take me long to make the decision to follow my inner prompting. I was accepted into a doctoral program the following July, with the goal of finding a way to "get my act together," of composing my *"Thunder Song"* so that I might sing Great Spirit's song.

In August of 1993, about three weeks prior to another planned visit to Sedona, I became very ill with an intestinal disorder. I was sicker than I have ever been in my adult life, with unrelenting diarrhea and vomiting. Unable to eat or drink anything but water for three days, I found myself in the hospital emergency room being treated for dehydration. During my illness, I had a strong feeling that I was going through some sort of initiation. It was as if there were a reason why I needed to fast for, as it turned out, exactly three days and three nights—something I have never done in my entire life and probably never would have of my own volition. I did not even attempt my normal self-healing techniques as I knew, in light of past experiences with Sky Hawk in Sedona, that there was a purpose to this illness, that I was being prepared for yet another step in my journey into the world of the shaman.

So on our subsequent visit to Sedona in early September, I was once again gifted by a visit from Sky Hawk. He appeared to me in a vision, dressed in his now familiar wolf skin, and this time, I was given my own animal skin to wear—the skin of a bear. I understood this to mean that I was now ready to come into the fullness of my shamanic power and that Bear was my power animal. As we chanted, danced and rattled to the drumming around the fire, I knew for the first time that Sky Hawk had been my father in a previous life when we were American Indians. He was a shaman in that lifetime and he had taught me (his son) then, as he did now, the way of the shaman.

At this point I was still questioning the validity of all of this. I had thought that my experiences in my visions were interesting and relevant, but I had no idea that, if researched, they would bear any resemblance to anything remotely related to authentic shamanic experience. All along, I had persisted in doubting and minimizing what was happening to me. Although I didn't realize the similarities at the time of the visionary experiences, while researching for a paper on shamanism that I was writing in the fall of 1993 as part of my doctoral work, I was truly surprised to learn that there were astounding similarities. I discovered that what I experienced in my visionary reality is totally consistent with what has been documented as a traditional initiation of a shaman. For example, Mircea Eliade, respected authority on shamanism and the author of *Shamanism: Archaic Techniques of Ecstasy*, maintains that "...one of the commonest forms of the future shaman's election is his encountering a divine or semidivine being, who appears to him through a dream, a sickness, or some other circumstance, tells him that he has been "chosen," and incites him thenceforth to follow a new rule of life. More often it is the souls of his shaman ancestors who bring him the tidings."[1] Marie-Lu Lorler, in her book, *Shamanic Healing Within the Medicine Wheel,* also states: "Another way to the calling is that of a sudden vision in which a spirit appears to the chosen one, most likely the spirit of one of the person's ancestors or of a deceased shaman, who passes on the responsibility of becoming a shaman. The call is also heard in dreams, in which the candidate, in a trancelike state, experiences the entire path of apprenticeship up to the ritual of initiation."[2] In addition, Eliade describes initiation rituals which involve the themes of suffering, (often in the form of being "cut"), death and resurrection: "Dream, sickness, or initiation ceremony, the central element is always the same: death, and symbolic resurrection of the neophyte, involving a cutting up of the body performed in various ways (dismemberment, gashing, opening the abdomen, etc.)." A future Yakut Shaman, for example, " 'dies' and lies in the yurt [a tent-like structure] for three days without eating or drinking." Among the Pomo, shamanic initiates "lie on the ground like corpses and are covered with straw."

It was the reading and researching into shamanism that I did for this paper that validated my visionary experiences, convincing me that something more than just an overactive imagination was at work here. Although completely unaware of this information at the time of my visionary experiences, and rather ignorant of Native

American spiritual practices as well, it became evident that my adventures with The Shaman were extraordinarily consistent with these descriptions. They were indeed authentic shamanic initiatory experiences that took place within the shamanic state of consciousness. I was, in other words, initiated into the world of the shaman by some internal mechanism that seemed to know everything about the authentic, traditional shamanic experience, of which I was consciously unaware. It was as if there truly were an Inner Shaman that led me along this path of shamanic apprenticeship and initiation into the world of the shaman—exactly as had been promised to me on that summer day by the pond when I first met The Shaman. If this were really the case and there were really an Inner Shaman within leading and directing me along a shamanic path and awakening a deep yet profoundly meaningful ancient consciousness within me, what does it all mean? What are the implications? How can I make sense out of all of this?

The answers to these questions begin to come into better focus when I look at what else was going on in my life at the very same time that my Inner Shaman was weaving its shamanic tapestry within me. Let me explain. In 1988 I had been diagnosed with an autoimmune disease, similar to lupus. At that time I was told by the medical profession that it was an "incurable" illness and all that they could do for me was to treat the symptoms as they occurred. They sent me home with the recommendation to take an aspirin every day and to call them if my condition worsened. In the fall of 1989, about three months after seeing Sky Hawk for the first time, blood tests indicated that my condition had indeed worsened considerably. My initial response to all of this was one of dismay, but after a short time, I decided that if the medical profession couldn't help me, I would have to help myself. I wholeheartedly accepted the challenge to "cure" an "incurable" disease. Setting a healing intention and a goal of complete recovery, I plunged headlong into this endeavor and so my journey into self-healing began.

Pursuing a holistic approach, based on the integration of body, mind and spirit, I accepted responsibility for my own healing and focused all of my energy to restoring myself to wholeness and health. I incorporated such things as psychotherapy, chiropractic, acupuncture, massage therapy, meditation, relaxation, bioenergetic work, psychophysical exercise, aerobic exercise, nutrition, visualization and a reconnection to nature into my self-healing regimen. I achieved amazing results for my efforts. What could have brought about the dramatic shift that I experienced in the way that I felt, both physically and emotionally? Was it the "holistic" path that I followed or the incredibly strong intent to heal that was responsible for the changes? I can't say for sure. But, there does seem to be a great deal of synchronicity between my improved health and the awakening of the ancient shamanic wisdom within me. So, I find that I must ask myself, "could this experience have anything to do with The Shaman and my apprenticeship to him?" Could I have been tapping into the shamanic consciousness and utilizing shamanic methods for self-healing on a purely unconscious level?

I am confident that there is a deeper meaning to it all, an unconscious message around which I need to shape my conscious reality. I now believe that the archetypal Shaman has been and continues to awaken within me, as it is in the external world as well, and that within the shamanic consciousness lie the secrets for both individual and planetary healing. The purpose of this study, then, is to explore my own healing journey and how it emanated from the shamanic consciousness within. It seems that my personal healing coincided on many levels with an inner awakening to the world of the shaman, and it is this synchronicity of healing and shamanic awareness that I will investigate here.

It has been as though I have a shaman deep inside, guiding and directing my way. My "Inner Shaman," as I call this inner consciousness, taught me all I need to know about the world of the shaman and how to navigate around in it. The Inner Shaman has

been both my teacher and healer, speaking from within and showing me the way to reconnect to my Inner Spirit. It is the Inner
Shaman who has shown me the healing path and has led me along
my healing journey. Through my visionary experiences, intuitive
understanding, and direct communications, which I have recorded
in writing, the Inner Shaman has taught me not only about the
world of the shaman, but about myself—from the inside out. This
inner voice has taught me how to reconnect to my source, to the
world of spirit, so that I would find the "medicine" that would heal
me. It has been under the teaching and guidance of the voice of the
Inner Shaman that I have proceeded on my journey of self-discov-
ery, self-loving and self-healing. As I have allowed the shamanic
consciousness lying dormant deep inside of me to awaken, I have
been able to soar to new heights, reach new dimensions and come
ever nearer to attaining the healing for which I have been searching. This is the essence of my journey.

As the shamanic consciousness has awakened within me, the
voice of the Inner Shaman has gifted me with an untold wealth of
wisdom and awareness. My inner teacher, Sky Hawk, through my
inner visionary experiences, has led me on a journey of self-discov-
ery and self-healing. Another inner teacher who has also been my
companion along the healing path has joined him. This inner
teacher identifies herself as White Buffalo Woman, the mystical
woman who, as legend has it, came long, long ago bringing the
sacred pipe as a symbol and reminder of unity to the Lakota Sioux.
She remains to this day a central figure in the spiritual way of the
Lakota and many other native peoples.[3]

It is the teachings of the inner voice of White Buffalo Woman,
which I have recorded and will be presenting throughout the book.
The teachings of Inner Shaman, White Buffalo Woman, are to be
found in the text written in *italics*.

*Metaphorically,* declares the inner voice, *the Inner Shaman is the
mechanism with which we all connect to Spirit. It represents humankind's*

*ability to travel into the world of Spirit as ancient peoples once did without a second thought, as shamans of all traditions have always done. This ability, for the most part, has been lost by the majority of people in modern western society, as so much emphasis has been placed on materialism and sensory experience. People have truly gotten lost in the physicality of their being and have forgotten their true nature as spiritual beings. Within the shamanic world view, Spirit and spiritual matters assume a most important role. We are now entering into a time period in which spiritual matters will once again be of primary importance. They will no longer be shoved into the background and left to rot. Spirit will become an everyday concept as it once was. Certainly the shamanic consciousness puts Spirit in its rightful place. Within this perspective there is an appreciation for the importance of Spirit and its incredibly vital role in our lives. This concept must once again become a well-known fact, not one that is hushed and spoken of only among a handful of awakened souls, but one that is known by everyone as a matter of course.*

*When one allows the shamanic consciousness to reawaken, one also reactivates this ancient mechanism for connection to the world of Spirit that has lain dormant for so long. It is by remembering how to use this resource, this innate mechanism (that humankind, for the most part, has forgotten how to use) that is the key to healing. The Inner Shaman is a metaphor for the divine connection to Source that exists within each of us. It is the vehicle that can take us to a place of oneness where insight and divine knowing are possible. It is here that all kinds of wonderful things can take place. It is here that healing can occur, for within this ancient shamanic consciousness lie the secrets to healing on all levels of being. The reawakening of this ability is what is occurring now. The Inner Shaman represents this awakening, the awakening of those who have been in a state of slumber, to a higher state of awareness that will enable healing, individual as well as collective, to take place. The reawakening of this consciousness is what humankind at this very crucial point in planetary history needs so desperately.*

In the chapters that follow I will share the gifts that my Inner Shaman, White Buffalo Woman, has presented to me. I will explore some of her teachings and examine a number of elements identified by this inner voice to be inherent to the shamanic world view, basic concepts that define and describe the world of the shaman and how it operates. I will then weave my own healing story through these elements, all of which have been identified by Inner Shaman as the keys to healing and transformation and have been profoundly relevant in my personal journey. My narrative will be presented through a series of stories and vignettes, which are not necessarily in chronological order, but which will come together to create a tapestry of the essence of the shamanic consciousness and my personal self-healing experience. I will begin by exploring in more depth just what a shaman and shamanism are all about. I will also include a "Healing Journey" for you to take at the end of Chapters Two through Ten. Each "Healing Journey: Activities for Going Inward" section will include a Journal Exercise, a Meditation, and a Ritual, all of which will help you to both awaken the shamanic consciousness within you and to deepen your personal connection to your Inner Shaman.

Come, let us take this journey together.

# CHAPTER ONE

# The Essence of Shamanism

IN RECENT YEARS, interest in shamans and shamanism has grown significantly. More and more people in contemporary society have become attracted to this ancient system which draws upon the worlds of nature and of spirit for its vital energy and offers to those who live and practice its ways a source of profound healing and connectedness to the Divine. Within this ancient consciousness there exists a completely distinct world view, one which perceives all things as being intricately connected in a great web of energy and acknowledges that there is an inner or spiritual realm of reality which affects and influences outward experience. Accessing and honoring this inner spiritual reality—the essential feature of shamanic practice—provides a connection to deeper parts of the self, helping to bring the seeker to a place of profound healing and inner peace.

Within this system, one comes into direct contact with knowledge that has been known for thousands of years by those who performed the shamanic functions within their tribal or communal societies. Entering into the world of the shaman provides one with the secrets and keys to healing, a profoundly important and relevant experience for today's world of global decay. It is, as I see it, the challenge of our times to extract the richness that emanates from the shamanic consciousness and to employ it for healing both ourselves and our world.

It is not so much the purpose of this study to investigate shamans and shamanic practice, however, but more to enter into and explore the essence of the consciousness that is universally found within shamanic systems. Nor is this primarily a study of traditional shamanism as such, although I will be referring to it and drawing from it throughout the book. It is rather a consideration of and reflection upon the shamanic consciousness that has emanated from within me, that has been awakened by the voice of my Inner Shaman.

What then is a shaman, and what characterizes the shamanic world and sets it apart from the modern day world? The shaman, as a universal archetype and a cultural tradition, has existed since the dawning of human history. Scientific evidence suggests that shamanic methods date back as much as twenty to thirty thousand years, making shamanism the most widespread and ancient form of healing known to humankind.[1] Nearly all primal societies around the world have had their version of the shaman who functioned as healer, teacher, peacemaker, tribal sage, administrator of sacred ritual, emissary between the seen and unseen worlds, and advocate for lost souls. Shamans were the world's first psychotherapists, first religious ministers, first magicians, first performing artists, and first storytellers.[2]

The shaman's duties included communicating with the spirit world, counteracting magical spells, and journeying to the three worlds of the shaman: the Upper World (the heavens and realm of the gods), the Lower World (the realm of the dead and souls), and the Middle World (the here and now) on behalf of members of the tribal community. Shamans, traditionally endowed with supernatural psychic powers, were able to heal, to diagnose clairvoyantly, to control the weather, to levitate, to be immune to fire, and to see into the future.[3] Appearing crossculturally, their role was tribally assigned and defined, but always embodying a common essence, which varied only minimally from culture to culture. In her book,

*Shaman, The Wounded Healer*, Joan Halifax identifies this "common thread" that appears to connect all shamans around the globe as the "shamanic mission," the essence of which involves awakening to other orders of reality, the experience of ecstasy, and an opening up of visionary realms.[4]

A shaman, as defined by Hawaiian shaman, Serge Kahili King, is a "healer of relationships: between mind and body, between people, between people and circumstances, between humans and Nature, and between matter and spirit."[5] Michael Harner adds to the definition by describing a shaman as "a man or woman who enters an altered state of consciousness—at will—to contact and utilize an ordinarily hidden reality in order to acquire knowledge, power, and to help other persons."[6] Jeanne Achterberg defines a shaman by both practice and intent, stating, "Shamanic practice involves the ability to move in and out of a special state of consciousness, a notion of a guardian spirit complex, and has the purpose of helping others." Shamans are individuals who are gifted not only with insight and wisdom regarding the human condition, but who also have achieved a good deal of understanding about the workings of spirit and the spirit realm. They use these gifts to perform their healing role. By any definition, in all cultures and in all times, it is the shaman who is the healer, the guardian of an extensive body of knowledge and methodology used for the attainment and preservation of health and well being both for self and the entire community.

Shamanism is not a religion, but rather a belief system that, along with a complex set of practices, convictions, values and behaviors, embraces its own characteristic world view or consciousness. Within this consciousness exists several fundamental assumptions that have been found to exist universally among shamanic peoples. Kenneth Meadows in his book, *Shamanic Experience*, identifies four assumptions that provide the infrastructure for the shamanic consciousness:

1.  There is a Supreme Intelligence or Ultimate Source—known as Great Spirit to Native Americans—which is everything that has, does, or will ever exist. This Supreme Intelligence, which is behind all things in existence, exists not only outside, but also inside all Creation. Everything that exists is one and the same; energy and matter are one.

2.  Everything is connected to everything else, with all things interconnected in a giant universal web of energy. Nothing exists in isolation; man is not alone but interrelated with all levels and forms of life. It is this awareness of a universal oneness or consciousness that makes it possible to link with, journey through and attain knowledge of all things.

3.  Everything is alive, and as such, everything has an organizing life force energy and awareness.

4.  There are inner realms of reality which both affect and influence outward experience. It is within these inner realms that dwell spirit helpers, guides and teachers with power to bring about change in the outer reality.[7]

Operating universally under this set of assumptions, shamans were, and are, travelers into the world of the unseen, the inner realm of spirit. The "shamanic journey" is the way in which the shaman enters into this alternate reality. Described by Michael Harner, author of *Way of the Shaman*, as "the centerpiece of shamanism," the shamanic journey involves moving from an "Ordinary State of Consciousness" (OSC) to a "Shamanic State of Consciousness" (SSC). Carlos Castanada[8] describes it as moving from one state of reality to another, from "ordinary reality" to "nonordinary reality."

16

The SSC may be described as a trance or transcendent state of awareness in which the shaman attains what is termed "shamanic enlightenment," the ability to see both literally and metaphorically in the darkness what others cannot perceive. While in the Shamanic State of Consciousness, the shaman journeys to the Upper, Middle and Lower Worlds for the purpose of gaining knowledge, acquiring power and helping others. During these adventures into the unseen world, which he or she consciously experiences and is able to later recall, the shaman obtains useful information, contacts and dialogues with teachers and guides, works with power animals or guardian spirits, meets and helps spirits of the dead, and assists individuals in making their transitions to the land of the dead.

It is the shamanic journey, or the "ecstatic experience," as Mircea Eliade terms it, which sets the shaman apart from others. He states: "... shamans do not differ from other members of the collectivity by their quest for the sacred—which is normal and universal human behavior—but by their capacity for ecstatic experience, which, for the most part, is equivalent to a vocation."[9] Eliade describes the shaman as the "great master of ecstasy" and equates shamanism with a "technique of ecstasy." He points out, however, that not just any ecstatic can be considered a shaman. A shaman specializes in a trance or state of ecstasy in which his or her soul is believed to leave his or her body in its magical flight to the Upper, Middle or Lower Worlds of the shamanic journey.

The shaman is able to move from one reality to the other, sometimes with the help of hallucinogenic substances found in sacred plants or sometimes with the aid of drumming, rattling, dancing and chanting, fasting, temperature regulation, or sensory deprivation, but always at will and always in complete control. He or she moves easily between the two realities, purposely and with serious intent, invariably acting in ways appropriate to whichever reality he or she is in at the moment. The shaman must be a master in functioning in both realms, and keeping "a foot in both worlds." The shaman believes that the non-physical reality is as real as the physical reality. There is no distinction between the two.

According to Inner Shaman: *What happens in the unseen world is every bit as real as what happens in the seen world. What the shaman experiences on his or her journey into the world of spirit is considered to be real in the fullest sense of the word, sometimes even more real than what occurs in the physical reality. The shaman must operate in this way. What he or she experiences on the journey is not considered to be "fantasy," or "imagination," but truly real. If the shaman does not believe this, does not operate within this belief system, then his or her work is truly in vain. The shaman must believe in what he or she is doing or his or her efforts are useless.*

Perhaps one of the most integral aspects of the shamanic consciousness is the notion of ritual as a way of marking the transformation of the shamanic initiate into the role of the shaman. The initiation process that all shamans must go through, has been thoroughly documented and described by Mircea Eliade in his book, *Shamanism: Archaic Techniques of Ecstasy.* According to Eliade, the shamanic ecstatic initiatory experience invariably encompasses "the universal theme of death and mystical resurrection of the candidate by means of a descent into the underworld and an ascent into the sky."[10] Eliade describes initiation rituals that involve the themes of suffering, death and rebirth, and, in one way or another, the cutting or mutilation of the body. Initiates are often ritualistically buried to mark the symbolic death. The ritualistic death is typically followed by a "resurrection" or rebirth, and sandwiched in between is always a period in which the candidate is isolated or separated or somehow identified as being different from other members of the community. Eliade enumerates these as: "(a) Period of seclusion in the bush; (b) Face and body daubed with ashes...to obtain the pallid hue of ghosts; funerary masks; (c) Symbolic burial; (d) Hypnotic sleep; drinks that make the candidate unconscious."[11] The intent of all of this being to facilitate the candidate's forgetting of his past life, of letting go of the old one, so that he or she can easily move into the new one. The shamanic initiation process goes to great lengths to ritualize and mark the end of one way of life and the beginning of another.

Fundamental to shamanism is the acquisition of power, for it is through the use of special powers that the shaman performs his or her role. Power, however, is not something that one earns or pursues, but rather it is a gift from the spirit and natural worlds. In Amber Wolfe's view:

> The world of the shaman is constantly moving. Everything in the shaman's world has its own special vibration, unique energy and power. The quest of the shaman is to achieve attunement with these vibrations and familiarity with Spirit. To accomplish this is to attain power. Still, the shaman knows that this cannot be pursued, only received. Power is a gift. That is the first wisdom of shamanism.[12]

In order to perform his or her work, then, the shaman relies on special, personal power that, in the shamanic view, comes from guardian or helping spirits. These guardian spirits, the fundamental source of power and knowledge for the shaman's functioning and protectors from the dangers that may be encountered on the journey, are often animals, known as power animals. Common to shamans the world over is the belief that humans are bound together with the animal kingdom through a sort of collective unconscious or non-local mind, making it possible to not only share consciousness with an animal, but also to actually become one.[13] As Jeanne Achterberg states, "When a shaman dons the skin of his power animal and dances around the campfire, it is the power animal dancing in the SSC, not the man and a skin in some theatrical rendition."[14] To wear the skin of an animal, then, is to actually become that animal and, by becoming an animal the shaman becomes something stronger and greater than him or herself. In so doing, the shaman is empowered to do his or her healing work.

*The shaman is an unparalleled symbol for the mediator between the phys-ical and the non-physical worlds. It is the shaman that takes flight and ventures into the other world of the non-physical reality to make contact with Spirit for the purpose of obtaining information that is only available from that other reality. This information is then used for the benefit of the indi-vidual or group that is in need of some type of healing. The shaman is never an ambassador of negativity, although he or she may oftentimes encounter such energies along the way. The shaman, by definition, has as his or her goal only the highest good of all concerned. Those who do the work of the shaman and have other ends in mind are not true shamans. The shaman is always seeking whatever information or truth that will help the situation, whatever it may be. This is done on an intuitive, clairvoyant, or psychic level, making the shaman a channel of spiritual wisdom, knowledge and understanding.*

Shamans see the world in a distinctly unique way. As Jean Houston attests, "The shaman perceives a world of total aliveness. Everything is full of life. Everything is profoundly interconnected. Everything has meaning."[15] *Shamans truly view the world through a lens of wonder-ment. They approach virtually everything they look at with a sense of awe, wonder, and curiosity. This precludes the possibility of judgment or censor-ship. They meticulously observe and report on what they have observed, adding a measure of richness in the way of interpretation. The world of the shaman is perceived as magical and in constant movement, always chang-ing and growing. This is true at the macro as well as the micro levels, externally as well as internally. Change is the call word for the shaman who believes that there is no such thing as stasis. Everything is in constant motion. The world is alive. All of nature is given a personified identity. There is no such thing as "inanimate" in the shamanic world view—virtu-ally everything is animate. The shaman's world is one of vibrancy and color; sensual richness abounds. There is a depth and richness to all that is per-ceived by the shaman, who actually perceives things in profoundly deep ways, both through the physical senses and the nonphysical ones.*

The shamanic world view sees all things as intrinsically related, a web woven of myriads of interconnecting relationships. In the Lakota Sioux tradition, for example, the words Mitakuye Oyasin, "All my relations," or "We are all related,"[16] reflect these native people's profound evaluation of the nature of the Universe. For the shaman, then, it is quite natural to communicate with animals, spirits or even rocks, since in the shamanic world view everything is connected, everything is one.

. It follows that in the shamanic world view, humans are seen as being one with all of nature. Paula Underwood Spencer describes Indian traditions as being "nature-inclusive,"[17] in which humankind is not seen as being separate from the rest of creation, but rather is seen in the context of an interrelated whole. The fundamental assumption that all things are interrelated naturally leads to the shamanic focus on the importance of attunement, balance and harmony. Spiritual balance, which is intrinsically linked to being in balance with the natural world, is seen as being the main purpose of life, crucial to both the physical and spiritual well being of the individual and the world.[18] And so the concept of health takes on a depth and richness of purpose not found in the Western world view, as Jeanne Achterberg so eloquently suggests:

> The function of any society's health system is ultimately tied to the philosophical convictions that the members hold regarding the purpose of life itself. For the shamanic cultures, that purpose is spiritual development. Health is being in harmony with the world view. Health is an intuitive perception of the universe and all its inhabitants as being of one fabric. Health is maintaining communication with the animals and plants and minerals and stars. It is knowing death and life and seeing no difference. It is blending and melding, seeking solitude and seeking companionship to understand one's many selves. Unlike the "modern" notions, in shamanic society health is not the

absence of feeling; no more so is it the absence of pain. Health is seeking out all of the experiences of creation and turning them over and over, feeling their texture and multiple meanings. Health is expanding beyond one's singular state of consciousness to experience the ripples and waves of the universe.[19]

Thus, within the shamanic system, health and wellness are seen as being in perfect harmony with self, with spirit, with all of nature, and with the very universe itself. Health is not defined in terms of the absence of pain, disease or illness, or in terms of a well-functioning "machine," as is often the case in the modern allopathic medical view. But rather, it is defined in terms of the presence of a dynamic balance between nature and spirit, between body and mind, between individuals and the universe.

If health is defined in terms of balance and harmony within the shamanic perspective, it follows that illness or disease can be seen as a consequence of disharmony of some sort in relationship with one's self, or others, and in relationships with the spirit world as well. The shaman interprets the manifestation of a physical or mental illness as a loss of equilibrium, the person has lost his or her personal spiritual purpose. This might be described in terms of "losing one's vision" or "not living one's medicine anymore."[20]

Seeing illness as a physical manifestation that something is wrong with the soul, the shaman first seeks to discover the root cause of the problem and then assists the sick one to realign with his or her spiritual purpose. Accordingly, as Lewis Mehl,[21] points out, for the Cherokee sickness was not a permanent state, but rather a territory to pass through, a purifying experience with the purpose of setting them back on their spiritual path. In other words, illness was viewed as a message from the body to examine one's way of life and make the necessary adjustments to get back on the right path. The ill person needs to understand the illness as a teaching, that every illness, injury or accident happens for a reason, and the message of the illness needs to be correctly interpreted. It is the role of the shaman to help patients decipher the messages which will indicate how they may have gone astray to a path that is not in keeping with their true destiny, and to remove the hindrances blocking their reconnection to the Source. Disease is always viewed, then, as a reminder to the individual that he or she needs to reunify his or her earthly existence with the Whole, with the cosmos. When thought of in this way, illness becomes an opportunity for transformation. In the words of a Hopi shaman, "Man has chosen the way of sickness to become healthy and whole once more."[22]

Inner Shaman has a great deal to say on this subject, giving very clear, and elaborate definitions and explanations of dis-ease, illness, health, healing and self-healing within the shamanic consciousness. She differentiates dis-ease from illness in that illness is a condition that may or may not result when a person is in a state of dis-ease.

*In the shamanic world view, disease is believed to be caused by a person being out of balance, or not in harmony with the SELF. Illness is a condition that results from being in a state of dis-ease, of being out of sync with one's higher, spiritual purpose. Dis-ease occurs when we are off-track, or not walking the path that we are meant to be walking. There is a dissonance between the ego self and the higher self. The two are not of one mind, not in resonance with each other. This means that the ill person is ill because something is not quite right at the level of spirit, the inner essence of the self that is the real person. Once this is understood and the appropriate steps taken to resolve the lack of harmony, the dis-ease will disappear. The shaman knows that to be whole, which is the essence of health, the person must walk his or her own path, the path that they came here to follow. If this is not what is occurring, then illness will inevitably appear. This is really a matter of spiritual concern. Illness is not merely physical, not ever. It manifests on the physical level only when the spiritual, mental and emotional factors have been repeatedly ignored and passed over. If one were truly in tune with one's spiritual life to the extent that awareness was open and constant, then physical illness would never occur. There would simply be no need for it. Illness,*

*I repeat, serves a very definite purpose or function. It is not just a random thing that occurs to some people and not to others. It is always a message from the high self that something is not right at the spiritual level. This could mean that the person is not living a life of truth, light and love, is not living a life of integrity. Then one symptom after another will appear to draw attention to this fact.*

*Healing invariably involves a form of integrity. When one's life is not in congruence with one's higher purpose, or when one's actions are not in line with one's beliefs or feelings, a tension or conflict is produced that will ultimately lead to some sort of dis-ease that can manifest in a variety of ways. Healing, then, is seen as a restoration of balance and harmony to the individual's physical-mental-emotional-spiritual system. The person must come into a place of peace and harmony with SELF at all four of these levels, regardless of on which level the dis-ease is manifesting. That is why one of the first things that must occur in order to heal is a shift in consciousness, a shift from ego-centered to spirit-centered thinking. This is the most important aspect of the healing process. Once this shift occurs the healing can then follow.*

*The symptoms that one experiences are messages from the god-self to the ego-self to wake-up, to pay attention to the greater picture. The person's symptoms are a way that the high self, through the body-mind, communicates to the conscious self that something is out of whack, something is not as it should be. When we are in tune with our body, we are able to read its warnings and avoid or quickly eradicate any illness that may come our way. When we consistently ignore the signs and messages that our body is sending us, serious illness may take hold. We will continue to get ill as long as the message is not understood and something done to act on it. If one thing is "cured" by surgery, let's say, but the message is not heard and heeded, then another illness will develop in another part of the body and so on and so forth until the person either gets it or finally succumbs to serious physical illness or even death. The shaman has always believed that this is the way things work. Modern medicine does not view illness this way. This profession insists on cutting one thing out at a time, eradicating symptom after symptom, without the slightest consideration of what the symptom is trying to communicate to the person. This has proven to be a great disservice to humanity, one that needs to be turned around soon.*

*This is why the notion of awakening is so important to the healing process. To awaken to one's higher self and what it is attempting to communicate, is what is required to attain the goal of resonance with the god-self. This is the inner understanding of the self in relation to SELF. This is the essence of healing, relating SELF to self at the deepest, most intimate level. When this is accomplished, the person is then in a state of integrity and a state of complete and total self-love. Once this happens, healing is possible, but only then. Love of the self for the self is the ultimate goal of healing. It is the only way for true and complete healing to occur. All healing is self-healing and all healing requires self-love. It is that simple.*

The role that the shaman plays in the healing process and shamanic methods are remarkably similar the world over, regardless of differences in culture and geographical separation. As Jean Houston so aptly puts it, "From the distant past to the emergent future and across the boundaries of all cultures, the depth culture of the shaman is shown to persist curiously consistent in many ways in both method and metaphor."[23]

*This common essence of the shamanic process has to do with the flight into the world of spirit and with the fulfillment of the role of healer by serving as mediator between the individual and his or her illness. Within the shamanic world view, the ill person must come to terms, or make peace, so to say, with his or her illness, and the shaman is the facilitator of that process. It is the shaman that helps the person to understand the meaning and function of the illness or dis-ease and how he or she is out of balance, or out of sync with his or her higher spiritual purpose. This is generally the main cause for all illness—a state of disharmony with one's spiritual goals and aspirations. This lack of harmony with self is what causes a person to lose power and become susceptible to illness or injury. To the shaman, it is not, as is commonly believed in Western thinking, germs, bacteria or viruses that cause the illness, but rather being out of tune with one's own instrument that causes the problem. The microbes are merely a mechanism through which the illness manifests in the body, but they are not the cause. The cause of all illness begins on the spiritual level and likewise, the healing or cure also originates at this level. Until one approaches the disease or illness from this level in one way or another, there can be no real cure, only a temporary remission or respite.*

*The real work of healing must take place in the inner dimensions. This is why the shaman is so important because he or she is the one who is skilled at traveling, getting around and functioning within this inner realm. The shaman is the one person who is at home in both worlds and can be the mediator between the two. He or she, however, does not do the healing directly, but goes into the world of spirit and returns with the keys that the ill person can use to open the door to healing. Yet the person in need of healing must be the one to turn the key. The shaman is unable to do that for the person. That is why all healing is considered to be self-healing.*

Within the shamanic consciousness, all healing is seen as self-healing. The shaman plays the role of an evocator of health, but ultimately, healing is up to the individual. In their book, *Secrets of Shamanism: Tapping the Spirit Power Within You,* Jose and Lena Stevens point this out:

> Master shamans know that ultimately, all healing is self-healing. They are good at naming the problem, targeting the problem area, contacting power animals or guardians, communicating silently, and staying out of the way. They do not deplete themselves nor do they falsely believe that they alone are able to heal. They are the go-betweens or midwives between the power of the spirit world and the physical landscape.[24]

In her book, *In the Shadow of the Shaman,* Amber Wolfe also strongly maintains that all healing is self-healing, attesting that:

> No one heals another. No one. All we can hope for, in helping another person's healing process, is to be a catalyst and a channel for the healing energies. We can catalyze these

energies with our training, our personal experiences, our heartfelt compassion, and our faith in the powers of self-healing. We can channel healing energies through ourselves and direct them to merge, awaken, and strengthen the healing energies of another.[25]

Of course, it would be important to note that numerous people who visit the doctor's office in modern day society believe that the doctor or the doctor's treatment will heal them. Similarly, it was not, or is not, uncommon for people living in shamanic societies to view the shaman as the source of the cure, and for this myth to be played out between the shaman and the ill person. The understanding within the shamanic consciousness, according to the voice of Inner Shaman, is that all healing is self-healing.

*As you know, shamans from all cultures from all over the world were looked upon as the healers or the medicine people of their respective tribes. They were respected, revered and sought out for their exceptional skills in this area. They knew how to enter into the world of spirit to find the answers that the sick person needed for the healing to take place, but they were limited in their ability to heal. They could provide insight, information, give herbs or "medicine," prescribe ritual or offer suggestions on how the patient might proceed, but ultimately it was up to the person who was sick to heal him or herself. The shaman knew that all healing is self-healing. No person, god or human, can heal another. This lies strictly within the realm of the individual. Jesus knew this. He did not heal the sick. The sick healed themselves by shifting their belief systems to open to the possibility of health. They were not magically healed by God or otherwise. Jesus provided energy or helped shift beliefs and then the person's own inner healer took over and the healing was effected. All of the medicine, therapies, surgeries, techniques, practices and what have you in the world are not capable of healing. Only the person's own inner healer is capable of doing that for him or her.*

*To say that one is a healer is a misnomer unless one understands "healer" to mean "one who facilitates self-healing in another." This is not to say that healers are useless or have no importance, for they most certainly do. It is the healer that provides the alternate belief system that the patient was unable or unwilling to provide for him or herself. It is the healer that evokes the patient's own inner healer to awaken and to rise to the occasion and do what needs to be done. It is the healer that sustains and nurtures the patient through difficult and challenging times, providing comfort and encouragement when times get rough. This relationship is extremely valuable. It offers the patient a model for entering into a similar relationship with the self, one that smacks of self-love, self-esteem and self-nurturance. This is what in the end will do the work of healing, not any herb or exercise or surgery. It is the action of the patient, the movement toward the direction of self-love, reflected in all of the different ways that the patient attempts to self-help, self-comfort, self-nurture or self-sustain, that does the healing. That is why some techniques work for some some of the time, but healing is really a totally individual affair. And it is entirely dependent on the person's inner state, not on any external situation, object or event. I will repeat, healing is an internal process, not an external one, ever. Healing begins on the inside, within the realm of what can be termed spiritual. It culminates in the physical cure if that is the destiny of the individual. Healing may or may not involve a physical cure, however, it may simply mean coming to a place of peace and acceptance of self and life.*

As Inner Shaman points out, within the shamanic world view, love plays a crucial role in healing, one that involves an interactive process between patient and healer. Michael Harner, in giving a description of the mechanism of the interactive process that exists between patient and healer, suggests that love and caring on the part of the shaman is an essential component of the healing process:

> Shamanism is a great mental and emotional adventure, one in which the patient as well as the shaman-healer are involved. Through his heroic journey and efforts, the shaman helps his patients transcend their normal, ordinary definition of reality, including the definition of themselves as ill. The shaman shows his patients that they

are not emotionally and spiritually alone in their struggles against illness and death. The shaman shares his special powers and convinces his patients, on a deep level of consciousness, that another human is willing to offer up his own self to help them. The shaman's self-sacrifice calls forth a commensurate emotional commitment from his patients, a sense of obligation to struggle alongside the shaman to save one's life. Caring and curing go hand in hand.[26]

The importance of love and caring in healing, so vital an element of shamanic methodology, is not a concept that is taught in modern day medical schools which tend to stress the importance of complete objectivity. However, as Larry Dossey in *Recovering the Soul* suggests, without these elements "medicine becomes a mere manipulation of tissue, an orchestration of chemistry." In discussing how healing takes place with psychic healers through the avenue of the non-local mind, Dossey, coming from a shamanic perspective, makes a strong case for the necessity of love in healing:

> When psychic healing takes place, the experience of love and nonlocality are so tightly connected that they cannot be teased apart. Healers experience a sense of holiness with that of wholeness, such that the universe seems Godlike, enchanted, and filled with love... The psychic healer does not have to deliberately strive to add the element of love to the healing agenda; rather, the love is endemic to the genuine nonlocal sense of wholeness. We are not speaking here about love as an emotion. Rather, this greater love is more akin to a deep, inner desire to reestablish completeness in the patient, the loss of which has expressed itself in the form of illness. Love for the patient is this yearning to help him or her to be whole, to be One. Without this love, healing simply does not occur.[27]

The shamanic consciousness offers a rich context in which to investigate the experience of healing. If, indeed, all healing is self-healing, and I believe that it is, then an investigation of what it means to heal the self would be valuable. So I invite you now to accompany me in an exploration of my personal healing journey within the shamanic consciousness.

# SHAMAN'S SONG

I hear his sweet song resound within my soul,
as the melodious lyric echoes through my heart.
The enchanting, haunting rhythm vibrates every cell in my body,
speaking to me in a strange new language, a foreign unfamiliar tongue.
Yet with every beat of the drum that pulsates through me
I hear the call to awaken.

The shaman's voice whispers, with a sweet unmistakable clarity,
"Awaken, dear one, to the light of the new day.
Take my hand and I'll show you the way.
Do not be afraid as you journey with me,
for I know the way that will set your heart free.
The path will be rocky, sometimes difficult to climb,
but hold onto my hand and, together we'll make it in time."

As I walk hand in hand with this Shaman within,
I feel my heart beat to the sound of his silent drum.
I let go of my fear and surrender to him,
trusting, without doubt that what he tells me is true.
Though the journey is fraught with danger and obstacles we find,
a light always glows in the darkness, illuminating the way.
As a beacon it shines, always bright, always true,
pointing the way to my soul's awakening.

Our adventure is marked by both challenge and trial.
Death and dismemberment sometimes crossing our path,
but the commitment to move forward within me is strong.
Ever onward I go, Inner Shaman by my side, into the light of the new day.
Awakened, refreshed, renewed, reborn, completely transformed,
I finally come to a place of inner healing and peace.
As the journey continues, for it never really ends,
I hear the Shaman's song echo inside once again.
It beckons me onward, helps me face each new day,
inviting me to fully participate in this journey called life.

"Awaken, dear one," I hear the voice whisper, "to the light of a new day.
Take my hand and I'll show you the way.
Do not be afraid as you journey with me,
for I know the way that will set your heart free.
The path will be rocky, sometimes difficult to climb,
but hold onto my hand and, together, we'll make it in time."

— M. S.

*August 24, 1996*

## CHAPTER TWO

# The Journey:
# Entering the World of Spirit

*THE SHAMANIC JOURNEY—the flight into the world of Spirit—is the most vital aspect of shamanism, and it is perhaps the most important thing that the shaman does. It is what sets the shaman apart from others. It is what gives him or her special status within the community, for it is the one thing that shamans do that others cannot. It is only the shaman who knows how to navigate the stream of consciousness from one reality to another, from everyday waking reality to an alternate reality in the realm of the Spirit world. It is only the shaman who has the knowledge and expertise to perform this task. The shaman has been trained in the workings of the mind and knows how to achieve the state of consciousness needed to visit the non-physical realms wherein dwells Spirit.*

*It is within this realm that the shaman does his or her healing work. It is here that the shaman journeys to find the answers to questions that will allow him or her to do the healing work that characterizes a shaman. It is within the journey that the shaman learns what to do, discovers what "medicine" is needed, and how or where to find it. This then is passed on from the shaman to the ill person who must then make the necessary changes or take the required steps to facilitate and elicit the healing. This occurs only after the ill person has surrendered and moved into a space of trust and openness to Spirit. If this does not happen, then healing cannot happen. It is that simple.*

*The shamanic journey is, as I have said, at the heart of shamanism. It is the vehicle for the journey into the world of Spirit. This "going into the world of Spirit" is what constitutes the essence of the journey. It is not so much the techniques or the different worlds that the shaman may visit, as the fact that the soul of the shaman leaves the physical body behind and travels into another dimension of reality, an alternate reality in which dwell the non-physical beings of the spirit world. This is what is most important about the journey. This is what is most significant about the journey.*

*When the shaman travels to the other realities, he or she leaves behind the attachment to the physical reality and ventures into a world in which none of the laws of the physical world apply. It is a world without fear and the limitations that fear imposes. In this dimension, you see, anything is possible. People can fly through the air or breath under water or go for extended periods of time without food or water, or eat and eat and eat without ever feeling full. This is a world without rules, without the confines and limitations of time and space, a world filled with a richness and luminosity that is not found in the physical world. It is here that the shaman can find the answers to problems that cannot be solved in ordinary, physical reality with all of its limitations. It is here that the shaman is able to have experiences that are unthinkable in ordinary reality, yet necessary to complete the task at hand, whatever that may be. In other words, the limitlessness of this world offers the opportunity to arrive at conclusions that are not possible to derive in ordinary reality with all of its physical laws and assumptions. The shaman leaves all of this behind, entering into a world where a totally different set of assumptions prevails, and is thus able to make sense out of what otherwise might seem totally senseless if operating under the rules and assumptions of ordinary reality. This is the magic of the shamanic journey. This is what makes it so powerful a tool for navigating a course while in the physical reality.*

*You see humans are non-physical beings who are currently inhabiting a physical body and, as such, are limited to a physical existence governed by physical laws and assumptions. But there is so much more to human beings, so much more of which they, for the most part, are not aware. The Shaman is aware of this existence beyond the physical, beyond what is perceivable with the five senses and ventures into this other existence as a way of learning how to walk the path of life and helping others to do the same. This is the gift that the shamanic journey offers to those who take it. By entering into the world of Spirit, the non-physical reality that has no bounds, no limits, no rules, one can find the keys to health, peace and happiness, the way to successfully navigate the earth walk and bring it into the physical reality of everyday life. This is the significance of the journey into Spirit. It allows the journeyer to find the path to wholeness, health, peace and happiness.*

*The shamanic journey, of course, can also be viewed as a metaphor for life's journey, for the journey of spiritual growth and evolvement. It is only through embarking on this journey that one can arrive at a place of oneness with Spirit. Only by walking this path can one reconnect to the Source. Only by making this magical flight can one awaken to the reality of non-dimensional time and space wherein lies the essence of all life, all truth, all love. This is the place of the sacred flame, which burns within each living thing. The journey is, of course, inward. It is a journey into the inner realms, the place of stillness and chaos, the place of oneness and aloneness, and the place of darkness and light, the place of love and fear, the place of TRUTH. It is only when one enters into this place that awakening and healing can occur. It is only here that the connection to SELF and to SOURCE is possible. This is the place of divine knowing, from which emanates the Universal Truths that lead one along the path. This is the place wherein lies the beloved of the soul, the essential self. It is only by entering into this space that one can come to a place of oneness with SELF. This is essential for spiritual evolvement to occur. This is a place where only the brave will venture. Those who are afraid will not survive the journey for it requires great strength and endurance. There are many perils and trials along the way, all of which must be faced with fearlessness and trust.*

MY JOURNEY INTO THE WORLD OF SPIRIT actually began long before that day in the summer of 1989 when I first met The Shaman, Sky Hawk. In looking back over my life, I remember that at quite an early age I would "go off" somewhere, on a journey not at all unlike that which a shaman undertakes, on a journey deep inside of myself. When I was a child in the 1950's, this was called day dreaming, and I recall doing quite a bit of it. I used to love to listen to music and get lost in a world of imaginary experience, in which the words of the songs took on a life of their own. One of my favorite pastimes was to swing on the swing that Dad had hung for me under the back porch and zone out into a world of aliveness and wonderment that existed within me.

Shutting myself off from the world behind the closed door of my bedroom was another way I spent a lot of my time, lost in the world of imagination, but a very real world all the same. I would daydream about most anything imaginable from the wonderful man I would someday marry to what it might be like to have lots and lots of money and live in a big house. Spending time inside of myself was, by far, my favorite form of entertainment. While spending this time within my own world of imagination, I was actually living an incredibly rich spiritual life, one filled with peace and joy—although, at the time, I thought it was merely daydreaming.

As the years passed, this pastime began to take on a spiritual quality. Born into an Italian-American family, I was raised in the Catholic tradition, attending parochial school and going to Church every Sunday without fail. From an early age, my religion formed a very large part of my life. It was an important part of who I was, although I kept this to myself. Feeling that prayer and religion were private and personal things, I would spend quite a bit of time alone in silent prayer and contemplation. But, my prayer was more than just reciting the Rosary Beads or reading from a book; it inevitably took on the quality of an imaginary experience.

Jesus was a very good friend of mine in the world of imagination that I had created within myself. We spent many, many hours together. I recall one Holy Saturday (the Saturday before Easter) when I was 13 or 14 that stands out to this day as one of the most profoundly wonderful moments in my life. I had gone alone to church to spend an hour in prayer, and I remember sitting there and thinking about Jesus and experiencing ecstasy. It was a moment of true connection with the divine, an intensely moving and deeply spiritual experience that has remained with me my entire life, an experience that I cannot even begin to articulate, except to describe it as "ecstasy." The journey inward led me to a very special world inside myself, one that I have longed to revisit my entire life.

As the years passed, my life followed a fairly typical pattern. I went to high school, met the man of my dreams, went to college, married that man of my dreams midway through college, became pregnant, quit college, had two children by the time I was 24, and did all of the things a "good" mother/housewife of the '70's did. But I felt an emptiness deep inside, a yearning for fullness and fulfillment that never seemed to go away. I continued to practice the Catholic Religion, but found less and less satisfaction from it. It never seemed to adequately answer some of the burning questions about life and its meaning. We are born, we live a tough life, we grow old, we die, and then what? We sit on a cloud somewhere playing a harp? It all seemed so futile, so meaningless. What had happened to that moment of ecstasy I experienced in that church so many years ago? How could I find ecstasy in my life NOW and not have to wait to sit on the cloud? Cleaning house, sewing, running PTA and Girl Scout meetings, chauffeuring kids around town, cooking and doing laundry didn't seem to bring me the deep spiritual experience that I so longed to have. Where was the ecstasy? Where was the meaning? Where was that rich spiritual life that I had had as a young girl? Was it lost to me forever?

It was during this period of intense emptiness and longing that I began to experience one physical symptom after another—migraine headaches, chronic lower back pain, swelling and coldness in my hands (later diagnosed as Raynaud's Syndrome), chronic anemia, lack of energy and chronic fatigue, all accompanied by anxiety and a mild depression that never seemed to go away. In my late 20's and early 30's it was all I could do to get through the day without collapsing on a bed or a couch at some point during the day. The emptiness and pain that I was feeling deep inside, at the very core of my being, had begun to manifest at a physical level. I don't recall ever making it through a day without some physical pain, or feeling so de-energized that I could barely function in my day-to-day routine. Feeling lousy was the norm; feeling good the exception. And still no answer to the question, "where was the ecstasy?"

Then, one day during the summer of 1981, I picked up a book entitled *What Dreams May Come*, that had been sitting on my shelf for a year or two; I had bought it at K-Mart for a dollar. It was a fictional story about a man who died and what happened to him after his death. The book described this man's journey to a place called "Summerland," and told of his experiences in adjusting to his new life in the afterworld. And then, at the end of the book, his soul was reincarnated, reborn into another human body to start another life on earth. The last lines in the book read:

> True life is a process of **becoming**. Death is a stage in this progression. Life is not followed by **un**-life.
> There is only a single continuity of being.
> We are part of a plan, never doubt that. A plan to bring each one of us to the highest level of which we are capable. The way will be dark at times but it leads, assuredly, to light.
> Never forget, however, that we pay for every act and thought and feeling we commit.
> One statement from the Bible says it all.
> "Whatsoever a man soweth, that shall he also reap."

People are not punished **for** their deeds but **by** them. If only everyone believed that.

If only every man and woman in the world knew—beyond a shadow of a doubt—that they would have to face the consequences of their lives.

The world would change overnight.[1]

I hung on each of these words and felt an astounding resonation deep within me with this new, yet strangely familiar notion. This entire book, and these last words especially, had made a deep and lasting impression on me, one that not only piqued my curiosity, but also opened up a new world of possibility. After reading this book, I felt excited and energized. Could it be possible that reincarnation is a reality? Could there be more to life, and afterlife, than I had been taught? Could it be that Life has a deeper meaning and that it is an on-going process of evolution, growth and becoming?

I remembered hearing about the reincarnation controversy in the 1950's when the Bridey Murphy story was all over the news[2]. I recalled being intrigued by the concept of having more than one life and asking my mother at that time if it could be true. She, of course, adhering to a very Catholic belief system, quickly put out the flames of my excitement about this possibility. The flames that had been extinguished so many years before had just been rekindled after reading this book. I began to come alive. I found myself searching bookstores and libraries for other books that had anything to do with the subject of reincarnation. My interest expanded to include anything of a spiritual or metaphysical nature. I read voraciously and, within the following year, I had read close to 100 books that dealt with these topics. I was beginning to find some answers to my questions about the meaning and purpose of life. I was beginning to feel some hope that perhaps there was more to life than the Catholic Church said there was, that quite possibly life was continuous and that there was a whole world in another dimension that I could tap into if I so desired. I was beginning to feel less empty. I was beginning to think that maybe, just maybe, somewhere, somehow, I could recapture the ecstasy!

With this hope and an overpowering curiosity about reincarnation, I began in my early thirties to explore lives that I lived in other times and other places with undaunted determination. I read book after book about past life recall. I prayed and prayed, asking that I might be given the gift of insight into my past lives. I prayed and waited and waited and prayed for the memories to surface. The breakthrough finally came after reading a book entitled *Past Lives Therapy*[3] in which the authors describe a technique for unlocking past life memories hidden in the subconscious mind. The technique was quite simple—merely identify a recurring, repetitive phrase that you habitually say, close your eyes, and repeat it over and over until an image from another lifetime emerges.

I tried this. I began repeating a phrase which was a theme in my life at the time (as well as my dreams), "I can't communicate," over and over again. I soon found myself as a young German soldier, sitting in front of a radio set in something that seemed to be a front line station. An intense battle was being waged all around. Unable to make contact with anyone by radio, I heard myself saying over and over, "I can't communicate! I can't communicate!" The next thing I recalled was the unmistakable whine of an airplane that had been shot down as it plummeted to the ground. Then an explosion…fire…smoke…burning flesh…and peace. I had been killed by an airplane crashing into the station in which I was operating a radio. I was nineteen years old. The year was 1943, four years prior to my birth into my current lifetime. I didn't quite know what to make of this memory, but it certainly explained why I had the lifelong, recurring dream of airplanes crashing into my house or nose-diving to the ground. It also explained why I had always been so uncomfortable with that whinny noise that airplanes made as they approached the airport that was not too far from the house in which I grew up, or why I become terrified of low-flying planes directly overhead. After having this past-life memory surface, the dreams of planes crashing have stopped (but I still don't like that whinny noise that airplanes make!).

This was the first of a number of past life memories that began to surface at that time. I found that all I needed to do was to go into a relaxed, meditative state and ask myself a question, like "When did the reason for this situation first exist?" with the intention of exploring a life in another time and place. I would invariably get an answer to my question. Then all I needed to do was to trust the images and information that would come. (Although I didn't know it at the time I first began this exploration, accessing information in this way is essentially the process and intent of the shamanic journey— journeying into another reality, visiting another world that exists in another time and place, in order to acquire information.) And so I began to have one memory after another. It was as if the floodgates had been opened and the waters began to pour through with great force. There was a lifetime as a woman in England in the early 1700's, one in Russia as a peasant woman, one as a woman in Polynesia one thousand years ago, one as a hunter who died in a blizzard, one as a young peasant girl killed by a wolf. One by one they emerged, each bringing insight, understanding and a measure of healing to an area of my life, each one helping me to know and appreciate myself more and more.

Perhaps the most important memory that came forth at that time, which largely contributed to my healing, was a lifetime as a woman during the Civil War era. Over a period of weeks and months the memories of this lifetime surfaced, bit by bit. With each new awareness I felt such a sense of resonance. Deeply feeling emotion after emotion as the memories emerged, I relived the joy, pain, grief, fear, and disappointment that was all a part of my experience in that lifetime. This resonance served to convince me that the memories were genuine, that I was not merely "making it all up." It all felt so real, at times even more real than memories that I had of past events in my current lifetime. It was the experience of having this particular past life recall that forever put an end to whatever doubts I may have had of the validity of my memories of having lived in other times and other places. (And, it was engaging in this process of past life recall that helped to cultivate my ability to "journey" in time and space, thereby preparing me for the shamanic journeys and visionary experiences that were soon to follow.)

The memories of that lifetime were very vivid and remain so to this day. As a child, I lived with my parents in the South, in Savannah, Georgia, in a big white house. Having three younger brothers, I was the oldest of four children. My mother died when I was twelve, and the young black woman who was our servant became my "nanny." Her name was Maddie. Maddie was my most beloved friend. My father, who was a Methodist minister, was opposed to slavery and so we had no slaves, but kept some black people as servants. Maddie was free, but chose to stay with us, as she considered us her family. When the time came for me to marry and leave home, Maddie accompanied me. I married a man who was about twenty-five years older than me. He was a very rich, successful businessman—"shipping magnate" are the words that came to me. We lived in the city. My husband and I had a cool, distant, and loveless relationship. We had a child, a boy named Mark. When Mark was four years old, the war broke out. I fell in love with a young man, a soldier in gray, and we had a torrid romance and love affair before he was killed in battle. I became pregnant with his child. When my husband found out that I was pregnant, knowing that it could not possibly be his child, enraged, he raped and beat me. He never touched me again after that encounter. The baby was a boy. I named him David.

I had a very close relationship with one of my brothers; his wife was my dear friend. He also died wearing a gray uniform on a battlefield bathed in the blood of young men. I hated slavery, and I hated the war. It was senseless, brutal and served no purpose in my mind. I prayed for its quick ending. When Mark was just six years old he became very ill and died. I recalled feeling such unbearable grief over the loss of my beloved child. Maddie was my support and sustenance during those painfully difficult times. My husband and I remained together, for appearance's sake, until his death, but related only minimally, coexisting in a sham of a marriage. I lived with my son, David, until my death in my mid-fifties. I was severely injured in an accident when I was thrown out of the carriage in which I was riding; I died at home in my bed several days later, with David and Maddie at my side.

The insight, understanding and awareness that I received as a result of this memory answered many questions I had about relationships that I had at the time. I unmistakably recognized virtually everyone in that lifetime in Savannah as also being in my current lifetime. Although the genders and relationships might have been different, friends and relatives of that lifetime were now friends and relatives in this lifetime. My husband then is my husband now. Maddie is my older daughter. My sister-in-law then is a dear friend now, and so on and so forth. Having this awareness helped me immeasurably to understand and heal current relationships. I have since explored and identified dozens of other past lives, each one shedding brilliant, healing light on my relationships. To this day, when I encounter a problem in a relationship I explore the possibility of the problem being a carryover of an unresolved issue from a former life. Often, this is exactly the case, and I have learned that gaining the awareness and doing healing work on the past life relationship helps to heal the situation in the current one. Entering into the realm of past life memories has been a significant step on my healing journey.

And so my life moved on. More years passed. I had begun to grow in many ways. I left the Church. It held no meaning, no relevancy in my life anymore. I had grown out of it. It had served its purpose. It had given me the start in life that I needed to pursue the path that

I was about to follow and unshakable faith in the unseen world of Spirit, but now it was time to let go and move on. I needed to be free of the fear, of the rules, of the limitations and of the inflexible doctrinal teachings of religion so that I could explore and expand my personal spirituality that was so very eager to spread its wings and to take flight.

Leaving the Church was perhaps one of the most difficult things that I have ever done, but I knew in my heart that it was what I was being called to do. The ending was accompanied by incredible inner turmoil and conflict, but I *knew* what I needed to do. Each time I attended Church services I felt sick. I invariably would develop a headache and stomachache during Sunday Mass. I listened to the message that my body was giving me and, following my heart, my intuition, I left the religion of my youth, of my parents, and of my parent's parents, and moved, all alone, into uncharted territory, with nothing but my inner voice to guide me. Holding ever dear those precious gifts I had received from the Church and letting go of those which no longer served me, I continued my unending search for Truth, for my truth. In so doing, I took a giant step on my journey into the world of Spirit.

Letting go of my old world view, I opened to a completely new one. My horizons were expanding. I was free to search and explore without the restrictions and limitations of "good and bad" or "right and wrong" imposed by the Church. My search for Truth led me along a path of intense investigation in pursuit of answers to the questions about life that burned in my heart. And so it was that in 1982 I returned to the world of academia to complete the education I had begun years before. I entered into this endeavor primarily as a way to satisfy my burning need for deeper understanding about Life. I also realized at this time that I had a fervent desire to answer some call that I vaguely heard from a wee, still voice inside me. Although I had no idea what I was being called to do, I was driven by an intense sense of mission to do something, somewhere. I was both driven and inspired by the words of a song that I had sung in church that echoed in my heart, "Here I am Lord. Is it I, Lord? I have heard you calling in the night. I will go, Lord, if you lead me. I will hold your people in my heart." So, in 1987 I received my Master's in Social Work Degree and began a new profession as a psychotherapist, a profession that afforded me the opportunity to continue to search and grow spiritually while helping others to do the same. It also allowed me to respond to the burning call that had been reverberating in my soul. I was now living a life of service to others, answering the call to "hold God's people in my heart."

As I began to practice my profession of service to others, I came to feel that I was finally in sync with my spiritual purpose, that I was finally doing, at least in part, the work that my soul had come to earth to do. I was beginning to feel much fuller, much more energized and satisfied, but still no ecstasy. My physical symptoms were beginning to slowly diminish, as I had set the intention of healing my life, of finding that ecstasy that I had lost so many years before. I attempted anything and everything that came along, chiropractic, one diet after another, exercise, vitamin and herbal supplements, meditation, therapeutic massage. I attended one self-help workshop after another, and read every book in sight hoping that each one would hold the answer or provide me with the key that would unlock the door to healing. I went to every extreme, left no stones unturned, all in an effort to heal my ravaged and tired body.

The real opening came, I believe, when in 1988 I was confronted by the challenge of "curing an incurable illness." It was then that I began to let go of my attachments to many of the things of the physical world so that I could open more and more to the spiritual. I became less focused on the mundane, everyday, material aspects of life and more devoted to pursuing spiritual, non-physical goals. This happened when I made the commitment to do whatever it would take to bring healing into my life, to dedicate myself to becoming whole once more. I was sick and tired of feeling sick and tired and

I was determined that there was something that I could do to change that situation. Led by the guidance of Sky Hawk, I came to realize that the "something" that was needed was to be found more so in the spiritual realms than in the doctor's office or a bottle of pills.

It was at this time that my journey inward took on a new and more vigorous intensity. I began to take meditation a bit more seriously and made it an integral part of my daily routine. Feeling like I really didn't know how to meditate at first, I began to listen to guided imagery tapes and found it fairly easy to visualize and go into a state of visionary experience. Soon I realized that I didn't need external guidance, that I could simply "go off" somewhere all by myself. After all, hadn't I mastered that skill as a young girl? So my meditations began to evolve into what I call "visions," which I would describe as a form of passive, internally guided imagery, as distinguished from active or externally guided imagery. I learned that while in a meditative state, all I needed to do was still myself, remain open, and wait and "listen." Not all of the time, but sometimes I would be gifted with a visionary experience.

I am convinced that once I opened myself to Spirit in this way, the door opened, Spirit entered and my life began to change significantly. In reflecting upon this, I realize that it wasn't merely *having* the visions that changed my life. It was *paying attention* to them and the messages that they held, and subsequently living my life accordingly that did the trick. It was, in other words, when I let Spirit into my life and began listening and following its lead that things began to shift for me. Is this not, after all, the essence of the shamanic consciousness? Is this not the very same thing that the shaman does in performing his or her healing art? This was the turning point for me—opening to Spirit, listening to its message, and living my life by making decisions based more on this inner wisdom than on logical thinking.

This, however, was no easy task. Coming to the place of accepting, believing and validating my experience was what seemed, for a long time, an insurmountable feat. In the beginning, I was filled with doubt about what was happening to me. I found it difficult to believe that both my visionary experiences and the inner voice that I was hearing were not merely my own thoughts creating a fantasy, spinning an interesting yet unbelievable yarn. I struggled with an inner conflict. Part of me felt that my experiences were so real and wanted to believe without question, and another part of me protested loudly that it was all so silly, so illogical, and that I would be a fool to believe. This has been my challenge—bypassing the logical, critical, unbelieving self and accepting without doubt, criticism, qualification or censorship both what I have experienced and the information that I have been given. I needed to let go of the need to know with my logical mind that my experience was true or real. I needed to trust that my experience in the spiritual realms during a journey or meditation, whether "real" or not, was valid, significant and useful. Even if I were "only creating a fantasy" the experience still has merit. Once I accomplished this, I was able to listen to my intuition—my inner wisdom—and to follow the guidance and direction of my inner teachers, my Inner Shaman, without question or doubt. In so doing, I have opened myself to a whole new world, the world of Spirit, the world of healing within the shamanic consciousness.

After this occurred, things started to happen and healing entered my life. My life began to turn around, slowly, yes, but noticeably so all the same. Today headaches and low back pain are a rarity, and I seldom feel fatigued or de-energized, almost never taking a nap in the middle of the day. Blood tests have indicated that the autoimmune condition, although not totally gone, is largely under control. I have found a sense of inner peace and joy, and even though I am not completely symptom free, I feel happy to be alive. The days of being paralyzed by depression and anxiety are a thing of the past, and life has taken on a new and vibrant hue. I have recaptured the ecstasy that was once mine! I have reconnected to Spirit, and in so doing, have found the secret to health and wholeness. Although my life is not without its "ups and downs", sometimes with one major challenge after another presenting itself, I am always comforted by the confidence that, with the help of Spirit, I can face any challenges that come along. And I think that this, more than merely the absence of physical symptoms, is what healing is all about.

I believe that it was the search for ecstasy, that deep, intimate connection and union with Spirit, more than anything else that helped to propel me along on the road to healing. My journey into the world of Spirit has led me along the path to healing and wholeness. It has helped me to journey through the darkness of night into the light of a new day, awakening to a new life, a life marked by oneness, wholeness and healing.

## HEALING JOURNEY:
### Activities for Going Inward

JOURNAL EXERCISE: Assessing Your Spiritual Journey

Journal writing can be a powerful tool to help you to access your inner self and your true feelings. One of the techniques that I like to use is what I call "Rambling Writing," a form of free association in which you just let yourself ramble on and on. Simply write continuously—without lifting your pen or pencil from the paper—for a specified length of time (two or three minutes) about a particular issue or question. Just keep writing, even if you're merely writing, "I can't think of anything to write." Simply let the words flow without judging or censoring what comes out. It is helpful to use a timer.

Here are some questions for "Rambling Writing." Write the question on your paper, set the timer and begin writing. For each question, write two to three minutes without stopping. Then go onto the next question. After you've finished, read what you have written—you might be surprised at what you've learned about yourself. (If it appears that you have not written anything significant or said anything of any value, don't be discouraged. Trust that what you have written has value no matter what. Often when we revisit our journals weeks, months or even years later, those things that seemed meaningless when we wrote them make perfect sense in retrospect.)

1. Where are you now on your spiritual journey?

2. What was it like when you first entered the world of Spirit?

3. What is your level of commitment to following your spiritual path?

4. How do you want to grow spiritually, i.e., what are your spiritual goals?

5. What obstacles stand in your way to achieving your spiritual goals?

6. What do you need to do to get beyond these obstacles?


GUIDED MEDITATION: Meeting Your Inner Shaman

Following is a meditation or guided imagery that you can either read and do on your own, or record on an audio tape in your own voice and play it back. (After you have finished your meditation, remember to record your experience in your journal.)

Sit in a comfortable position with your eyes closed, preferably with your back straight and both feet on the floor.

Begin to pay attention to your breathing, finding a deep, slow and rhythmic pattern. With each breath in, imagine that you are drawing in relaxation, with each breath out, letting go of tension. You might see all of your cares, concerns, and matters of your everyday life turning into bubbles that softly float away out of sight. Breathing in peace and relaxation and breathing out tension and stress, you feel your body relax more and more as you continue to breath. You are going deeper and deeper into a state of perfect relaxation, so that your mind is empty and your thinking is clear. With each breath you take you are letting go more and more, going deeper and deeper into a state of peace and relaxation.

Imagine now that it is a beautiful, sunshiny summer day, early in the morning. You are out alone for a walk in the woods. You walk along a path that is familiar to you, allowing your senses to drink in all of the beauty that surrounds you. You feel the warmth of the gentle morning sun overhead as it peeks through the branches of the tall trees that surround you. You smell the scent of pine trees and hear the sound of the wind gently rustling the leaves as it moves through the woods. You take in the beauty of the wild flowers that dot your path and a colorful butterfly playing near them. You can feel your feet on the earth, cushioned by a padding of soft pine needles, as you move almost effortlessly through the forest.

As you continue to walk along the wooded path, you see a clearing ahead of you. You walk into the clearing and find yourself attracted to a small pond that you notice in the center of the clearing. The water in the pond is clear and clean, a brilliant shade of dark blue glistening in the morning sun. The light reflecting across the pond catches your eyes and invites you to gently close them. As you close your eyes you immediately get an image of someone, a person or being that you vaguely seem to recognize, but know for sure to be your Inner Shaman. You notice in detail what this being looks like. This being identifies itself to you and tells you why he or she has come. You spend some time alone with this being, your Inner Shaman, listening carefully to what he or she has to say, knowing that you will vividly recall your experience and any messages given to you. [Allow two to three minutes of clock time for this.]

Before your Inner Shaman leaves you he or she places a gift in your hands. Look down at what you are holding and notice what it is that you have been gifted with. Thanking your Inner Shaman for the gift and for coming, you say good-bye and make plans to meet again soon.

Slowly you begin to leave the clearing and find your way back along the wooded path that leads you through the woods. You return back to your normal waking state feeling renewed, refreshed and alert, and very grateful for the experience you have just had.


## RITUAL: Embodying Your Spiritual Goals

Ritual is another important tool for you to use. It is a way to integrate what is happening on the spiritual level with everyday life. It involves some form of symbolic acts or ceremony, which can be very simple or very elaborate. What is most important is your intention.

Now that you have clearly identified your goals and intentions for your spiritual journey, it is useful to embody them in physical form as a way to recognize and honor them as sacred. Here is a very simple ritual that will help you to do that.

Create an altar which is meant to honor your spiritual journey. If you already have an altar, rearrange or add to it so that you create a section that honors your spiritual journey. Here again, an altar can be as simple or elaborate as you want it to be. (I have a number of altars all around the house. They generally consist of candles, crystals/stones, things of nature like pine cones or dried flowers, figurines and any sacred objects that I am inspired to put on it. For example, on my desk, next to my computer where I do my writing I always have a lit candle, a picture of White Buffalo Woman, a crystal, a small fetish of White Buffalo, and my rosary beads. This is a small, simple altar.)

You can put anything on your altar that you choose, but be sure to include an item that represents each of your spiritual goals, and any other aspect of your spiritual journey that you would like to include. The item might be a crystal, a twig or a flower. What it is doesn't matter as long as it has symbolism and meaning to you. You might want to have a theme of some sort, such as an altar that includes only things of nature, or only different kinds of candles, or a collection of angel figurines. Let your creativity and imagination lead you. The important thing is to in some way embody your spiritual goals in physical form and honor them by creating a sacred space or altar on which to put them.

Then ritually lay each object on your altar, and as you do, make a commitment to work toward the goal which that particular object represents. You might light candles and play music, sing, dance or do whatever feels right as part of your ritual. Remember the ritual can be as simple or elaborate as you would like. What matters most is your intention.

# NEW DAY

I remember the days of old,
when life was dark and cold,
when nothing fit, nothing worked.
Those days are gone, gone forever.
Now I walk in the light of the sun,
I have entered into a new day, a new way.
Empowered, unshackled, unafraid.
I walk unashamed to be the self that I have come to be,
proud to stand with my head held high,
touched by life's challenges,
yet unscathed by the pain that comes my way,
knowing that it is I who makes the pain,
and it is I who saves the day.
I now know that I am more than I ever knew,
more, much more than meets the eye.
Creator of my destiny, maker of my day,
I can face the day without fear, as I now can find my way.

— M. S.

*April 27, 1995*

CHAPTER THREE

# The Acquisition of Power

*TO THE SHAMAN, power is a matter of opening to the gifts of the spirit world. It is, in other words, not a matter of personal power so much as the opening to the power of the other realms and allowing it to work through oneself. Power is generally believed to come through the attraction of the spirit of an animal, known as the power animal. The shaman views this animal or animals as its source of power in performing his or her healing art. It is the power animal that guides the shaman while on the journey into the other realms, and it is the power animal, in many instances, that teaches and instructs the shaman while there.*

*It is an ancient concept or belief that all power comes from within. This power that comes from within is ultimately of divine origin. It can be activated and added to through the use of certain objects, called power objects, or through calling on the power of the spirits of animals. Many shamanic traditions utilize the animal in this way to a great extent, while others, like Huna, use it minimally. What must be understood here, however, is that the belief is always that the power is of divine sourcing. It never originates from the object or the animal or the shaman. These are only channels or vehicles for the energy, or power, to move through. Once the power is moving, the shaman, through his or her training and expertise, has the ability to orchestrate its usage. He or she knows how to focus it and utilize it for maximum benefit, always for the good of the group, self, or individual. Anyone who calls him or herself a shaman who misuses power also misuses the identity of shaman, for a shaman is a healer motivated always by love, serving as a channel of divine energy to move through for the benefit of others, never for their detriment.*

Those who misuse power are more properly called "sorcerers," and they are not included in our discussion of shamans.

This notion of power seems somewhat paradoxical, as the shaman believes that power comes from the spirit world, while at the same time maintaining that all power comes from within. The concept of oneness with the greater circle accounts for this paradox, as there truly is no separation at this level between the individual and the spirit world. They are one and the same. The spirit of the animal becomes one with the spirit of the shaman and enables the shaman to do things that are ordinarily seen as being outside the realm of what is considered to be normal. It is the power animal that provides the connection between the two worlds; it is what enables the shaman to become the bridge between the two realities.

Within the shamanic world view, illness is believed to be caused by a loss of power at some level of being. It is the loss of power that allows one to succumb to illness or to be weak enough to allow an injury to occur. Disease is not about germs. It is about becoming weak or losing power. That is the basic cause of all illness. In other words, a person falls ill when he or she has lost his or her vital power to the extent that he or she becomes vulnerable to the microbes or the cancer cells or the accident, etc. The spirit, or vital energy, is drained or has leaked from the person to such an extent that a weakness occurs that allows the illness to take hold. In the shamanic world view this is called "soul loss." Soul loss occurs when a part of the person's vital energy or life force leaves the body in response to a trauma or other painful, scary or uncomfortable event. It is believed to go to another dimension, to non-ordinary reality, and to hide there so it does not have to deal with the traumatic situation. The soul part may return on its own or it may remain in non-ordinary reality until it is found and retrieved by a shaman in a process known as "soul retrieval."

Power is always an issue in any disease, and reclaiming one's power is central in shamanic practice. This brings us to the notion of responsibility. In the shamanic perspective each person is ultimately responsible for his or her state of health or dis-ease. Illness is viewed as a loss of personal power. If personal *power originates from the spirit world, then, when one is disconnected from Spirit by being out of harmony or balance in one way or another the individual is seen as being responsible for this and needs to make the appropriate changes.*

*It is most important to make clear, however, that when we speak of responsibility for our health and healing, we are not in any way inferring blame or fault. What we mean is that there is something that we did, thought or believed that has in one way or another attracted a certain situation to us. This may have originated on any of the four levels—physical, mental, emotional or spiritual—but it always has its connection to the spiritual. When one is out of sync with his or her spiritual purpose there is always an imbalance that occurs, as there is a lack of congruence between the actual situation and the intended one. Here is where responsibility comes in. We have the responsibility to learn what our true purpose on earth is and then to do our utmost to stay in tune with it, to harmonize and get in sync. We must learn to walk in balance and harmony with what we truly are. When we do not do this we lose power, give into dis-ease and become ill. But, when this happens, we are not innocent victims who have played no part or had no participation in creating this situation; we created it all by ourselves, however unaware or ignorant we were, but we created it all the same.*

*True healing will only occur when we realize this is the situation and accept the responsibility, and not blame it on a virus, or any other external factor, and then take appropriate steps to change what needs to be changed. This is what constitutes healing. It is about doing whatever it takes to undo the mess that we have created in our lives by not staying in tune with our spiritual, divine purpose. This is the core of the problem. Shamans have always known this, have always performed their healing craft through the window of this belief, focusing from this perspective. That is why they have always been successful. They do not employ magical means so much as common sense. They understand that life is very simple. We have a life purpose, and when we stray from that purpose we set up a state of conflict, imbalance, and disharmony, and then dis-ease of some sort appears. It is that simple. They do not need to know about all of the varieties of bacteria, virus and the like. To the shaman, disease is not about microbes. It is about being off your life course, out of sync with your life's plan, out of harmony with your true self.*

*When this is the case, a variety of negative feelings arise and enter into the picture. These contribute to the problem and help to strengthen its stronghold. But, always the main reason for illness is loss of power which occurs when you are giving away your power by not accepting responsibility for your life. That is what it all boils down to—accepting responsibility for your life. It is that simple. In order to do this, one must be in contact with Spirit, or at least with their inner selves. If this is not the case, then it is impossible for the healing to take place. I will repeat. Unless one is in tune with his or her inner, spiritual self, at some aware or unaware level, healing cannot take place. Many people are in touch, but they do not know it or call it by another name. But unless one is in touch with this essential spiritual self, healing cannot occur. That is why shamanism is conducive to healing—it encourages, supports, and facilitates connection to Spirit. That is the essence of healing—connection to Spirit. It is that simple.*

*If what I have just said is truly the case, then we are not innocent victims of illness. We are not innocent victims being zapped by bacteria, a virus or God, for that matter. Cancer is not the insidious monster that attacks us from the outside by surprise. More accurately, it is a wake-up call that tells us in no uncertain terms that we best take a good, hard look at how we are living our life or it may soon be over. It presents both a challenge and an opportunity to learn and to grow, but cancer, as all illness, is never random or without a purpose. We get exactly what we need to teach us what we need to learn.*

*The temptation to "blame the victim" is strong, but this is not at all what this is about. It is more about heeding the call to "get with the program." It is about becoming empowered, not about giving our power away by blaming. To be a victim is to give away power; to become empowered is to accept responsibility. This is the fine line that must be defined in the matter. Blaming ourselves for becoming ill is about as useful as holding our breath. All that it does is stop the flow of energy that is vitally needed at this time. It is a con-*

*striction or shutting down of sorts that can only lead to more complications, the most likely one being depression, commonly defined as anger turned toward the self. This is not what responsibility for self is about. It is merely accepting the fact that there is something out of line, something that is not working as well as it might that needs some minor fine-tuning. It is that simple. No judgment is necessary. We do not need to become the judge, jury and executioner in this situation. We just need to stand back and observe the situation from a place of wonder and curiosity without entering into the process of judging, and then do the work that needs to be done so that healing can occur.*

*It is here that responsibility for self becomes vitally important. It is here that one finds many who feel that they are totally powerless, feeling like helpless victims who have no resources or any other recourse but to sit and wait for someone or something outside of themselves to take over and rescue them. It is most important that people become aware that they and only they have the power to heal themselves. The same holds true for maintaining health or preventing illness. The power to do so is within the individual. The inner shaman can direct the person as to the course that should best be taken for his or her healing journey. Listening to one's own inner body wisdom is an essential element of healing. The inner shaman that exists within each person is the metaphorical link to accessing this inner wisdom. As it is the shaman's role to journey into other worlds to get information or wisdom, so it is the inner shaman who will find a way to access or activate the patient's inner wisdom so that healing may occur. It is vital to understand this. Healing must begin with a shift in awareness or consciousness. This is related to heeding what the inner shaman has to say so that the person will make changes in his or her life that will alleviate the reason that the illness occurred in the first place.*

*Virtually the same holds true for dis-ease in other areas of one's life, be it emotional, relationship, career, or financial areas. When a person fails to accept responsibility for having at some level, in some way, created whatever the situation is that exists, then he or she is powerless to change it. But when a person understands, without blaming or getting into self-judgment, that he* or she created the situation, then healing that situation is possible. Until this occurs the person is locked into the victim trap that promotes blame and passing the buck. Pointing the finger at God, your parents, your boss, your spouse, or whomever will not change the situation. It will merely keep you deeply entrenched in your victimhood. Accepting personal responsibility for creating it, however, will bring both the awareness and the understanding that will pave the way for change to occur.

When we fail to accept responsibility for our life situation, when we live our life caught in a victim belief system, we give away our power; we are powerless. Accepting responsibility for our life is what gives us the power to change it.

The whole notion of power, as I have said, is quite paradoxical. We must learn to relinquish our power at one level in order to acquire it at another. This means that attaining true power requires one to completely surrender and trust in Spirit, for as I have already said, power is opening up to the gifts of Spirit. As the shaman must surrender to the power of the power animal in order to be empowered by it, we must also let go of the fear that enshrouds the ego and move into the place of total surrender and trust that allows this to happen. This is when true empowerment can take place; this is when true healing can occur, for they are really one and the same. The awareness and activation of the principle of surrender and trust is an essential element for healing. Without this component, healing cannot take place because fear will still be present preventing that from happening. Surrender and trust demands the abandonment of fear, which keeps you locked in your cage of disharmony, dis-ease and illness. When this does occur, however, wonderful things can happen.

IN LOOKING BACK OVER MY LIFE, it is apparent that I was a top-notch victim right from the start, having learned very early on to respond to life with a blaming, "poor me" attitude. I think this is why I spent so much time in my room "day dreaming." I retreated inside of myself because for one reason or another I felt sorry for myself because someone (Mother, a teacher, my older sister, etc.) had done something "bad" to me. In some cases, I am sure this was an accurate account of what had transpired. It didn't take long, however, for me to make the decision that this is the way life is—people dump on you and then you get to blame them for their misdoing and feel sorry for yourself as well. And, I learned early on that playing the victim role and feeling sorry for myself was comforting and even somewhat pleasurable.

I also learned at a tender age that it was rewarding to be a victim, especially when being a victim involved getting sick. This was the only time that I could count on Mother being warm, loving and nurturing. When one of us kids was sick, she was the best mother anyone could ask for. She waited on us hand and foot, lovingly nursing us back to health, oftentimes even sitting on the bed with her rosary beads in hand. The best thing about being sick, however, was that Mom never got angry with me; she never yelled, or even slightly raised her voice. She was as patient and nurturing as a mother could be. My sister and brother and I were all quite good at finding ways to be sick. After all, there was a pretty hefty reward for being victimized by those nasty microbes—Mother's undying love and attention for as long as the symptoms persisted.

My upbringing in the Catholic religion also supported my development as a victim. The Church in those days taught that suffering was desirable and even necessary for the repentance of sins. This went a long way in promoting the establishment of what I call the "victim-martyr syndrome," which I learned to fully embrace. Martyrs, after all, had to suffer unthinkable pain and death, but they were rewarded by eternal glory in heaven and canonization into the realm of sainthood—a true reward for their victimization I should think. I was taught that to deprive myself and indulge in some form of self-punishment (although it was not ever termed that exactly), especially during the Lenten season, was desirable and pleasing to God, whose own son through his suffering and death on the cross was quite the quintessential victim himself. In actuality, this victimization of Jesus was the cornerstone upon which all of Christianity was founded. So, my young mind reasoned, there must have been something quite substantial to this victim thing.

The Church routinely categorized everything as either "good" or "bad," creating a judgmental belief system that supported this duality and its companion, blaming. This also went a long way in providing a foundation upon which to build a world view that maintained that being a victim was exactly what God wanted of us. The "good" ones were usually the victims and the "bad" ones were the ones who victimized the victims. Taking the whole religion thing very seriously, I was determined to do what God wanted, no matter what the cost. And, thinking the only way to be "good" was to be a victim, I played the victim role out to its fullest. This naturally meant that in order to be "good" I also had to be "right." Allowing myself to be "wrong" or to make a mistake was unthinkable. That's where the blaming and the unwillingness to own or accept responsibility for just about anything came into the picture. For me, playing the victim role meant that I had to always be "good" *and* "right"; accomplishing that magnificent feat usually required blaming someone or something outside of myself for whatever I may have done that didn't work for me. When following this line of thinking, it becomes quite impossible to ever admit to self or anyone else any form of wrongdoing; apologizing is something that is absolutely out of the question. I was trapped in a self-made victim role, unable to take responsibility for myself and armed with only a finger pointed at something or someone else to help me through life. I became very good at this blame-game, at this victim role. I got to blame others, feel sorry for myself and elicit the sympathy (and, if I got really lucky, perhaps even the "love") of others. However, the price I paid for always blaming something external for all of my woes and never owning responsibility for my life, was continually giving away my power.

This was dramatically evident in the early years of my marriage, or, more accurately, the first twenty years. I was firmly entrenched in the victim pattern of thinking and responding to the world. By the time I got married at age twenty, I played the victim role enthusiastically within my marital relationship. Of course, in order to be a victim you need a victimizer. So my husband, Tom, and I quickly developed an unconscious myth and the accompanying behavior pattern based on the notion that I was the "good" one and he was the "bad" one. I was the victim and he was the persecutor. We unwittingly played this out to the extreme. The more "bad" things he did, the better I looked and the more I got to blame him for all of my, and our, problems. Of course, he did his share of blaming as well. We did this dance of the "good guy vs. the bad guy" quite well together, constantly blaming each other for our troubles, with neither of us ever assuming responsibility for the problems that plagued our marriage.

We played this good guy/bad guy dynamic out so fully, that one Halloween early in our marriage, we embodied it in our party costumes. Tom dressed as a red devil, complete with goatee, horns, tail and pitchfork, and I was attired as an angel, dressed in lily white, accented with a golden halo and gossamer wings. We won the prize at the party for the best couple costumes. If the other partygoers only knew that these get-ups were not costumes at all—they were true manifestations of this aspect of our relationship dynamic.

Playing my role in this dynamic provided an excellent excuse for me to maintain my strong need to always be "right." Within this interactional pattern, it became impossible for me to ever own a mistake, and I virtually never apologized for anything. After all, he was the identified "bad guy" and I was the identified "good guy." Tom was the one who always needed to apologize, not good little ole me. I was not about to shift roles either. It would create too much confusion. Anyway, I loved being the "good" one. I didn't have to accept responsibility for anything, and I got to whine and cry a lot too.

So we went along like this for twenty years. I was terribly unhappy, and reflecting on the number of times that my husband threatened to divorce me during those years, I would venture to say that he wasn't too happy either. I felt victimized, completely powerless and hopelessly trapped, terrified that he would leave me, yet miserable in the relationship. In true victim style, I held onto anger about everything that Tom ever did that I had judged to be bad or wrong in the past twenty years, allowing an immense well of resentment to develop. I was filled with anger and resentment, and the longer I stayed within the victim belief system that I created, the harder it was to let it go. Letting it go would mean that he wasn't so bad or wrong after all. I was trapped in my victim system, unable to do anything but blame him. I felt as if there were nothing I could do to improve things so I pointed my finger at him and waited for him to change. I certainly didn't need to change because I was the innocent victim. I pointed my finger at him for twenty years, and for twenty years this behavior was completely ineffective in creating the happiness that I yearned for in my life and my marriage.

Almost a year after getting my master's degree and moving into a new home, the stress in our twenty-year marriage reached a crisis stage. One evening in the winter of 1987, following a loud and hurtful argument, I recall giving my husband an ultimatum: "Either we get a therapist or a lawyer!" He agreed, although reluctantly, to go for marital therapy. It turned out to be the best decision we ever made.

It was during the course of therapy over the next nine months that I began to awaken to the possibility that maybe the victim role that I had played since childhood needed to be reevaluated, and perhaps even changed. Although our therapist had the tendency to annoy and aggravate me, ruffling my feathers, you might say, (and I think I had the same effect on him), he helped me to do just that. I can't remember any brilliant things that that man said or did, but I do remember that his main tactic was not allowing us to blame each other. It was that simple. He kept us from blaming each other and, in so doing, forced us to look at our own responsibility in creating the mess that was our marriage. I was totally frustrated by this approach, since blaming was my only mode of operation; I knew no other way. But, in the course of treatment, as frustrating and unsettling as it was, I was able to move from the place of a victim into the place of an empowered person with, I may add, more than a few ruffled feathers to show for my efforts.

I will never forget one particular session in our therapist's small and brutally untidy office that, I believe, was the turning point for me. I had received my Master's Degree in Social Work several months prior and thought that I knew it all. I understood all of the "system's theory" that was taught in social work graduate school, and that the two partners in a marriage do a dance together, each one contributing to the situation. I had that all down pat, at least on an intellectual level. But that particular evening, as I continued to indulge in the blame game, the therapist badgered me and badgered me, telling me that he knew I was much smarter than I was indicating at the time. Then, all of a sudden, came one of those wondrous moments of awakening, of receiving an insight in the grand "AH HA!" manner. I realized at that moment, at a profoundly deep place within myself, what all that mumbo jumbo I had learned in marital treatment class meant. Something deep inside clicked, and I finally got it! It finally occurred to me that I had participated in creating our situation, and that didn't necessarily implicate me as a "bad guy," (for to accept myself as a "bad guy" at that time would still have been a stretch) but simply as a "participant." Furthermore, I realized it did no good to blame either myself or Tom, but rather to simply pick up the pieces and move on, together creating a way that worked better for both of us.

It was a moment in which I felt a rush of power, for if I had helped to create the situation then maybe there was something I could do to change it. It was also a moment of release, of freedom, of awakening. Wow! What a new way of looking at things! Could it really be true? Could I finally undo the victim shackles that had bound me since childhood? Could I finally allow myself to make a mistake and give up the unrelenting need to always be "good" and "right?" Could I grow to become responsible for my actions, for my participation in the relationship, without judging myself as "bad" or "wrong," and could I maybe even learn to apologize if or when that was appropriate? Could I stop blaming my husband for my unhappiness and accept responsibility for creating my own happiness?

Yes, yes, yes! I was finally able to do all of those things, and so much more. As each day passed, my relationship with my husband improved dramatically. We moved along on a path of healing our relationship, as we both began to stop engaging in the blame game and accepting personal responsibility. I learned that it was all right to make a mistake, that I didn't always need to be perfect. As I gave that gift to myself, I found that it was also much easier to give Tom a break and to not expect him to be perfect all the time either.

It was shortly after ending marital therapy, early in 1988, that I happened upon a book, which completely supported this new world view, and helped to move me further along on the path to empowerment. The book was *You Can Heal Your Life*, written by Louise Hay.[1] In the book, the author makes the most outrageous statements, saying things like "The point of power is always in the present moment," "The thoughts we think and the words we speak create our experiences," and "We are 100% responsible for everything in our lives." She also pointed out the importance of the words that we use, that our vocabulary helps to create our reality. One of the words she said needed to be totally eliminated is "should." Using this word sets us up to be "bad" if we don't do what we "should" do. This whole line of thinking went a long way to support my budding new perspective,

66

one that propelled me out of the helpless, impotent victim role into becoming a self-responsible, empowered human being!

How did this new way of viewing the world, from the eyes of an empowered person instead of from those of a victim, translate into changing my life, into healing my life? In pondering this question, my initial response is that shifting from the limiting consciousness of a victim to the expanded consciousness of a self-responsible, empowered person gave me a sense of freedom that I had never experienced before. I was no longer caught in the victim trap, and I was now free to make other choices that reflected my expanded vision of the world—a world in which at some level and in some way, I created my own reality. I felt that I was no longer a reed being tossed around by the wind; I had become the wind. Or, to use another metaphor, I was now in the driver's seat, in complete control of my vehicle. I felt a sense of power and control that was alien to me, a feeling that was very strange and new, but one that I quickly came to resonate with. I was now playing by a new set of rules that went along with the new consciousness that I had moved into, a set of rules that emphasized that I always had a choice and that my power was to be experienced by making my choices. The choices that I now made were reflections of this new awareness, this new consciousness that held that there are absolutely no victims and no need to blame. Because we create our own life situation, in one way or another, we have the power to make the necessary changes in our lives.

This new consciousness allowed me to not always be perfect, to make mistakes, to let go of anger and resentment, to forgive myself and others, and to suspend my judgment of myself and others. In so doing, I was able to cease the endless blaming that was the first and foremost rule of the victim consciousness that I had subscribed to for so long. The result was that I began to feel so much better about myself. My self-esteem and self-love both began to grow, day by day. I was truly coming into my power, a phenomenon that I found to be exciting and exhilarating on the one hand, and just a bit scary on the other, for it meant that, ultimately, I was responsible for my life. I could no longer blame anyone or anything external to myself for my life's situation.

The nine months Tom and I spent in marital therapy brought the notion of responsibility for self to my conscious awareness, but the transition from the helpless victim to an empowered person had gradually been taking place at a more unaware level prior to entering marital therapy. I had already begun to enter into this consciousness of freedom and self-responsibility, as evidenced by the fact that I had taken the major step of leaving the Catholic Church just about two years earlier. After years of personal inner turmoil over what the Church's role would be in my life, I had come to the realization that when it came to matters of my personal "salvation", it was really up to me to find my way. No one, not Church, priest or God was going to do that for me. As a matter of fact, when I left the Church I threw away the entire notion of "salvation" and replaced it with the notion of a journey home. I needed to find my way home with, of course, some assistance and guidance from Spirit. This, however, involved assuming personal responsibility for listening to Spirit, that small voice within my heart, and following its bidding. This was quite different from my old pattern of relinquishing all responsibility for finding my way by doing exactly what I was told—by allowing my life's course to be determined by a person or institution external to myself. I would no longer live my life by adhering to a dogma of beliefs prescribed by the Catholic Church that spelled out the one and only way to get to heaven. Neither would I exclusively follow the "word of God" written only in the Bible, not within my heart. This would be a quite different approach; it would require a whole new way of navigating life. It took a lot of courage to make that break, to venture into an uncharted territory with only my inner voice as my guide. Although unaware of Inner Shaman as such at the time I left the Church, isn't that what the whole notion of Inner Shaman is truly about? Doesn't Inner Shaman teach that life is essentially a journey home, a journey of healing and wholing, a journey of reconnection with our spiritual selves, a journey into oneness? I would have to answer this one in the affirmative.

And how did entering into this newfound consciousness of self-responsibility and empowerment, this consciousness intrinsic to the shamanic world view, play itself out in the healing of my physical problems? Perhaps the single most important aspect of this facet of my life is that when I was diagnosed with the "incurable" auto immune disease shortly after completing marital therapy, I did not experience the situation from that of a powerless victim. In the past, I would have responded by feeling sorry for myself, by blaming, and by looking for the "cure" to come from some external source. Instead, I accepted full responsibility for my own healing and, feeling a sense of power, I courageously embarked on my healing journey, a journey that has taken me a long way along the path to wholeness. Here, of course, is where the guidance of my inner voice, my connection to the world of Spirit has led the way. But, letting go of the structure and security of the old, familiar, external guidance of the Church, the Bible, or anyone I saw as "the authority" was still a little scary. Listening exclusively to the inner voice and the guidance it provides takes a good measure of courage, letting go of the fear of "making a mistake," or "not being right" in the eyes of others.

Here is where the paradox that Inner Shaman speaks of comes into play. Here is where on the one hand I felt like I was now in control, but on the other hand that I needed to learn to let go of my need to control. The difference being that my ego, or "my little local self," as Jean Houston would say, needed to move aside and let the "captain of the ship," my higher self, take over. For me, the one who was so firmly rooted in the need to be "right" so as not to be judged bad or wrong by others, this required a good deal of letting go—letting go of fear. I was told repeatedly by my inner voice that I needed to "surrender and trust" in order to let go of the fear. Surrender and trust, I was told, was an indication of higher spiritual development and was that not my goal? In order to come fully into my power I needed to surrender and trust. In order to completely realize my full potential, I needed to relinquish the need to control at the level of conscious ego and allow the other-than-conscious, grander part of myself to lead the way. I was told that at this level I would find true, authentic power, not merely the illusion of power. Wow, what a paradox indeed! What a challenge!

I went through a number of years in which facing and letting go of my fears was a prominent issue in my life. The Universe, however, did not give up on me and provided me with one opportunity after another to face and transcend my fears and move into a higher place, a place where I gradually became more comfortable with the idea of "surrender and trust."

I recall one vision that came to me during a time of extreme personal challenge that helped to drive this message home. Sky Hawk led me down to the river and told me to get into the canoe that was sitting on the shore. I got in and sat at one end of the canoe. I was very carefully covered with a warm and cozy buffalo skin and made to feel quite safe and comfortable. Bear joined me and took a seat at the opposite end of the canoe. The two of us were then pushed off into the river, floating downstream, *without any paddles!* We were set adrift without any way of steering or controlling the canoe. We were at the mercy of the water. I was told that I needed to learn to stop fighting, to surrender and trust that the water would take me exactly where I need to go. I got the message! That image has been with me ever since.

Perhaps my most memorable story relating to the notion of surrender and trust, however, occurred during the summer of 1994. While visiting Sedona in late May, I had been guided in a meditation to attend Brooke Medicine Eagle's Deepening of Spirit Camp, an event that involved sleeping in a tent for two weeks and included a two-day solo vision quest in the wilderness of Montana. I had read Brooke's book, *Buffalo Woman Comes Singing*, in which she describes what took place at Spirit Camp about two years before. I absolutely loved the book and what Brooke had to say resonated strongly with me. When I finished it, I made a firm commitment to someday attend this camp. I (at least my little local self) hadn't planned on attending that particular year, but it seemed that Spirit and my higher self had other plans for me—"someday" had arrived. This was going to be a real stretch for someone who had camped only one night in her entire life. But, by that time I had learned to listen to what Spirit was telling me and to follow its lead. I was already practicing this surrender and trust thing, at least to some degree. So in mid-June I registered for the camp, which was to begin the first week in August, giving myself just about six weeks to prepare.

The first thing that cropped up when I sent my registration and non-refundable deposit off in the mail was *fear*, big-time fear, the likes of which I can't remember ever having faced. Some of this fear, or perhaps even all of it, was quite justified. After all, I was leaving the security of my home. I was venturing out on my own, to a place I'd never been before. I would be engaging in activities I never had done before and spending two days alone in the wilderness with no food, tent or any other of life's amenities. If that were not enough, I would be completely alone in the very same place that bears, cougars and mountain lions call home! I quickly became obsessed with the idea of meeting one of these creatures face to face—alone, in the middle of the night. This whole thing was a stretch for me, as it would undoubtedly be for most people. So I gave myself a break—my fear was reasonable, but how to get beyond it was the question at hand.

One of the things I did to prepare myself for the trip was to read some of the books on the reading list that Brooke had provided. One of the books that caught my attention was *The Seat of the Soul*, by Gary Zukav, a book that had been sitting, unread on my bookshelf for at least a year or two, just waiting for the right moment to be read. That moment had arrived. I had long believed that the Universe provides us with what we need, when we need it, and reading this book at this time was just what I needed.

Zukav's message of what it means to become spiritually mature struck a chord within my soul, and addressed the issues I was currently dealing with—power, fear, surrender and trust. His main thesis was that we, as a species, are evolving and moving away from pursuing external power, power that is based on the perceptions of the five senses. We are instead evolving into a species that pursues authentic power, a power that is based upon the values and perceptions of the spirit. This idea spoke to me. His presentation was very simple, yet deeply profound. He made simple statements, but statements that were loaded with powerful truths. As I read the book I found that I could not read more than a paragraph at a time without stopping to ponder and digest what he had written. He made statements that felt as if they had been written just for me to read at that moment in time: "Authentic empowerment is not gained by making choices that do not stretch you." "Behind fear is powerlessness." "You lose power whenever you fear. That is what a loss of power is." "Challenge your fears."

Zukav was speaking directly to my frightened ego self, saying precisely what it needed to hear and encouraging it to move fully into that place of surrender and trust. Perhaps the statement that resounded the most dramatically for me was this:

> Try looking at life as a beautifully well-organized dynamic. Trust the Universe. Trusting means that the circumstance that you are in is working toward your best and most appropriate end. There is no when to that. There is no if to that. It is. Release your specifications and say to the Universe: "Find me where you know I need to be." Let them go and trust that the Universe will provide, and so it shall. Let go of all. Let your higher self complete its task.[2]

Is this not exactly what I needed to do—let go of my fear, surrender to the Universe and my higher self, and trust that all would work to

my highest good? In order to calm my frightened ego self, I interpreted this to mean that I would NOT be eaten by a bear or a
mountain lion. That, I reasoned, would not serve my highest good—
not at all. So I was able to move beyond the fear of being eaten alive
in the wilderness and began to feel some measure of calm.

In those last few weeks before going off to camp, Spirit was also giving me all of the support that it possibly could to assist me in
transcending my fears and experiencing the fullness of my power by
surrendering and trusting. One morning in late June, I sat down to
meditate and soon found myself in the middle of a full-blown vision,
one of those prized gifts from Spirit that come when I least expect
them.

In my vision I was leisurely walking through the forest with Sky
Hawk. (By this time, five years after first having met The Shaman,
Sky Hawk, Bear and Wolf were regular visitors to my visionary experiences.) It was a glorious day, with the sun shining brightly
overhead, and it seemed that I had not a care in the world. We were
following Wolf, who was doing a superb job of navigating through
the thick woods. Suddenly, Wolf just stopped and sat down, at which
point Sky Hawk looked at me and told me quite unequivocally to
take off my clothes. I looked back at him in surprise and responded,
"Excuse me, I don't want to take off my clothes." Sky Hawk, persisted, insisting that I needed to take off my clothes; I persisted in
resisting the whole idea. We bickered back and forth for a while
until I finally made a deal with Sky Hawk that I would take my
clothes off only if he would take his off as well. He agreed and we
both disrobed. I laid my clothes on the ground next to Wolf and
stood looking at Sky Hawk with a "so now what?" look in my eyes. Sky
Hawk said, "Now go!" I looked at him incredulously, and responded,
"Go where?" He said, "Just go!" We went back and forth, once again,
with me not at all understanding why I needed to do this ridiculous
thing that he was asking of me and very strongly resisting. I finally
gave in and said, "But where will I go?" Sky Hawk looked at me with

wisdom in his eyes and responded quite simply, "You will know when you get there."

And so I reluctantly set off on my own, naked, into the forest having no path to follow, no one to lead me, not having the faintest idea as to why I needed to go, and feeling quite fearful and very angry about having to do so. As I walked along, my internal dialogue went something like this: "Why do I need to do this? I don't understand. Who does he think he is to send me off like this, alone, with no clothes, and no guide. Where is Bear? I never go anywhere without Bear. This doesn't make any sense. He wants me to go somewhere, but he doesn't tell me where or how to get there and he expects me to just comply without a question. Well, this makes me furious!" The inner dialogue went on like this for a while as I struggled to find my way through the woods. Then finally, I said to myself: "Just stop fighting it and go with it. Stop judging and scaring yourself and just see what happens. Trust that Sky Hawk knows best. He has never led you astray before."

At that very moment of surrender, at the moment that I let go of my fear, anger and confusion, my need to be in control, my need to make sense out of it all, I saw before me what looked like a searchlight. It seemed to be lighting a path before me; I decided to follow it. The pillar of light led me up and around. Spiraling up and up, I slowly made my way up the side of a mountain. As I approached the top, I noticed that the pillar of light was beginning to change form; it was shifting into a spiral of light. When I reached the top, Bear was sitting there, waiting for me. I felt so comforted knowing that he was near and that I was no longer alone. Then, I noticed that the spiral of light was shifting once again. The light was swirling and swirling, appearing to be doing some kind of a dance and, as it danced, it was taking on a shape or form. I watched intently as the light finally took form. At first glance, it looked like it was an animal, a white lamb. As I looked at the lamb, I heard a voice that said, "It's not a lamb; it's a white buffalo calf." I stood there, somewhat dazed, watching as the white buffalo calf looked back at me, gazing deeply into my eyes. I felt such incredible love and wisdom emanating from those eyes, which seemed to see deep into my soul.

As the white buffalo calf and I gazed at each other, I noticed that it was now beginning to shape-shift once again. Soon I saw standing before me a beautiful Indian woman dressed all in white. I knew that this was White Buffalo Calf Woman, the legendary figure who brought the sacred pipe to the Lakota peoples long, long ago, the White Buffalo Woman that Brooke Medicine Eagle writes about. I stood in amazement, feeling a rush of excitement that she would honor me with her visit. She told me to lie face down on the ground, and as I did, she began to speak to me. She told me all that I needed to know to help me to prepare for my vision quest. In so doing, she gifted me with untold peace and calmness.

When she had finished speaking, she quickly shape-shifted once again into the swirling spiral of light, which soon faded away. I followed Bear down the mountain where Sky Hawk and Wolf were waiting for me—right where I had left them. I put my clothes back on and Sky Hawk gave me a big hug and a smile that said more than any words possibly could.

That experience was the first time that White Buffalo and White Buffalo Woman came to me in vision. They both have been coming to me on a regular basis ever since, continuing to gift me and empower me. When I finally embarked on my wilderness adventure in Montana several weeks later, I left with a strong sense of faith and trust that the Universe would take care of me. I was given more than a few opportunities during that time to practice surrender and trust. In so doing, I opened myself to receive the incredible gifts that came to me during those two weeks. The actual two days of the vision quest were most challenging, but White Buffalo Woman came to me repeatedly and helped me to get through the difficult times. On August 20th, two days after returning home from Spirit Camp, Miracle, a white buffalo calf, was born in Janesville, Wisconsin. Her birth, viewed by Native Americans as the fulfillment of an ancient prophecy heralding a time of peace and unity among all peoples, was well publicized. When I saw her on TV for the first time, tears began to roll down my face as she looked like a lamb to me, exactly as the white buffalo calf that I had seen in my vision six weeks earlier had looked. At that moment, I felt so blessed, so connected to Spirit.

The message of the vision was quite clear. It was, of course, a wonderful metaphor for life's journey, for my journey. It pointed out to me the importance of letting go of my reluctance and resistance to listening to Spirit and following its lead. I clearly saw that when I was able to trust Spirit enough to completely surrender to it, my path was illuminated and wonderful things happened. Inner Shaman points out that "power is opening to the gifts of the spirit world." As a result of letting go and trusting, I was able to open to the gifts of the spirit world and to make the connection with Spirit that I needed to heal an aspect of my life at that time. After this experience, my fear and apprehension about going on my vision quest melted away. This is the essence of healing, attests Inner Shaman—connection with Spirit. This vision has taught me, that it is only possible when I surrender and trust. I have since worked very diligently to heed the message of this vision and to remember to surrender and trust in Spirit, in the Universe, in my higher self. Since that time, when times get difficult and challenges come my way, I remind myself of this vision and somehow find the courage to keep going, knowing that once I surrender and trust in Spirit my path will be illuminated, and healing will follow.

# HEALING JOURNEY:
## Activities for Going Inward

JOURNAL EXERCISE: My Relationship to Power

Using the "Rambling Writing" method, write in your journal in response to the following questions:

1. In what ways do I lose power?

2. How do I give away my power?

3. How do I feel about owning my power?

4. What role does fear play in my relationship to my power?

5. How can I reclaim my power?

GUIDED MEDITATION: Surrender and Trust

You are leisurely walking through the forest with your inner teacher, your Inner Shaman. It is a glorious day, with the sun shining brightly overhead, and it seems that you have not a care in the world. Suddenly, your teacher just stops walking and sits down, and instructs you to take off your clothes. You begin to strongly resist these instructions, complaining that you don't want to take off your clothes. Your teacher insists that you must do as he or she says. You bicker back and forth for a while until you finally give in and decide to follow your teacher's instructions and you disrobe. Then, looking at your teacher wondering what this is all about, you hear him or her say, "Now go!" "Go where?" you ask, to which your teacher responds, "Just go!" Once again, you strongly resist not at all understanding why you need to do this ridiculous thing that is being asked of you. You finally give in and say, "But where will I go?" Your teacher looks at you with wisdom in his or her eyes and responds quite simply, "You will know when you get there."

And so you reluctantly set out on your own, naked, into the forest having no path to follow, no one to lead you, nor the faintest idea as to why you need to go, and feeling fearful and angry about having to complete this task. As you walk along, your internal dialogue sounds something like this: "Why do I need to do this? I don't understand. Who does he think he is to send me off like this, alone, with no clothes and no guide. This doesn't make any sense. He wants me to go somewhere, but doesn't tell me where or how to get there and he expects me to just comply without a question. Well, this makes me furious! It also feels very scary." Your inner dialogue goes on like this for a while as you struggle to find your way through the woods. Then finally, you say to yourself, "Just stop fighting it and go with it. Stop judging and scaring yourself and just see what happens. Trust that your teacher knows best. She has never led you astray before."

At that very moment of surrender, at the moment that you let go of your fear, anger and confusion, your need to be in control, your need to make sense out of it all, you see before you what looks like a searchlight. It seems to be lighting a path before you, and so you decide to follow it. The pillar of light leads you up and around. Spiraling up and up, you slowly make your way up the side of a mountain. As you approach the top, you notice that the pillar of light is beginning to change form; it is shifting into a spiral of light. When you finally reach the top, you notice that the spiral of light is shifting once again. The light is swirling and swirling, appearing to be doing some kind of a dance and, as it dances, it takes on a shape or form. You watch intently as the light finally takes on a form, and, at this moment, you are gifted with a healing vision from Spirit, an experience in which you are told or shown all that you need to know to assist you in restoring power in your life. You listen closely and watch intently as the vision unfolds. [Allow two or three minutes of clock time for this experience.]

Now, recalling the information that you have been given in this healing vision, you follow the same path down the mountain and meet up with your teacher who is waiting for you right where you had left him or her. You put your clothes back on and your teacher gives you a big hug and a smile that says more than any words possibly could.

And now, recalling all that you have experienced and all that you learned, you slowly come back to the present moment and place. You return to your normal, waking consciousness feeling alert, renewed, and revitalized.

RITUAL: Letting Go of the Victim Consciousness

In your journal or on a piece of paper, make a list of all of the ways that you have been, and still are, a victim. Note the times when you don't accept responsibility for your life, when you blame things outside of yourself for your experiences, and when you get into "whining and crying" about your life rather than doing something about it.

You might start the list by writing: "I AM A VICTIM WHEN I:" and then itemize the different ways you get into being a victim. Your list might look something like this:

I am a victim when I:

• blame my husband for my unhappiness.

• hold my parents responsible for "making me the way I am."

• complain about "my lot in life" but do nothing to change it.

• blame the kids for my headaches.

• spend all of my time taking care of others and then complain I have no time for myself.

• blame God for giving me a big nose.

• etc., etc.

Now, it's time to do some housecleaning, letting go of these victim patterns that no longer serve you. Searching through your house, garage, basement, closets, cabinets and drawers, find a material item that represents or symbolizes each item on your list, and discard it. That's right, throw it away, toss it, let it go. As you put each of your material items in the trash or a bag headed for Goodwill, set an intention of letting go of your victim thinking, behaviors and feelings. Affirm to yourself as you let go of each material item that represents a victim aspect of yourself:

I let go of the need to be a victim!
I reclaim and own my power!
I accept full responsibility for my life!

And, then begin to live this new consciousness each day, and see how much lighter you feel!

# SONG OF HEALING

Oh, Mother, I sing to you.
My heart hears your cry of pain.
I know no other way to answer,
but with the beating of my drum.
As I play my drum to ease your pain,
our hearts become as one.
Together we call to Great Spirit
to bless our song of love.
Beater in hand I play your song;
I beat the beat of love.
I feel the sound of our heart's duet
as the song resounds within.
I sing a song of healing,
for you, Sweet Mother, and for me.
I ask forgiveness for my part in the wounding,
and I hear you call my name.
Oh, Mother, I hear you call.
My heart cries out with yours.
I know no other way to comfort you
than with the sounding of my drum.

— M. S.

*May 1, 1995*

## CHAPTER FOUR

# Creating Balance and Harmony

*THE NOTION OF BALANCE in the shamanic perspective has to do with being in a state of right relationship to yourself, your natural environment, other people and the spirit world. What right relationship means is that there is an equal exchange of energy. The energy is not moving in one direction only, but is freely moving back and forth. It occurs on the micro and the macro levels, from the cellular level to the planetary level. All life is dependent on this free flowing exchange of energy. When there is an imbalance of this energy exchange, then problems or dis-ease can occur. The most obvious example of this is how human beings have shifted the energy exchange with mother earth to be almost totally one-sided by taking, taking, taking and almost never giving back. This has caused a grave imbalance, the effects of which you are now beginning to feel in the way of strange weather patterns, severe storms, and upheavals in the form of earthquakes and volcanoes virtually all across the planet.*

*Since your bodies are microcosms of the macrocosm, the same things are happening within each of you. This is happening at the personal level, both individually and collectively. And so the imbalances that you have created in the earth mother are the same within you. The fast-paced lifestyles, with fast food as king and the resultant poor nutrition, along with the lack of proper exercise, are taking their toll in the health of your people. You are seeing more and more illnesses like cancer and AIDS that were not known to your species several hundred years ago. These are the dis-eases of imbalance. You as a people have created them, and a host of others, by not living in right relationship with all that you are in relationship with, and that means that you can reverse this by coming into right relationship. This is what coming into balance means.*

*Right relationship also includes the notion of harmony, of two or more things existing together in the absence of conflict, in a state of peace and tranquillity. Harmony means that things are functioning smoothly, in a state of synchrony and congruence that creates a pleasant effect, an agreeable energy. The world of nature is a perfect example of harmony. All of the creatures of the wild know how to live harmoniously with each other and with their environment. Similarly, indigenous peoples have also traditionally managed to harmonize with nature, knowing instinctively that respect and reciprocity were elements of harmonizing with the natural world. Unfortunately, modern society has, for the most part, lost this reverence for nature and has developed a lifestyle that is not at all in harmony with the Earth Mother. Humans have instead chosen to disrespect, discount, and dishonor her, maintaining an attitude of dominance and control over her rather than one of co-operation and mutuality. Humans have forgotten that they are part of the earth, that the earth is their mother. Humans are, after all, the only species that can be so disharmonious that they engage in warfare or destroy the natural environment.*

*The notion of harmony, when taken to the individual level, is also related to the matter of finding a way to exist without conflict, in a state of peace and tranquillity with self, others, nature and spirit. The shamanic perspective maintains that the absence of balance and harmony in one's life, then, contributes to the loss of power, and thus helps to create dis-ease, as it tends to block the flow of energy. Restoring balance and harmony to one's life is seen as a key to healing.*

*As you know, there are four levels of being in which you as humans exist: the physical, mental, emotional and spiritual. There are also other imbalances that grow out of your society's value system, one that places the mental and physical aspects of your being at the top of the priority list and almost totally ignores the emotional and spiritual aspects. This creates an imbalance that is also affecting you on individual, collective and planetary levels.*

*Getting back into a state of balance and harmony at this level requires grounding and centering in the core of one's essence. This involves a deep connection to spirit, to the divine essence within. There is really no separation, but when one is under the illusion that they are separate or cut off from the divine source then this may result in dis-ease. Being connected to the spiritual part, the divine part of self, is at the heart of the matter. If one wants to heal on all levels of being, this is essential. The truth of the matter is that this is where all dis-ease originates. It comes from a disconnection from self, from the source, from the divine, from our own essence. (This is the loss of power that we have previously referred to.) When we find a way to reconnect, the dis-ease is healed.*

*You see, the imbalance comes because the flow of energy from the source to the self is somehow blocked. This creates a back up of sorts and, thus, the imbalance. When the energy is allowed to flow freely, balance is once again restored. It is as if one had two balloons attached with a tube. The desired state is for both balloons to be equally full, with a free exchange of air between the two. If the tube becomes blocked, however, one balloon fills up with more air than the other and an imbalance is created. The secret is in keeping the tube open so the air can move freely from one to the other. There must be, in other words, an exchange of energy from lower self to higher self, and from entity to source, or there will be an imbalance and dis-ease will follow. There must be a lifeline to supply the power source. This is the essence of what the shamanic consciousness teaches us; the shaman knows how to bridge the gap from the physical to the spiritual. Of course, bridging this gap by bringing the spiritual aspect back into the picture is what I have been talking about all along, and it is what the whole notion of the Inner Shaman encompasses.*

*When we speak of balance, it is almost impossible to discuss it in individual terms only, for it is not merely an individual affair. You exist in a very fragile and sensitive planetary ecosystem that also includes all of these four levels, as well as the individual, collective and planetary ones, and so imbalances at any level are felt on all levels. Humankind has been doing a fantastic balancing act, so to say, for the past several hundred years, as it has created more and more imbalances in the natural environment. The effect of*

*this is that the structures, both micro and macro, that have been thus creat-
ed are very top-heavy and are ready to crumble and fall over at any moment.
Restoring balance so that the structures do not topple is the only way out.
This is essentially the current challenge that you as a species are facing—how
to restore balance to a severely imbalanced ecosystem that exists both within
you and outside of you.*

*This is why self-healing is so very important, because in order to heal the
larger circle of life it is vitally essential that healing take place on the individual level first. Once this happens, the larger circle will automatically heal.
What holds true inside your bodies holds true in the body of mankind and
within the body of earth mother. Native peoples have always held this primary truth as sacred. This is why a return to the shamanic perspective that
values this world view is what is needed at this time. When you heal yourself,
the larger circle also heals, and conversely, when you neglect, abuse or subject
yourself to imbalances the larger circle also suffers. It is that simple. But this
is a totally alien concept for your western society's minds to comprehend. It is
not the way that life has been lived for the past thousand years. But, do not
be discouraged. The power is within each individual to turn this around by
healing the self. When enough have awakened to this understanding and
have healed the imbalances in their lives, the same will occur in the larger circle as well. People need to awaken to the concept that it is each person's
responsibility to create balance and harmony in their lives and to not sit pas-
sively and wait for everyone else to do it for them. This must begin at the
individual level or it will not occur. This is what we are striving for, and this
is what can and will happen if humankind heeds the wake-up calls that are
all around them and takes the appropriate action to restore balance and harmony within themselves, their social systems, and between themselves and the
earth.*

INNER SHAMAN makes some very pertinent points on the issue of balance and harmony. She holds that, according to the shamanic world view, the maintenance or restoration of health requires the creation of balance and harmony. To be in a state of balance and harmony, she claims, means to be in right relationship with virtually everything around you. Right relationship, furthermore, means that there is an equal exchange of energy and that harmony (peaceful, congruent coexistence) is present.

When I apply these concepts to my life and explore where in the past my life was most lacking in harmony and balance, in what area the exchange of energy was most lopsided, the area of social relationship jumps right out at me. I was a codependent for many, many years. Actually, I was not just a codependent; I was a Master Codependent. (My high-level performance as a codependent was rivaled only by my unexcelled skills in the victim role!) Balance and harmony cannot be, by any stretch of the imagination, considered to be characteristics associated with codependency.

Codependency is an unconscious pattern of continuously accepting responsibility for the needs and feelings of others. It generally involves endlessly counting the wants and needs of others before self, caretaking, focusing on helping "fix" other people and their problems, and some form of conscious or unconscious manipulation for the purpose of attaining reciprocal caretaking and love. Instead of finding a way to meet his or her needs directly a codependent will try to take care of someone else's needs with the hidden expectation that the other person will reciprocate and take care of his or her needs as well. What generally occurs, however, is exactly the opposite. There is not reciprocity and that, of course, results in an unequal exchange of energy. When this happens, as it usually does, anger and resentment tend to build up as the one person keeps attempting to get "love" and nurturance, following a hidden, usually unconscious, agenda. This hidden agenda, however, is not effective in getting the person what he or she wants; his or her needs are virtually never met. This breeds anger and resentment. When caught in this pattern, the codependent, not knowing any other way, keeps trying harder to get the love and nurturance that he or she needs by caretaking even more, and feeling more and more angry as his or her needs are not met. This pattern goes on and on in circular fashion, and is at the core of many unhealthy, unsuccessful relationships.

This pattern of codependency, like the victim pattern, can be traced back to my childhood. From an early age, I recall always trying to please other people, especially my mother who presented me with a definite challenge in that area. Sometimes I could please her and sometimes I couldn't, but I never gave up. I simply tried a little harder the next time. Somewhere along the way, I developed a world view that held that love was something that needed to be earned, and if I wanted others to love me, I needed to work very hard and "earn" their love. So, the pattern of trying to earn love by pleasing others and taking care of their needs at the expense of my own developed very early in my childhood.

One of the behaviors from my childhood that reflects this was that I was never able to say "No." If someone asked me to do something for them, I virtually always said "Yes," whether I wanted to do it or not. Saying "Yes," and saying it with a smile on my face became like an automatic, knee-jerk reaction.

During my childhood, we lived on the second floor of a two-flat. My aunt and her family lived downstairs. In order to get downstairs into the back yard I had to walk through my aunt's back porch. My aunt, Aunt Loretta, was an overweight diabetic who had the gift of being able to sweet talk me into doing just about anything for her. I can't tell you how many times when she would be sitting in her kitchen (which was adjacent to the back porch), she would "catch me" as she saw me coming down the stairs and ask me to do something for her. Her requests ranged anywhere from going to the delicatessen, to washing her kitchen floor, to tying her shoe. She would usually reward me for my efforts with some coins. But, I didn't do it for the money. I did it because I didn't know how to say "No," and I didn't know how to say "No" because I wanted and needed her to love me. Saying "No," to my way of thinking, would have jeopardized that goal. I truly do not recall ever turning her down, no matter how I may have wanted to refuse when I had other things on my agenda.

My agenda, even back then, just never came first; everyone else's did. I had such an intense need to please others, to win their love, that my wants and needs right from the start, took a back seat. It seemed to work back then. It seemed to get me the love and attention from my family that I so desperately wanted and needed. To my aunt and her family, I was a little "darling." They always made a big fuss over me and thought I was the best thing since sliced bread. Aunt Loretta played the piano and would often play and sing at family gatherings. She would invariably play and sing a song just for me, "Margie, I'm always thinking of you, Margie..." Since my people-pleasing behaviors seemed to work so well at home, I did the same thing at school, with the teachers, with my peers, with virtually everyone I came in contact with. After all, it seemed to indisputably work in getting me what I needed, so why would I want to give up such a good thing?

At school, the ante was raised just a bit. I attended Catholic school, both elementary and high school. Here the added dimension of needing to be the "good girl" made this behavior pattern even more desirable. Discounting myself, always saying "yes," taking care of others, invariably volunteering to help out, etc. worked very well in gaining the approval of the nuns that I so desperately needed. It also earned me the reputation of being the "good child," the kind that God finds most pleasing and, oh, how I wanted to please God! To be selfless was considered a virtue; to be selfish was a sin. The implicit message was clear—it's not okay for you to have wants or needs, let alone to ask for them. So, if you want your wants and needs met, you need to find a secret or covert way to do that. Saying "Yes, Sister!" was definitely the thing to do. (I think I used to say it so much that I probably even said it in my sleep.) I learned that if I went through life saying "Yes, Sister," I would eventually get the love and approval that I needed.

This pattern worked so well that when I was in eighth grade, I was given the distinct honor of crowning the Blessed Mother at the annual May Crowning, an honor that was only bestowed upon some-one who was considered to be the cream of the crop. In all seriousness, this was truly a privilege and an honor that I hold dear even to this day. Unfortunately, however, it further solidified and reinforced my budding codependent behavior.

Of course, when I got married and left home, this pattern was first and foremost on my repertoire of relationship skills. The pattern was simple—discount your own wants and needs and tend to the other person's wants and needs so that you can secretly get your wants and needs met. It made such perfect sense! And, as I said before, it really worked, or, at least, so I thought. There was one seri-ous flaw—it *didn't* work in the long run, because it created a serious imbalance in the relationship. Codependency is simply not an exam-ple of being in right relationship. By its very nature, it sets up an unequal exchange of energy and thus the imbalance. As Inner Shaman attests, imbalance causes dis-ease. The dis-eases that kept cropping up in my life were anger, resentment and chronic depres-sion, among others which contributed to the unhealthy and unsatisfying relationship that I had with Tom for the first twenty years of our marriage.

I remember believing in the early years of my marriage (and actu-ally verbalizing to other people) that my main purpose in life was to make my husband happy. I cringe at the thought of it now, but, in those days, I truly believed this, and I lived my life according to that dictum. With this classic codependent belief system prompting my behavior, I sincerely felt responsible for his feelings and tried my utmost to make him happy. This was a set-up for failure.

The sad thing is that I tried and tried, but the harder I tried, the more I failed. Judging by the amount he was drinking in those days, Tom was not happy. Neither was I, and at some deep level, I genuinely felt responsible. If he wasn't happy, how could I possibly be? According to the game plan that I had followed since my youth, I got my needs met only if I managed to take care of other's needs first, so if I wasn't succeeding in making him happy, where did that leave me? It left me in an impossible situation. I wasn't getting the love and attention that I so yearned for, and I wasn't able to do anything about it. It was a vicious circle. I tried to please Tom, I failed, he wasn't happy, I didn't get the love I needed, I felt angry, that pleased him even less, I tried harder, and the cycle repeated itself on and on ad infinitum! Simply stated, we were not in right relationship, with ourselves or with each other. Consequently the relationship was not right.

The codependency went hand-in-hand with the victim-martyr syndrome that I also suffered from, and together they spelled trouble. I found it difficult to be a mother of two children and a codependent victim-martyr at the same time. It required me to do an almost impossible juggling act. As a mother, I followed the same dictum as I had with my husband, devoting my life to taking care of my children's every want and need, rescuing them, attempting to fix all of their problems. I did whatever it took to operate under the rules of social interaction that I had learned as a child, which had appeared to work for me then. As a young mother, however, it seemed that all I did was give, give, give and I never got anything in return. I still hadn't learned to say "No." Sadly enough, I even felt the need to go that extra mile to please my children so that they would love me. Of course, the codependency really fed into the victim-martyr role, because the more I gave and got nothing in return, the more I got to feel sorry for myself, and the more I got to whine and cry.

No wonder I was tired all of the time and suffered from chronic fatigue. No wonder I was always angry and continually struggling with depression. No wonder TMJ and migraine headaches were part of my daily routine. No wonder lower back problems caused me continuous pain. I spent so much of my energy attempting to do something that I didn't have the power to do—make other people happy—that there was nothing left to give. My body was crying out, giving me a wake-call that it took much too long for me to hear. Not knowing any better, and not being a quitter, I kept trying and trying, harder and harder, until the well had just about run dry. I was out of balance, my relationships were out of balance, my life was out of balance, and I was sick, so very sick, sick and tired, tired of trying to do something that just couldn't be done, and not knowing any other way.

My body was only reflecting the illness that was deep inside, the dis-ease that had robbed me of my spirit, of my vital energy, of my power—the dis-ease that results from a lifetime of discounting the self at a very deep level. My illness was truly of the nature that Inner Shaman describes when she talks about dis-ease being a result of disconnection from one's inner self, from one's spirit. How much more disconnected from self and spirit can one be than to live a lifetime of discounting and dishonoring the wants and needs of the self?

Then one day I began to wake-up. I think it was about the same time that Tom and I were in marital therapy and that I began to move out of the victim consciousness and become self-responsible. As I walked the path out of the victim consciousness into the consciousness of self-responsibility, I was beginning to realize that I was responsible for myself, not for the rest of the world, just for myself! *The only person that I had the power to make happy was myself; others needed to do that for themselves.* Yes! What a grand awakening that was! What a totally new way of looking at the world!

And with this awareness at some deep level within, I was able to take the first steps out of the codependent pattern that had entrapped me since childhood. I was able to let go of my childhood beliefs about the way the world worked in favor of a set of beliefs that were more in keeping with my new consciousness, the consciousness of empowerment and self-responsibility. I was able to stop the endless circular patterns that got me nowhere and nothing. I allowed myself to have wants and needs, and to even ask for them. I could say "NO!" when that was what I wanted to say. I was able to let go of the unrelenting need to please other people in the hope that would get me the love that I needed. I gradually began to bring my life back into balance.

Today, I live my life based upon a different set of rules, rules that are more consistent with the notion of right relationship. During graduate school, I had taken a weekend course on couple's communication. I don't remember too much from that class, but one thing has stayed with me, which I teach to all of my clients. There are basically three ways in which two people can relate. One can be described as "I count me, I don't count you." This is a situation where one, or both, people continually thinks only of him or herself and never the other person. The second is "I count you, I don't count me." This, of course, describes codependent behavior perfectly, where one person consistently discounts the self in favor of the other person's wants or needs. The third one is "I count me, I count you." This one, at first glance, might appear to be "selfish," based on the fact that it suggests counting the self first. But, after some thought, it becomes quite clear that it really isn't possible to genuinely consider someone else's needs if you haven't tended to yourself first. This brings to mind the instructions given when traveling on an airplane: "In the event of a sudden drop in cabin pressure an oxygen mask will come out of the ceiling in front of you. Passengers traveling with small children put your own mask on first and then assist your child." In my codependent days when I traveled on an airplane, I thought this was scandalous. What proper mother would think of herself first? Today, it makes perfect sense. This third situation, "I count me, I count you," is the one that describes a balanced exchange of energy and that results in what Inner Shaman refers to as being in right relationship. I have found the "I count me, I count you" technique to be the best, most effective technique in creating healthy, satisfying relationships.

Today "I count me, I count you" is the dictum that guides my life. I now make a habit of checking in with my feelings, wants and needs, before even considering those of others. In considering myself first, I now am able to make conscious choices about whether I want my wants and needs to take a back seat to those of the other person, as sometimes is necessary for the give and take required for a relationship to work. As long as it is a conscious choice, not an automatic reaction, and as long as there is a balance in the "I'll scratch your back, you scratch my back" routine, this is consistent with right relationship. Putting this into practice has certainly helped to make my relationships right, as it goes a long way toward eliminating conflict and creating a peaceful and harmonious co-existence.

Righting external relationship patterns was one way that I have helped to create balance and harmony in my life. Righting internal relationship patterns within myself was another. As Inner Shaman points out, there needs to be an inner balance between and within each of the four levels of our being—physical, mental, emotional and spiritual. There must be a free-flowing, harmonious exchange of energy here or dis-ease can result. We need to be in right relationship with all of these aspects of the self.

In looking back at this matter in my life, I can see that things were severely out of balance for a long time between my physical and spiritual aspects. The restoration of that balance and alignment was a large part of my healing process. Finding a way to live in my body and follow my spiritual path has been one of the greatest challenges of my healing journey.

As a child growing up in a Catholic family in the 1950's, I was taught that my body was something to be ashamed of, something to be hidden and covered up. The body was certainly not to be valued since physical bodies were the cause of sins—"sins of the flesh," as they were called. Its primary value was in being "the Temple of the Holy Spirit," not in being the physical vehicle for our soul's human journey on this earth. We were taught to deny the body, to deprive it of "earthly pleasures," both in repentance for our sins and so that our reward in the afterlife would be that much greater. Denying our bodies was pleasing to God, while indulging them was not pleasing at best, and mortally sinful at worst. Such was the case with sex, one of those "earthly pleasures," which was sanctioned only for its pro-creative function within marriage. Its role in the physical expression of human love and affection, and as a pleasurable, natural and satisfying shared human experience wasn't recognized. The implicit message in all of this was that the physical body was something to be "respected" and tolerated, but definitely not celebrated, honored, and loved. It was only our immortal soul that mattered because the body would eventually die and only our souls would remain. If we had lived a life of "earthly pleasure," we would be sure to live an afterlife damned to the eternal fires of hell. So, if what happened to our souls was all that really mattered, and our bodies were the source of sin, we were caught in a double bind—we needed to find a way to disown our bodies while trying to live in them at the same time.

Remarkably enough, I managed to find a way to do this. I'm not sure exactly how I did it, but I do know that for many years I disowned my body; I was virtually never in it. Being out of my body had its merits, as it helped me to develop my spiritual, psychic and intuitive self. However, the challenge remained—how to find a way to be truly spiritual and fully present in my body. I can remember being so out of touch with my body that at times I could go for hours ignoring a headache or back pain, vaguely recalling noticing the pain many hours before but not really feeling it until much later. I think that this is also one of the reasons why I spent so much time out of my body—it was generally the source of pain, and rarely pleasure.

As I began to grow and develop spiritually, it became more and more evident that to be spiritual did not at all mean to forsake or disown the body. It meant, instead, to embrace it, to honor it, to pleasure it, to celebrate it. It required that I learn how to live fully and completely in my body, grounded in my physicality while at the same time fully attuned to my inner, spiritual self. It required finding a workable balance between the two.

In making my way along the spiritual path, I came upon a number of techniques that helped to ground and center me in my body, while enabling me to spend the time in the spiritual realms that I so craved. Perhaps the technique that was the most useful to me was the Master's Psychophysical Method, a blend of movement and consciousness work, which is a re-education of the body-mind system. Based on the Feldencrais Method with a sprinkling of yoga, the Psychophysical Method teaches you how to tune into your body and to listen to what it is telling you. In studying this method, I learned how to scan my body and to be fully aware of what was going on with it, noticing minute details and slight variations as they occurred. I also learned how to enter expanded states of consciousness while remaining present in my body. I have practiced this method for a number of years, with positive results. The spinal movement exercises (which I do just about daily) have helped open up my back by allowing the energy to flow freely up and down my spine. I believe this has helped to alleviate my lower back and neck pain.

Prior to coming to this place of balance between my physical and spiritual selves, short of feeding and bathing my body, I paid very little attention to it unless it was crying out in pain, which it did on a regular basis. Then I would swallow an aspirin, antihistamine pill, or an antacid tablet and be on my way. This usually shut it up for a while, but the underlying reason for the pain I was experiencing was never addressed; I never gave it the attention that it was crying for.

One of the reasons for this was that I was a card-carrying "Supermom," the kind that went without stop from morning till dropping into bed at night. I was living such a fast-paced lifestyle that there just wasn't time to pay attention to my body. Although I was a stay-at-home mom until my return to school in 1982, I packed my life to the brim with endless activities—Girl Scout leader, PTA board member, room mother, church activities and volunteering, cleaning, cooking, baking, sewing, bowling, tennis, chauffeuring the kids to and from school and their after school activities, and lots of shopping. I was always on the go—running, running, running. There simply weren't enough hours in the day to do something as frivolous as paying attention to my body's wants and needs. Although these were the days when I felt chronically fatigued, I pushed myself to keep going, whether I felt tired or not. When I felt so exhausted that I could almost fall over, I gave myself a thirty minute nap on the couch and then was on my way again.

During these "Supermom" days in my late twenties and early thirties, I went from doctor to doctor, trying to find out why I felt so tired all of the time. No one had an answer for me. A chiropractor that I was seeing in 1978 thought that perhaps my problem was hypoglycemia (low blood sugar) and suggested that I eliminate refined sugar and flour from my diet. I tried this for eight or nine months. When I didn't get any significant results, I gave the diet up and went back to my old eating habits, which included lots of sweets and refined carbohydrates. (I later discovered that I did not suffer from hypoglycemia. To date I have not been given a medical diagnosis regarding the fatigue. I can only speculate that, at the physical level, the chronic fatigue was related to stress, adrenal failure and the autoimmune condition.) I continued to feel tired most of the time, to push myself to keep going, and to ignore my body's cry for help. I knew something was wrong, but I was completely unaware that a balance between my physical and spiritual selves was part of what was needed.

After my spiritual awakening began in 1981, I gradually started to become more health conscious. It was a slow process. But, by the time I was diagnosed with the autoimmune condition in 1988 I was ready to heed the wake-up call. I finally began to listen to my body and heard the message it had been trying to tell me for so long—pay attention to me! I came to the realization that this was the only body I was going to have in this lifetime. If I wanted it to be healthy I needed to take responsibility for seeing that that occurred. I began in earnest to direct my energy to that end and began to give it the tender love and care that it was calling for. I had thought for a long time that self-healing only involved positive thinking and saying affirmations. I came to understand that these were only parts of the picture. Without attending to things at the physical level as well, all the meditation, visualization, prayer and spiritual practices in the world weren't going to heal me. I needed to roll up my sleeves and go to work on the physical level.

And go to work I did. I began to reevaluate my lifestyle and consider new and better ways to live in my body, ways that were more consistent with balance and right relationship, as Inner Shaman suggests is essential to health. (Of course, at this time I didn't have this information in black and white as I do now. It was purely an intuitive knowing that was emanating from my Inner Shaman, who at the time I didn't even know existed.) Once I was able to stop focusing on everyone else and to say "no" occasionally, I began to slow my "life in the fast lane" pace down quite a bit, focusing on stress reduction and stress management. I set aside regular time to just relax my body, sit and stare, contemplate, meditate or simply dissociate. I began to go for regular massage therapy. What a wonderful way to relax, while my body was being soothed and pleasured at the same time! I believe massage therapy has been a part of the regimen that has been instrumental in eradicating my lower back and neck pain as well. I began to experiment with different types of vitamin, herbal and nutritional supplements until I found a combination that seemed to be in proper balance. In addition to the daily psychophysical movement exercises, I also began to walk one to three miles a day, outside in good weather or inside on a treadmill in not so good weather. As I began to pay more attention to my body, I was really beginning to live in it, not just visit it occasionally. And, it felt good!

One of the major areas that I began to reevaluate during this time of expanding health consciousness was nutrition. In the area of nutrition, I was, like many other moms in the '70's and '80's, a fast food freak—the faster the better, both at home and on the run. Fast, prepared foods—from a box, a can, a freezer, or a jar—anything that could go in the microwave and be on the table in ten minutes or less was the order of the day. I put Twinkies in my children's lunches and bought gallons of diet soda, along with sugar coated cereal, hot dogs and lunch meat, and bags and bags of chips—potato chips, Cheetos, tortilla chips, pretzels, we loved them all! Anytime Tom was out of town or working late and wouldn't be home for dinner, I packed the kids in the car and off we went to a fast food place for dinner. We alternated back and forth between Taco Bell, Burger King, Pizza Hut, Wendy's, McDonald's, Arby's, and, yes, even White Castle's I had a lot of indigestion in those days. I wonder how the kids survived?

Then, one day, I made a major change in my diet; I gave up red meat. In 1986, my chiropractor had been treating me for some of my many complaints. In an attempt to help detoxify my overwhelmed liver, she suggested that I go on the Pritikin diet, a bare-bones regimen that drastically limited the intake of fat. Of course, red meat was not on the list of suggested foods, nor were too many other of those culinary delights that I had previously made the mainstay of my diet—cheese and dairy products, fried foods, processed foods that contained preservatives or artificial anything, white flour and sugar, essentially all of the things that made eating so enticing. Giving up red meat was not easy for me. There was nothing that I liked better than a medium-rare filet mignon with a baked potato smothered in sour cream and sauteed mushrooms on the side. To this day I occasionally find myself looking with longing at the filet sitting on my husband's plate when we're eating out. I do find it humorous that the very last meal I had that contained red meat was a White Castle hamburger. What a fitting ending to a life-long pattern of eating red meat at least once or twice a day!

Following the chiropractor's advice I remained on this diet for about eight or nine months. At the end of the diet, I went back to some of the old ways, but I never returned to eating red meat. At that time, I was given a firm directive from my inner voice to give up red meat entirely, and I began cooking and eating more chicken, turkey, and fish. When I went from serving red meat almost daily to not at all, my husband and daughters readily accepted that red meat was not going to be served at home, and it didn't create a problem. However, it didn't go over so well with my extended family. My father had worked as a meat cutter all of his life, and roast beef had always been the center of attraction at virtually all of our family get-togethers. Refusing to cook or eat red meat created a stir, but eventually they all got over it as well.

For the following seven or eight years (after being on the Pritikin diet) I would go back and forth, attempting to find a balance that worked for me. For a few months at a time, I would watch my intake of the "forbidden foods," and then I would fall back into the old habits again. In 1994, following the appearance of arthritis in my hands, I made the firm resolution to watch my intake of the foods that caused toxic build-up in the body (especially those containing high fat content, preservatives, artificial ingredients, caffeine, MSG, and any form of hydrogenated oils). I began grocery shopping at a health food supermarket that had recently opened near my home, and I have managed to adhere fairly closely to these dietary restrictions up to the present time. I drink only spring water and herbal teas—no alcohol, no soda. I haven't completely eliminated refined flour and sugar from my diet, but I do limit my intake of sweets.

It seems to be agreeing with me. I have come to relate to my body in a way that indicates that my body and its health and comfort are vitally important to me. I am willing to make what small sacrifices are necessary to take care of it properly. I now eat food that will nurture and sustain it, not poison and toxify it. No more ignoring and abusing it. No more running it ragged and rewarding it with a Big Mac, coke and fries followed by an antacid tablet to relieve my indigestion and a Tylenol to alleviate my headache. (But, I must confess I still have a little chocolate now and then!)

In some respects I might be considered to be one of those "health nuts," but I don't think of myself that way. I believe that the way that I am living my life is not "nuts" at all. It makes perfect sense to me to put forth the time, energy and effort that it takes to have a healthy body. The unconcerned, unconscious, unaware and disconnected way that I used to live was what didn't make any sense primarily because it just wasn't working! I view myself as someone who has found a way to bring a measure of balance into my life—by coming into right relationship with my body, and by bringing my body into right relationship with the food that it ingests. Accomplishing this, together with righting external social relationships has helped to create balance and harmony in my life. I have learned that following a spiritual path does not require me to ignore, deny, discount and disown my body. It requires just the opposite—to embrace, own, honor and care for my body. To follow a spiritual path I must live fully in my body while, at the same time, being fully in tune with my inner, spiritual self. Finding this balance between my physical and spiritual selves has helped to move me further along the path toward wholeness and healing.

## HEALING JOURNEY:
## ACTIVITIES FOR GOING INWARD

### JOURNAL EXERCISE: Right Relationships

The notion of balance in the shamanic perspective has to do with being in a state of right relationship to yourself, your natural environment, other people and the Spirit World. What right relationship means is that there is an equal exchange of energy. The energy is not moving in one direction only, but is freely moving back and forth… Right relationship also includes the notion of harmony, of two or more things existing together in the absence of conflict, in a state of peace and tranquillity.

Using the "Rambling Writing" method, assess whether your relationships with (1) yourself, (2) your natural environment, (3) other people, and (4) the Spirit World are in "right relationship." In assessing each of this four areas use the following questions as guidelines:

- What relationships in this area are not in "right relationship?"

- How are these relationships out of balance, (i.e., there is an unequal exchange of energy)?

- How are they lacking in harmony (i.e., conflict is present)?

- What are the undesirable effects of this imbalance?

## GUIDED MEDITATION: Balance and Harmony

Sorting through your tapes and CD's, select a piece of music (preferably instrumental) you would describe as being balanced and harmonious that would be appropriate as background music for meditation.

> Start the music and sit back in a comfortable and relaxed position. Close your eyes and begin to focus on the music. Allow yourself to deeply sense the music, having as complete a sensory experience of it as possible. Visualize what the music might look like if you could see it, what it might taste like if you could taste it, and what it might smell like if you could smell it. Experience the music in your body, giving special attention to its balance and harmony. Listen intently to its harmony and notice what that feels like in your body. Feel the vibration of the music, and imagine that it is balancing and harmonizing every cell of your body.

> Then allow the music to take you to a safe, relaxed and harmonious place within yourself. Feeling as if you are one with the music, invite your Inner Shaman to be with you in your safe inner place. After greeting each other, ask him or her what you need to do to restore balance and harmony to those parts of your life (identified in your journaling exercise) which are not in "right relationship." Then simply be open and "listen" to the answers, insights, visions or knowings that come to you. [Allow several minutes to do this.]

> (Each person will experience this differently. You may get visual images. You may hear something, feel something, or simply have a sense of "knowing." Whatever experience you have is perfect. Do not censor or judge your experi-

ence. Simply trust that it is the exact experience that you need at the moment. If it seems as if absolutely nothing is happening, don't be discouraged. I believe even though we may not be having a conscious experience at the time, we are "downloading" information at an unconscious level that will surface at a later time.)

Affirm to yourself that you will recall everything that you learned during your visit with your Inner Shaman, and thanking him or her for the insights and answers he or she has provided, begin to take your leave. Allow yourself to hear and feel the music once again, and begin to feel yourself coming back into your body and back into everyday awareness. When you open your eyes, you feel refreshed, bright and alert, grateful for the experience that you have just had.

## RITUAL: Creating Balance

Setting a healing intention, embodying it in a material object, and then affirming what you wish to occur in your life already has come to be can be an important component of healing an aspect of your life.

Choose an aspect of your life that is lacking in balance that you would like to bring back into balance. Using different sizes of beads and a cord or string, create a necklace or bracelet or anklet that represents or symbolizes this aspect. The goal is to create a necklace that is *balanced* and *symmetrical.* When putting each bead in place affirm to yourself: "*(State the aspect that you want to bring into balance)* is in a state of balance and harmony." Then create your own ritual centered around the wearing of the necklace. For example, if the aspect of your life that you wish to bring back into balance is your finances, you might wear your necklace each time you go shopping, sit down to pay bills, or plan your budget as a reminder to keep your expenditures in balance with your income. If the aspect is related to diet and nutrition, you might wear the necklace every time you eat as a reminder to eat balanced meals.

When not wearing your necklace, hang it in a place of honor or place it on your altar, repeating your affirmation whenever you look at it.

# GENTLE WIND

I stand among the pine trees, needles at my feet.
Above I see their green vibrant majesty,
below I feel their sweet downy softness.
Although alone, I somehow know that I am not.
For the gentle wind whispers to me,
"We are one, dear child, we are one."
The tree reaches out to me and jolts me into awakening
and suddenly I know that I am never alone.
"We are one, dear child, we are one," I hear again,
as the gentle wind whispers once more,
"I am the breath of the creator.
I embrace you with my touch,
and kiss you with my soothing caress
to let you know, dear child, that we are one."

— M. S.
*April 27, 1995*

## CHAPTER FIVE

# We Are All Related

*EVERYTHING THAT EXISTS IS ENERGY. WE ARE ALL RELATED in that we are all part of the same field of energy that is ALL THAT IS. We are virtually all connected by the fact that we all exist in an ocean of energy. Just us everything within the ocean is connected so are we; everything that exists is connected in this way. It is really very simple. Separateness is at once an illusion and a perceived reality, as we are both separate and connected. We are all one, yet we maintain individual identities. This is the grand scheme of things and is a part of the great mystery that is life. The apparent paradox is easier to understand when one considers the magnitude of the universe and the vast variety of life and life forms that abound throughout. How can we presume to believe that we are all that there is? There is so much more than human consciousness. The mystery of Oneness surpasses the ability of the human mind to comprehend and it must be taken at a level of faith, but it is the truth all the same. We are all one, we are all connected, we are all one in the Great Mystery, the Great Creator-Spirit.*

*Native people call this notion the Web of Life and refer to this concept of Oneness as the Great Circle of Life. The premise that everything is energy is not held by indigenous peoples only, however, it has been substantiated by quantum physics, as you know. Not only is everything nothing more than energy at various stages of density, but everything exists within a vast field of energy, implying that there is no such thing as separateness. Everything is within the same soup, so to say. Within the pot exists a liquid that contains chunks of things. The chunks have an illusion of separateness, but they exist only within the larger context of the soup. The carrots, celery, potatoes, etc.*

*may have the illusion of being distinct entities, which in some respects they are, but in the grander picture they are all part of the same soup. It is vital that all people come to understand this concept. There is really no such thing as separateness. WE ARE ALL RELATED! WE ARE ALL RELATED! We are all existing within the same soup. We are all made of the same substance. We are all connected at very deep levels.*

*In addition, we are all essential elements of the soup, for without the car-rots the soup would not have a certain sweetness, and without the onions it would be too bland, and so on and so forth. We are all necessary and we all have a certain purpose and function to perform within the soup. Those who believe that certain ingredients are more important than others are sadly mis-taken. Each grain of salt is as vital to the taste of the soup as each chunk of celery, for together they make the whole. The same is true of all of creation. Mankind is no more important than the flies, rocks or trees. Each of Creator's creatures is equally important in maintaining the ecological balance that is necessary for the health of the entire system. That is why with so many species currently dying off the earth is becoming more and more imbalanced.*

*This is all about energy, all about the notion that we are all one. What we do to one part of the system we do to all parts, for we are all connected. The same is true of the body that you dwell in. Once again the micro/macro con-cept that everything in the universe is hologramatic comes into play. What is true for the larger picture is also true of the smaller one. What happens at a cellular or atomic level is analogous to what happens at the level of solar sys-tems. There is a grand, universal plan that all of nature follows and it is essentially based on the notion that we are all one, that we, be it planet, solar systems, ants, cells or atoms, all exist in a unified field, and the same prin-ciples of relativity apply at all levels. That is why when we learn to walk in balance with each other, healing will occur, for it is about more than just individual healing. We are all metaphors for the grander scheme. This is true down to the minutest particle that swirls around the nucleus of an atom to the vast solar systems that swirl within galaxies. This notion has long been known and understood by indigenous people. Here, again, is found the macrocosm-microcosm concept. As within, so without, as above, so below. This is a basic universal principle that all life follows.*

*Let me say more about this micro/macro concept. This is about the notion that everything is connected and that within the universe there exist infinite other smaller universes. It is like looking into a mirror that is facing another mirror. The image that you see goes on and on into infinity. So, too, is the universe. From the smallest particle to the entire infinity of ALL THAT IS, there is an order and a programming or coding that exists for all things. That coding is a programming for life, change, movement, for evolution from smaller to bigger, lesser to greater, lower to higher, etc. This is universal law. It is the way that the universe operates, and within this system there exists a hierarchy of sorts, kind of like nesting boxes, with universe within universe within universe on ad infinitum. This is what I mean when I refer to the hologramatic universe. Within each part exists the whole and within the whole exists all parts.*

*Think of it like a story within a story. The tiniest atomic particle, each individual cell, each person, plant, animal, each family and social system, each political, economic, religious system, each nation, each planet and star, each solar system, each universe must evolve to its highest potential. This is universal law. This is the way that the universe has been designed.*

*Why this is so important to understand right now has to do with the fact that the entire universe is about to make a quantum leap into a higher state of being, a movement into an even higher state of consciousness. What is occurring on Planet Earth is central to this shift that is occurring universally. It is as if earth is at the center stage of this grand drama, but it is not alone. The entire universe will be affected, as WE ARE ALL RELATED— even at this level. At all levels this is true. WE ARE ALL RELATED in Great Spirit, Great Mystery, ALL THAT IS. When it comes to healing, then, it is essential to understand that "when I heal, you heal, and when you heal, I heal, and when we heal, the great WE heals." Each individual, then, must work toward healing, becoming whole, so that the greater system can heal as well. If you want the earth to heal, then you must heal yourself first. This is how Mother Earth will heal and this is the only way.*

*What is happening at the moment, then, is that humankind is on the brink of a quantum shift into a higher state of consciousness, into the next level of an infinite amount of levels of possibility, of potential. This is the meaning of evolution. This is the meaning of life and the purpose of it as well. We are all meant to evolve and become all that we can become and the "We" is not limited to humans alone. It refers to everything that exists from atomic particle to galaxies. Everything is set in motion in the direction of growth and evolution. Those individuals or systems that do not participate in this movement out of fear, disinterest or apathy will cease to exist in physical form. They will become devitalized as they will be in a state of what is called entropy, a situation in which a closed system actually converges in on itself and depletes itself due to lack of vital energy being generated by the system. Only those who are in a synergistic state, one of energy generativity, will thrive and grow and move in the direction of evolution. This is the natural law.*

*I know that this sounds like a lesson in quantum physics, and in many ways it is, but it is necessary to understand these concepts as they are at the basis of what is occurring. They are also very shamanic in nature, as shamans have always understood that everything is alive, and that everything is related. This is essentially what we are talking about here. This is also related to the notion of power. The shaman knows that when a person looses power or energy, they will get ill or even die—entropy—and that wholeness or healing involves a restoration or a generativity of energy—synergy. That is why shamanism and quantum physics are very much related.*

*Now, remember when I said that evolution to a higher state of being is the universal law? Well, there is more to this than meets the eye. It is more than just evolution, it is about growth and expansion and opening and "wholing" and healing. These are the things that support evolution. Stuckness, illness, depression and the like do not support evolution. They are entropy supporting and will eventually lead to the death of the system or organism. That is another reason why healing is so vital at this time. Those systems that do not heal will self-destruct due to entropy. Self-healing must be learned by as many people as possible so that healing can become more and more widespread in the next decade. The eradication of symptoms, as helpful as it appears, is not enough. Healing involves so much more than merely this. Eradication of symptoms involves surface issues only. Healing involves going into the depths and eradicating root causes for whatever the problem may be. This is very shamanic. In fact, it is the very essence of the shamanic journey. The shaman travels into another reality to get information about this very thing so that the person may then use the information to address the root cause of his or her problem.*

*Shamans have always known the great truth—that we are all one, that we are all connected—and have walked their healing path in the light of this knowingness. This awareness is what makes it possible for healing to take place. Understanding this great truth presents a belief system in which anything is possible, since we are all connected. It is this connection that the shaman calls forth in doing the work of healing. It is this connection to the ALL that the shaman evokes from within his patient. It is this connection that provides the healing field, the space in which the healing can occur. The connection to spirit and to the greater circle of life is what empowers both the shaman and the person to be healed. Without this connection, the shaman has no power. Without this connection the shaman cannot weave his or her healing tapestry. Without this connection, there would be no healing. "Mitakuye Oyasin"—WE ARE ALL RELATED!*

THESE WORDS OF INNER SHAMAN take on a deep level of relevancy as I consider the course of my healing journey, for connecting with the world of nature, with "all my relations," was one of the most important steps I have taken along the way.

I grew up in the south side of Chicago. As mentioned earlier, we lived in a two-flat that was sandwiched in between other two-flats, with only about ten or twelve feet separating each building. We had a small back yard, with one small tree adjacent to the garage, some grass and a border of flowering plants—peonies, mums, geraniums—and in the corner a patch of raspberry bushes. In the front yard there was a large old elm tree, some grass, a sidewalk and a concrete front stoop with a flowerpot on the ledge. This was what my world of nature consisted of for the first years of my life. I knew no other world.

Neither of my parents were outdoors people so, with the exception of visiting my uncle's summer home in Indiana several times a year, we never went on any outings in nature. My mother actually discouraged me from being outside during the summer because of my allergies. I got the message from her that being outside was not good for me and that nature, with all of its pollen, dust and molds, was bad because it made me sick. The same was true for the winter months. It was bad to be outdoors during the cooler weather because I would "catch cold" from getting a chill, or get an ear infection from the wind blowing in my ear. I grew up believing that the natural world was something to be feared—it was hazardous to my health.

The same went for animals. I didn't have a pet growing up and my mother, at the allergist's bidding, discouraged me from being near animals because it would probably give me an allergy attack. This, together with the fact that I had been bitten by a dog as a young child, contributed to the aversion and fear I felt for animals. I avoided them like the plague, freezing in terror if a dog should come up to me to smell me or lick me, and never, never extending my hand to pet one. In short, I grew up as disconnected from the natural world as I was from my own body. Consequently, for a good portion of my life I avoided nature, the outdoors and animals. I ignored, disowned and failed to live in the natural world, just as I had my body.

I recall somewhere in my late thirties beginning to wake up, just a little, to nature. I was seeing a therapist at the time, and one of the things she suggested I do was to begin to "take in beauty." She pointed to the beauty of the outdoor world as one possible source of beauty, a rather novel idea to me. I took her advice and began to notice the natural world around me. I experienced this beauty for the first time in my life—the brilliant colors of red, yellow and gold glistening in the glorious light of the sun. I had seen it all before, but I had never experienced it, and there is a difference between merely seeing and really experiencing. It was autumn, a season that I generally dislike because it means winter won't be far behind and, oh, how I hate the cold Chicago winters. In focusing so much on my not liking what autumn signified for the first thirty-seven years of my life, I had not allowed myself to experience its magnificent beauty. Since that time, I have continued to take in and fully experience the beauty that is nature, whenever and wherever I possibly can.

Another awakening occurred several years later. My younger daughter, Sherri, who was then approaching her fifteenth birthday, absolutely loved animals. She had been the kind of child that would get excited to see a squirrel run up the tree in the park or to hear the gentle cooing of the mourning doves which nested in our back yard. She was also known to cry hysterically if a gold fish died. Sherri had been asking for a dog since she was able to say the word "doggie," and, persistent child that she was, had never given up on that request. One day she and I were at the shopping mall and she dragged me into the pet store. She showed me this little Yorkshire Terrier sitting in the cage with a forlorn look in her eyes. I knew right away that I was in trouble. The main reason was that not too long before this my inner voice had told me it was time for me to make animals my friends. I knew I couldn't fight this one, for I would have been not only fighting my daughter, but the Universe as well. We got some information about the puppy and went home to see if we could get this one by Tom. After all, Sherri's birthday was coming in just two weeks and this would be a wonderful birthday gift for her. That evening all four of us (Tom, Sherri, Debbie, and I) returned to the pet store to check this whole thing out. We left, less than an hour later, with a new addition to our family. We named our new puppy, Brittany Ann.

I was, even to that day, terrified of animals, especially dogs, and even more especially big dogs. I had been bitten by a German Shepherd as a small child. During my late twenties, while riding my bike in the neighborhood, I was again bitten by a big German Shepherd. It wasn't only big dogs that terrified me, however. If my sister's dog, a twenty-pound toy poodle, even came near me I would cringe in fear. I never touched her and if she licked me, I would begin to hyperventilate. Having a puppy in the family was challeng-ing at first. But, to my surprise, it wasn't long before I fell totally and completely in love with Brittany. She became like a third child, like my new baby. It was then that I finally experienced what it was to love, and be loved by, an animal. Up to that point I couldn't even imagine how people could love animals. They were, after all, "just animals," something to be feared, and something right up there with my body and nature in terms of undesirable things. Now I knew first hand what it was like to love an animal. Brittany and I have a very special relationship. (Although Brittany was originally bought for Sherri, when she went off to college two years later, Brittany was all mine!) Her undying, unconditional love has given me so much. Her presence in my life and the spiritual opening and healing that resulted has been such a gift to me. What a difference this little ten-pound creature has made in my life. She has been one of my most important teachers. I hope she knows how much I truly appreciate what she has given to me. Since Brittany came into my life, I have begun to love and appreciate all animals, to see them through a different set of eyes. I have begun to view them as part of the great Web of Life, deserving of our honor and respect, and to celebrate them as the magnificent creatures of Great Spirit that they are. And today, ten years later, thanks to Brittany, I am no longer afraid of dogs, no matter how big or small they are.

My reconnection to the greater circle of life continued to take place in a number of ways, perhaps the most significant being my connection to Mother Earth and the natural world. The vehicle for this transformation was my ever-increasing interest in Native American spiritual concepts and traditions, which had been sparked by my first vision of Sky Hawk. While the traditions of each tribe are unique and different, Native Americans generally view the earth as a living entity, as truly our mother, and as such, something to be cared for, honored, and respected. They see Great Spirit as being present in and revealing itself through the natural world. Their indigenous lifestyle, close to nature, reflects these beliefs and is marked by harmony and balance. From this tradition comes the concept of oneness and connection of which Inner Shaman speaks.

People of European heritage, in what has come to be called Western culture, have over the centuries come to view the earth as an inanimate, lifeless object, something to be used and even abused for the benefit of humankind. It does not view God as being present in nature, only as the creator of it, which maintains a notion of duality and separateness. This is the belief system in which I was reared. I spent a large part of my life not appreciating the earth's beauty or magnificence, taking it for granted and never tuning in to Earth Mother's spirit. The more that I have been exposed to Native people's concept of the Web of Life, the more I have come to value and accept its simple wisdom, and, in so doing, I have come closer and closer to Mother Earth and to All My Relations.

Several years back, I had a powerful experience that brought the notion that we are all one home to me in a big way. While hiking with my family in Sedona at Christmas time, 1993, I fell and cut my knee. My daughter and her fiancé noticed a plant nearby that they thought was an aloe vera plant. They suggested that we cut off a piece and apply the aloe vera gel to my knee to take the sting away and help it heal. I told them to ask the plant if it was okay to do so, which they did, and then they cut a piece off. Finding no healing gel inside, we soon realized that, although the resemblance was there, it was not a very large aloe vera plant at all. (We later learned that it was, instead, an agave plant.) We brought the cut-off part home and it sat on the countertop for the rest of the week. Right before leaving to return to Chicago, I flippantly threw it in the garbage without a second thought.

The following May, Tom and I were hiking in Sedona when I saw some wild grasses that I thought would look nice in a vase that I had in our townhouse. So I cut some of them, and put them in my back pack in such a way that they were partly hanging out. As we walked along, I noticed that they were bending and breaking and would not survive the hike, so I once again flippantly tossed them on the ground without another thought and went on my way. Later that day we were hiking on Bell Rock, and as I walked near an agave plant (a succulent type plant with very hard, pointed arms with razor sharp tips) it seemed to reach out and cut me. I was wearing shorts at the time and received a nasty cut, about six inches long, on my right lower leg. As I looked down and saw the blood dripping down my leg, I had a powerful awakening. I immediately recalled the agave plant that I had been a party to cutting five months earlier and I intuitively knew that my cut was somehow related to that event. I knew that I had just received another wake-up call, a message from the Universe, but I was not completely sure what the message was.

The next day, while meditating in Boynton Canyon, the answers came. I had a vision, and saw the image of an Indian, wearing a long feathered headdress, who identified himself as Black Elk (a renowned, deceased Native shaman of Lakota Sioux heritage). He spoke to me and told me that the cut I received was no accident. It was, in fact, a message from Spirit to teach me a valuable lesson. I wrote in my journal: "Black Elk said that we are all one, all connected, and when you cut a plant, you cut yourself, and when you hurt an animal, you hurt yourself. Animals and plants need to be treated with honor and respect and always in proper balance, taking only what you need." He said that it is all right to take from nature, but only if you respect and honor what you take. By mindlessly tossing both the agave plant cutting and the wild grasses away (even after I had asked permission to cut them) I failed to honor and respect these plants, and in so doing, flagrantly disrespected this guideline. This experience helped me to move out of Western thinking that objectifies the natural world and sees it as existing purely for our material use, into the Native perspective which holds that everything is alive, everything has spirit and, as such, demands honor and respect, because *WE ARE ALL RELATED.*

Black Elk also told me that the cut I received from the agave plant showed me what happens when we do not respect nature, that there will be consequences. My actions had their consequences, with a gentle reminder from Spirit that my behavior was not acceptable. He helped me to realize that what happened to me, because I cut the agave plant and pulled the grasses and disrespectfully discarded them, was exactly what will happen to humankind collectively if we do not learn to respect nature and to accordingly maintain a balanced relationship with it. This is what humankind needs to learn—to honor and respect all of nature, all of life, because we are all one, all related—if we are going to survive. It is, according to Black Elk, the only hope for the future of the human species. I learned a valuable lesson from that experience. I have a scar on my leg as a lasting reminder. Today, when hiking near an agave plant I unquestionably respect it, always keeping a good distance and blessing it as I pass.

During our next visit to Sedona the following October, I was gifted by Spirit with another vision that addressed the notion of honoring Mother Earth and all that she provides for us. The vision helped me to deeply experience the connection that ancient indigenous people had to the Earth. They were connected to the land and knew on a very deep level that they were a part of it. I gained a strong sense that these people knew their place in the grand scheme, how they fit into the great Web of Life. In my vision, I was a young child who lived in an ancient Native culture. I was participating in a sacred tribal ceremony honoring corn and acknowledging its importance. Following is the journal entry I made after my experience:

> The meditation began with an image of corn. I am a young female Native American and I am participating in a ritual of some sort honoring corn. Corn is a "giver of life," a very important part of Native people's lives. Everyone, including the children, fast from food during the ritual. This is a sacred ceremony that lasts for several days. It gives honor to the corn and the earth. I think it has something to do with giving back to the earth in thanksgiving for what it has given to us. I have a feeling the giving back involves planting—the whole tribe participates in some way in the planting of the corn.
>
> I have an incredibly strong sense of the harmony of these people. Their lives are so much in sync with nature and the cycles of life. Everything is part of the great rhythm with Nature, Spirit and Self. This is what health is. U.S. culture is so disconnected, so out of harmony and balance with this rhythm of life that the whole society is dis-eased. Native people have long held the secret to health and wholeness through honoring and maintaining this harmony and balance with the rhythm of life.

Perhaps there is an important lesson in this vision for all of us. If we are to heal ourselves and our sweet Mother Earth we need to return to the harmony, balance and rhythm of the cycles of nature and live our lives, both individually and collectively, in sync with them. We need to live in such a way that honors the notion that, as Inner Shaman says so clearly, *WE ARE ALL RELATED.*

Another profound experience that I have had in realizing that we are all one and in deeply connecting to Earth Mother, occurred during an all women moon lodge (sweat lodge) that I had the opportunity to participate in several years ago. It was an experience of deep connection to both the earth and to the other women in the lodge. Sitting around a pit of large red-hot rocks in the small tent-like structure of the sweat lodge, bodies touching, I felt truly connected to my sisters, the other women in the moon lodge. For the first time in my life, I sat naked on the earth, feeling the moist dirt beneath my skin. For the first time ever, I felt deeply connected and one with Mother Earth, the feminine energy that she brings forth, and with my sisters who sat in the circle. Together we sang, prayed, laughed, shared our joys and our pain, delving into the essence of the feminine. Each one of us was deeply touched by the experience. Sweating, singing and sharing, together in the womb of Mother, we were truly of one spirit—with each other and with the Earth—reflecting the reality that *WE ARE ALL RELATED.*

Another equally powerful experience that I had in connecting with Mother Earth took place during my solo vision quest while at Brooke Medicine Eagle's Spirit Camp in the summer of 1994. Resting continuously on the earth for two days, alone with nature, alone with spirit, I made a deep and lasting connection with the earth.

Prior to our vision quest we were given very specific instructions on what we were to do during those two days. We were allowed to bring only a tarp, a sleeping bag, warm clothing, and water. We were to set up an eight foot circle, marked by four stones, each one the color of one of the four directions (yellow for the East, red for the South, black for the West, white for the North). This was our circle of power, and marked the area in which we were to remain confined for the two days. Brooke had suggested that if we felt comfortable in doing so we should allow ourselves to be naked at least part of the time. Since the weather was extremely hot and sunny, this sounded like a great idea to me.

The first day was an experience of ecstasy in the arms of Earth Mother. I wrote in my journal:

> The day was really quite blissful. I was comfortable, had very little hunger and lay around all day feeling cradled in the arms of Mother Earth. Being naked I felt like a new-born baby, held, nurtured, loved and supported by my mother. It felt as if I was immersed in the earth, completely one with her. Oh, how sweet! I felt very safe and protected by Spirit, so that when darkness came I was not afraid at all.

I was truly deeply connected with the earth and Spirit that day, truly in a place of harmony and oneness, the likes of which I have not experienced before or since.

And, I think that what I wrote in my journal, "...so that when darkness came I was not afraid at all," holds the key to the healing. It was because of this incredibly strong feeling and knowing that I was connected, one with Spirit, one with Mother Earth and Father Sky, that I was not afraid. It is in the letting go of fear that we become empowered and it is the empowerment that heals. When I am truly connected to the Greater Circle, when the dark times come into my life, I know that I do not have to fear because I am not alone. Being able to live my life without fear is one of the most important aspects of my healing journey.

The notion of separateness is only an illusion that our minds create; it is not reality. We are always connected and part of the

Oneness that is Life. But when we fear we limit ourselves, for we restrict, constrict and limit the flow of energy that moves through us. This is what creates the illusion of separateness, as fear virtually closes the door to the Greater Circle and to Spirit. Spirit does not go away—we shut it out through fear.

There was another experience that I had several years prior to this that dramatically illustrates the notion that we are all connected and that when we feel connected, we can let go of fear. It was during the Desert Storm War, a period in my life when I was dealing with one fear-related issue after another. I had been watching the TV reports on the progress of the ground war all day and all evening. My husband was out of town that night and I was all alone in the house; well, Brittany and I were alone. I had a very bad cold and was sleeping rather fitfully. Shortly after falling asleep, I was suddenly awakened by a loud noise. I didn't know what it was, but it frightened me. I tried to calm myself down by telling myself that it was "only a basement noise," you know the kind that the furnace or water heater makes.

I soon fell back to sleep, only to awaken several hours later, about 1:30 A.M., coughing profusely and in a complete state of terror. I sat up in bed and reached for some cough drops that were on the nightstand next to me, and remained sitting up while the cough drop melted. As I sat there, the terror became more and more pronounced. My heart was pounding and I was literally frozen in fear. I didn't have a clue as to what exactly I was afraid of, but I was paralyzed by fear all the same. I sat there too afraid to even move a muscle.

I was in therapy at the time and my therapist had always said that it would be okay to call her any time of the night or day if I really needed her. "If I ever needed her before, I needed her now," I thought. The only problem was that I was so paralyzed in fear that I truly could not move. I could not get my body to move several feet across the bed to pick up the phone on the other night stand, let alone walk into the next room to get her phone number. So instead, I thought to myself that I would send her a telepathic message, telling her I needed her and asking for her help. Shortly after sending this thought out, I saw—and I was still awake, sitting up in bed—a blue "gassy" looking being come into my room and lay down on the bed next to me. It was her, my therapist; she was there. I truly recognized her essence and felt her presence. She said some things to me and asked me some questions and just lay next to me for a while. My fear soon dissipated and I fell easily off to sleep, dreaming about the two of us walking together somewhere.

The next morning, remembering what had happened, I didn't know what to make of the whole thing. I was certain that I was not asleep, nor was I dreaming. I was sitting up in bed, with my eyes wide open and I saw this blue being come into my room, something that I had never before or since experienced. Two days later, when I saw my therapist for a session, I told her of my experience. She told me that she too was awakened by her coughing about 1:30 A.M. that morning and that as she lay awake in her bed she sensed a blue light leaving her body and she didn't know what to make of it at the time. Now it all made sense and she knew where the blue light had gone.

This story clearly demonstrates that we really are connected to each other at very deep levels, so much so that when we call out—to Spirit, to the Universe, to each other—for help, it does come, and that when we experience this connection, our fear is abated. Once again, separateness is merely an illusion; connection is the true reality, for *WE ARE ALL RELATED.* This experience was extremely healing and empowering for me. It enabled me to take a giant step forward in moving through fear by deeply instilling in me the notion that, just as Inner Shaman attests, we are all connected.

There was another major shift in my life around this time that made my reconnection to nature and to the earth possible while at the same time helping me to move through the issue of fear. It was when Tom and I first started making trips to Sedona, Arizona. Prior to our first visit in 1991, my idea of a vacation always included fun in the sun and surf. I love the water and, consequently, whenever we planned a vacation, I always pushed for the ocean view room on a beach somewhere, preferably somewhere in Hawaii. Lying on the beach getting a tan and sipping strawberry daiquiris was my idea of paradise. Tom had wanted to visit the Grand Canyon for years and I had resisted, always managing to get my way with the ocean view room. Anyway, this year I finally gave in and reluctantly agreed to give the Southwest a try, even though there would be no ocean view rooms to be found. We ended up staying in Sedona, Arizona for our vacation. I'll never forget my reaction as we approached Sedona and the magnificent red rock terrain came into view. The awesome beauty of the red rock formations literally took my breath away. Mother Earth was in her most splendid glory, and I quickly knew I was hooked. I fell in love with this magnificent place. I didn't even miss the ocean view, for the view was spectacular enough without it.

Tom also fell in love with Sedona and we made a true connection to it, returning again and again, eventually buying our own town-house there. It has been during these trips to Sedona that I have deepened my connection to the earth and nature so profoundly. It has also deepened Tom's and my connection, for it is during the time that we spend together in Sedona, close to the Earth Mother, that we are able to come together in ways we have never been able to before. It has been a time of coming together in which we both support and encourage each other to confront our fears by trying new things.

An experience that we had on our second visit to the red rock country, in May of 1992, best illustrates this. We had been hiking in the area of Boynton Spires, and stopped to rest. I went off by myself to meditate, and as I did so, I was aware that Tom was sitting about thirty feet away, occupying himself by playing with some stones on the ground. After my meditation I walked over to Tom and saw that he had constructed something out of the stones that I had thought he was "playing with." I asked him what he had made and he in turn asked me what I thought it was. I replied, "It looks like two little medicine wheels joined together by a line of stones." He said, "That's right, but what does it mean to you?" I thought for a moment and said, "Is it the connection between the two worlds— the spirit and the physical world?" He replied, "Sort of, but it's more." And then, I was flooded with a wave of understanding and said, "It's you and me, isn't it? And it's the two worlds as well—the physical for you and the spiritual for me." He shook his head in affirmation and took me in his arms and we both cried. Then we simply sat together on the earth, in silence, both of us deeply feeling this connection between us that has come as a result of our connection to this magnificent place. Tom had simply embodied the connection that he was feeling in a stone formation. He had embodied his understanding of a coming together of two people who are so different, a true coming together of the two worlds—the physical and the non-physical.

I have always tended to be internally focused, preferring to spend my time with my head in the clouds with my spirit friends, and not feeling at home in the physical world. Tom, on the other hand, is externally focused and very grounded in the physical, feeling uncomfortable in the non-physical realm. What he recognized and shared with me is that here, surrounded by the beauty of the natural world, we have found a way to come together in a way that we had never been able to before. In Sedona, we are able to take each other's hand and enter into each other's worlds, worlds that are unfamiliar and a bit scary for each of us, but in so doing we have found a way to compliment and balance each other. He leads me into his world and I lead him into mine. He has taught me how to walk through the physical wilderness, and I am teaching him to enter into the wilderness within. This has allowed us to connect and share in ways that we have never done before and has given us both the opportunities to move through our fears of unfamiliar worlds. Tom has learned to talk to rocks and I have learned to climb them.

I was not, as I said, an outdoors person, but with Tom's help, I quickly became one. Tom and I bought hiking boots, backpacks, and water bottles and took up hiking as our major pastime while visiting Sedona. This has opened up another world to me, one filled with challenge and adventure in the wilderness—a totally new experience. I began to do things I had never done in my life and to stretch myself to do things that my fears had always stopped me from doing in the past. Things as simple as walking across a stream on a log or stepping stones, climbing up steep rocks, walking along a path precariously close to a 400 foot drop, all became major challenges. I was terrified of doing these things, not only because I had never done them, but also because I had never felt safe and comfortable in nature. At first, some of these things were incredibly scary to me, but Tom would always encourage me and cheer me on until I moved through my fear and achieved whatever the goal was. He still does that to this day. Nowadays I feel safe and comfortable in nature and I feel blessed to have come so far from the days when I never even noticed the earth's beauty or appreciated a sunset, or the scent of a flower, or the magnificence of one of God's creatures. I have begun to live in the physical world and have found that it is truly a wonderful place to be.

The empowerment that came from this reconnection is significant. I am reminded of a Native American verse that I once heard that attests to this:

> Within and around the earth,
> within and around the hills,
> within and around the mountain,
> our authority returns to us.

So, opening up to the world of nature in the wilderness surrounding Sedona and stretching myself beyond my normal limits has restored my "authority" to me. It has enabled me to seriously address the issue of fear in my life. What I have found is that facing and moving through my fears at the physical level, in these ways, has helped me to do the same at other levels, in other ways. This has been one of the most important components of my healing process, enabling me to grow and expand in ways I never dreamed possible. It opened up new universes of possibility to me, universes that I dared not enter before because my fear held me back. It is as if I have begun to live, really live, for the first time in my life—to be alive in the World and to be conscious and aware of my place in it and my connection to it, without fear. Knowing that *WE ARE ALL RELATED* and that I am truly one with *ALL THAT IS* has gifted me in many ways.

## HEALING JOURNEY:
### Activities for Going Inward

JOURNAL EXERCISE: We are All Related

The natural world has always been an inspiration to artists and writers. It seems to me that the beauty of nature speaks to us, filling us with a sense of connection and inspiring us to capture on paper the feeling of Oneness that we are experiencing in that moment. On one of my visits to Sedona, while sitting in stillness beside Oak Creek during a moment of Oneness, the rushing water inspired me to write this poem:

## LISTEN TO THE SOUND

Listen to the sound, listen.
The river calls my name.
It invites me to partake of its cool, clear essence.
River running strong and free, show me the way,

Listen to the sound, listen.
Hear the ancient words,
the truths of long ago echo through the canyon.
Canyon proud and deep, show me the way.

Listen to the sound, listen.
Raven's squawk startles me,
awakens me to its song of peace and beauty.
Raven singing true, show me the way.

Listen to the sound, listen.
Wind rustling through the tall pines,
whispers a magical tune of sacred mystery.
Pine tree standing tall, show me the way.

Spend some time alone in nature, allowing yourself to feel a sense of Oneness with all of creation. Take your journal along. Sit quietly, and just listen. Be open. Listen with all of your senses. Let nature speak to you. She might speak to you through a sight, a sound, a feeling or an insight, but trust that she will speak if you will listen. "Listen to the sound, listen . . ."

Then, write a piece of poetry or prose in your journal that reflects your experience. Just listen and write what comes into your mind. Don't think about what you're writing, just listen and write. If you're thinking that this won't work, just try it. You might find that you'll be pleasantly surprised, for, after all, *WE ARE ALL RELATED.*

## MEDITATION: Outdoor Walking Meditation

Spend some time alone outdoors walking around in silent meditation. As you walk, taking in the beauty that surrounds you, allow yourself to connect with all of nature. Experience the earth beneath your feet, the sky above your head. Take in deep long breaths of air as you feel the wind blow gently around you and the warmth of the sun upon your face. Pay attention to the plant life, perhaps even noticing some vegetation that you have never noticed before. Hug a tree. Look for signs of animal life; listen to the sounds of the birds. If you are near a body of water, drink in its vital energy with your spirit.

When you feel as if you have deeply connected with the natural world around you, select a plant, tree, animal, body of water, or rock to bond with. Spend some time getting to know it, experiencing it as an observer. Touch it, hold it, smell it, listen to it. Examine it thoroughly; sense it completely. Then, imagine that you are it, feeling your energy merging with its energy, until you feel as if you and the tree, plant or rock are one. Experience the world the way it would. If you have merged with a tree, feel your branches swaying in the wind, or if you chose a bird, see the world through the eyes of a bird. When you feel totally at one with it, begin to converse with it. Ask it questions. If there is a particular issue that you are working on, a decision that you need to make or question you want an answer to, ask it for advise. Listen to its response. Allow it to gift you with its wisdom, taking in all that it has to say.

When you feel complete, thank it and say good-bye. Slowly pull your energy back to yourself and disengage from it, feeling yourself coming back into ordinary, everyday awareness. Remember to record your experience in your journal.

RITUAL: Making Sacred Soup

*Native people call this notion the Web of Life and refer to this con-*
*cept of Oneness as the Great Circle of Life… there is no such thing*
*as separateness. Everything is within the same soup, so to say.*
*Within the pot exists a liquid that contains chunks of things. The*
*chunks have an illusion of separateness, but they exist only with-*
*in the larger context of the soup. The carrots, celery, potatoes, etc.*
*may have the illusion of being distinct entities, which in some*
*respects they are, but in the grander picture they are all part of the*
*same soup. It is vital that all people come to understand this con-*
*cept. There is really no such thing as separateness. WE ARE ALL*
*RELATED! WE ARE ALL RELATED! We are all existing with-*
*in the same soup. We are all made of the same substance. We are*
*all connected at very deep levels.*

Once again, go out into the world of nature and find a spot that seems to call to you, one that feels very comfortable for you to spend some time in making "sacred soup." If you already have a favorite spot, perhaps you would like to go there. Using stones, twigs, acorns, pine cones, seashells or whatever is available, construct a circle, which represents the soup pot. Make the circle any size you like, but one that is large enough for you to stand in. Then, walk around the area and collect things from nature to represent the ingredients in the soup—earth, air, wind, fire, sun, moon, stars, mineral, animal, plant, human, Spirit, etc.— making it as inclusive as feels right to you. As you place each ingredient in the "pot" (cir-cle), affirm to yourself, "*WE ARE ALL RELATED.* We are all existing within the same soup." When you have added all of the ingredients that you wish to include, enter the circle yourself, remembering to state your affirmation of connectedness to all things, seen and unseen. Once inside the circle, allow yourself to do whatever feels right at the moment—singing, dancing, drumming, praying, or just being still. But, whatever you do, make it your intention to honor the Great Circle of Life, the great soup in which we all exist. Honor, celebrate, give thanks and pray for the healing of the "soup."

When you feel complete, end your ritual in a way that feels appropriate. You may leave the circle in place, and visit it regularly. But, remember that you have created a sacred space and, if left intact, it needs to be kept sacred. You may also disassemble the circle, collect the elements or ingredients, and put them in a basket or bowl to place on your altar as a daily reminder that *WE ARE ALL RELATED*.

# POWER IN MY SOUL

I can feel the power.
It stirs deep within my soul.
Sometimes it frightens me so.
I can feel the power.
I want to learn to use it,
but it seems so elusive.
When will I become one with the power?
When will I let go and surrender to it?
I know that is what I must do,
but sometimes it frightens me so.

— M. S.

*July 7, 1995*

## CHAPTER SIX

# Energy in Healing

*ENERGY IS THE SOURCE OF ALL LIFE. It emanates from the one Source of all energy, all power, all life, the consciousness that you call God or the Creator. God is the energy and much, much more. The Creator shares itself with you as a way to further expand its experience and to continue to unfold more and more, in accordance with the Divine Plan. The unfoldment of ALL THAT IS is what this is all about. Do not believe those who tell you that God is perfect and, as such, does not change. God is ever changing and yet always the same. God is a magnificent paradox of mystery and incomprehensibility, at least for humans at your current level of awareness. To reiterate, then, God is the source of all energy.*

*The nature of energy is that it is always flowing. Energy, to be in a healthy state, must be constantly freely flowing and moving, always in a state of balanced and harmonious flow. It must be constantly moving or it stagnates. Stagnated energy is what can cause dis-ease, pain or illness. When the energy begins to stagnate in any area of the body it can cause one of these problems. This is a basic concept that most indigenous peoples, including the Chinese and Hindus, have known for centuries. Western medicine has yet to acknowledge this principal, but it will have to take a closer look very soon.*

*Everything consists of energy. All matter is a form of energy that has been condensed. Physical matter is the densest form of energy, while light is the least dense. Light has a high, fine vibration, while matter has a low, dull vibration. This does not mean that one is better than the other is, but that they are different. Matter and light can be likened to below and above, or the earth and the sky, the body and the spirit, female and male. What occurs in the*

135

*human body is the coming together of these two vibrations of energy, the body and the spirit. As this occurs life form comes into existence. The joining together of the dense, dull energies with the high, fine energies is what gives us life.*

*Within the human system, this coming together, this interface between the two energies takes place in energy centers commonly called chakras. There are a number of these energy centers in the body, each one having a different vibratory rate or frequency. These centers are the control centers, so to say, for the physical expression of life force energy. They are spinning vortexes of energy.*

*There are seven major chakras located in the body and a number of others located outside of the physical body. Our discussion here will be limited to these seven chakras located in the body. It is from here that the body receives its programming. The energy coming from the material or physical spheres (the earth) and the energies coming from the unseen world (the heavens), come together creating life and energizing the system. Each chakra is associated with a different vibration, which in turn is associated with a different color, sound, endocrine gland and function within the system.*

*The first chakra, the root chakra, located at the base of the spine, has the color of red and is associated with survival issues and rooting in the material plane. It is where we are anchored to the earth and where we are energized by her. The second chakra, the spleen chakra, is located just below the navel and is of the same vibratory rate as the color orange. It is associated with issues of identity, sexuality and creativity. The third chakra, the solar plexus, is located just below the rib cage and is of the color yellow. It is related to issues of power and emotional energies. It is the place of personal power. The fourth chakra, the heart chakra, is located at the heart area and has the color green. It is the center of love, forgiveness, healing, compassion, joy and grief. It is the spiritual center of the body, while the second chakra is the physical center. The fifth chakra is the throat center and has the color blue. It is the center of communication and creative expression. The sixth chakra is the third eye, located between the eyebrows, and it has the color of indigo. It is the center of psychic knowing, intuition and inner vision. The seventh chakra is the crown chakra, located at the top of the head, and its color is violet. It is the connec-*

*tion to the higher realms, to the heavens. It is the place where we are energized by the spirit world, as the first chakra is the place where we are energized by the physical world.*

*This all fits into the shamanic perspective in that the shaman knows about the necessity for maintaining a balanced energy flow. The shaman is constantly aware of the energy exchange that must go on between people and people, nature and people, and within the individual and spirit. This balanced exchange of free flowing energy is what gives life to all things. When the flow is completely stopped, that particular life comes to an end. When it is partially blocked illness or dis-ease occurs at some level. This is why energy can be a vehicle for healing. In virtually all cases, energy must be manipulated at some level for healing to take place. There must be a shift in energy to bring the system back into balance. Unless this takes place there can be no healing. A shaman knows that this must happen, that energy must be flowing smoothly and harmoniously throughout the system, as a river flows through its banks. If the flow is blocked at any point, the blockage must be opened so that the energy can flow freely again. This is basic to the repertoire of any healer.*

*The reason that I mention this is that this notion is vitally important for the well being of the system. When these energy centers get out of balance or begin to malfunction, dis-ease can result. The energy must be moving freely through the body and through these centers at all times. When it is blocked pain or illness occurs. Shaman healers have always had an understanding of the role that energy plays in the human system. They know that energy must be moving and balanced for the health of the organism. Shamans also know how to orchestrate the energy to help effect healing. Kahunas (Hawaiian shamans) are masters at using energy to heal, as are shamans of many other traditions. The shaman understands the vital importance of the role that energy plays in both the health and the dis-ease of the body, and has learned how to manipulate the energy so that balance and flow is restored.*

MY FIRST EXPOSURE TO THE NOTION OF CHAKRAS and the body's energy system did not come from Inner Shaman. It came, oddly enough, from Shirley MacLaine. During the mid 1980's, actress Shirley MacLaine made quite a splash, stirring up skepticism and controversy in Hollywood, with her book, *Out on a Limb.*[1] In it, she literally went "out on a limb" in telling the story of her spiritual awakening and the changes that ensued in her life as a result. My spiritual awakening was seemingly paralleling Shirley's at the time, and I was taken-up with her writings and the message she conveyed—essentially that we are one with God. Before the days of Inner Shaman, this was a rather novel idea for me, not to mention the rest of the population, but it was an idea that every cell in my body resonated with none the less. Greatly impressed and influenced by her message, I thought of Shirley MacLaine as a role model. She was one of my most important teachers. I read all of her books, viewed her made for TV movie based on *Out on a Limb,* and I even attended her weekend "Finding Your Higher Self Seminar" in 1987.

During this seminar, Shirley devoted a good deal of time to teaching about the body's energy centers. I can still see her standing on the stage before 1200 people pointing to a large chart with the outline of the human body and seven colored circles—red, orange, yellow, green, blue, indigo, violet—representing the seven chakras. She led a chakra balancing meditation and several experiential exercises as well. By the end of the weekend I had acquired a basic understanding of the nature, function and purpose of the chakra system. This marked the beginning of my quest in the area of energy healing. My appetite had been whet and I wanted more.

Shirley's teachings brought to my awareness the importance of the chakra system in maintaining health and healing, for it is through the chakras that we integrate body, mind and spirit. Good health, she claimed, is dependent upon the proper alignment and functioning of these vital energy centers. "An imbalance in the chakras disturbs and blocks the flow of energy within the consciousness and properly functioning physical health becomes distorted."[2]

I found this notion intriguing and set out to learn as much as possible about the body's energy system and its implications for healing, reading voraciously all that I could about the chakras and their role in healing. The chakras, as defined by Anodea Judith and Selene Vega in their book, *The Sevenfold Journey*, are "centers of activity for the reception, assimilation and transmission of life energies."[3] Each of the seven chakras corresponds to parts or organs of the body, an endocrine gland, and bodily processes, such as breathing, digesting or procreating. At a psychological level, each of these energy centers relates to a different life issue, such as survival, sex, power, love, communication, imagination and spirituality.

The function of the chakras is very closely related to the emotions, which affect the flow of energy through them. When an individual has an emotional disturbance, it becomes translated into an altered flow of energy to the corresponding chakra. Significant unresolved emotional issues in any one of these areas can result in chakra dysfunction, leading to a deprivation of nutritive energy flow to the region of the body, glands and organs associated with that particular center.[4] For example, grief is associated with the heart center. This is where the term "heartbroken" comes from in regards to grief over a loss. Someone who is experiencing grief for extended periods of time is likely to develop a heart problem if the unresolved emotional energy results in a blockage in the heart chakra.

The free flow of energy, both through the entire system and individual centers, is thus necessary for health at all four levels of being—physical, mental, emotional and spiritual. Since this is an interactive system, the chakras do not exist or function in isolation and the condition of one chakra affects all the others in the system as well. When the energy flow is blocked in an individual chakra it can be said to be either excessive or deficient. A deficient chakra has very little energy moving through it, which means that the corresponding body part, organ, system or activity associated with it is also energy deficient or blocked, thus capable of causing a malfunction in that particular area. A blockage in the first chakra, for example, might manifest as hemorrhoids or constipation. An excessive chakra is also blocked, because in effect it does not know how to let go and thus restricts the flow of energy through it, becoming too cluttered to be optimally functional. It is also possible for a chakra to be out of balance within itself, that is, deficient in some aspects and excessive in others. Whether excessive or deficient, a blocked chakra throws the entire chakra system off balance, as it makes the optimal flow of energy through it impossible. This can result in a variety of dysfunctions within the body.[5]

This awareness opened up a new world of possibility for me. I thought that perhaps, since I had so many symptoms, issues and problems at different levels, finding a way to release blockages and balance my chakras would prove to be beneficial. For the first time in my life, I began to pay attention to my body's energy system (something that I previously didn't even know existed) and its potential role in creating wellness and healing in my life. By this time, my healing journey was well under way, with the chronic fatigue and headaches showing some improvement, but lower back pain was still presenting a major problem and the autoimmune condition had yet to be diagnosed. Healing continued to be a major priority in my life. Setting out on a new leg of my journey, I moved into a period of energy healing.

By the late 1980's, with my healing focus having taken on this new perspective, one colored by the body's seven energy centers and the relationship they held in my healing process, my healing intentionality shifted. I now had a new priority of balancing and aligning my chakras. In looking back, it appears that I concentrated on one chakra at a time (essentially beginning with the first and making my way on up), dealing with issues related to that particular center. This wasn't something that I consciously set out to do, but in retrospect that's what happened. The notion of "We Are All Related" applies to the chakra system as well, so this did not happen in a strictly linear fashion. There was a simultaneity and overlap in chronological time during this process, but there were definite time periods during which my main focus was primarily on the issues linked to one or another of the chakras. In general, the process involved my focusing attention on the energies associated with a particular chakra and setting the intention to heal issues related to it. The Universe seemed to take over from there, providing opportunities to address where the healing work was needed. All I had to do was to respond to each opportunity by challenging myself to take risks, experimenting with new behaviors and being open to the changes that would follow. Over the years, this approach to healing has proved to be tremendously beneficial.

First chakra issues deal with survival, fear, safety in the physical world, groundedness and connectedness to the earth. Located at the base of the spine, the root center energizes the legs, feet, base of spine, hips and pelvic region, providing overall strength and support to the entire body. Some dysfunctions resulting from first chakra imbalances include: obesity, eating disorders, hemorrhoids, constipation or diarrhea, knee troubles, frequent fears, inability to focus, and "spaciness."

When I began my psychotherapy early in 1989, I searched for a therapist who was knowledgeable of the body's energy system and its relationship to healing. I found one that fit these criteria, and the first issues that popped up were related to root or first chakra energies. We plunged right in. It was during this "root chakra phase" of therapy that I addressed the issues of fear, owning my physical body and connecting to the Earth as discussed in earlier chapters. It was apparent from the start that I simply didn't want to be in a physical body—a classic first chakra issue. Early in treatment, during a guided imagery session in which I was regressed to a fetus, I discovered that I didn't want to be born. Leaving the freedom and expansiveness of the spirit realm only to be constricted in a physical body with all of the accompanying limitations was very disconcerting. That seemed to be consistent with the fact that for my entire life I was disconnected from both my body and the physical world around me, preferring to "space out" rather than be fully present in the physical realm. At age forty, that issue had yet to be resolved. Living fully in my body, being grounded in the physical, had always been a challenge. As previously discussed, through exercise, psychophysical movement, guided imagery, chakra meditations, exploring nature, and so on, I began to feel more grounded and connected to my body and the earth. I lost the feeling of not wanting to be on earth, gradually coming to a place of embracing life with a newfound enthusiasm and aliveness.

The second chakra, sometimes known as the spleen chakra, is associated with the expression of sensual emotion and sexuality. The notion of duality leading to relationship presents itself in this center, as well as the concept of polarity—of female and male, yin and yang.[6] This center is linked at the physical level to the spleen, urinary bladder, large and small intestines, the appendix and the sacrum. Imbalances in the spleen chakra can lead to such disorders as colitis, irritable bowel syndromes, bladder tumors, sexual dysfunction, sexual anorexia or sexual addictions, emotional instability, and low back pain.

When I began to work on the second chakra in conjunction with my psychotherapy, I dealt primarily with healing relationships. I continued to work on relationship issues with Tom, which we began in our marital therapy the year before, but which still needed more fine-tuning. While dealing with the energy of this center, life also presented me with an opportunity to face, resolve and heal some long-standing extended family relationship problems. I went through a time of both external and internal turmoil as a result, but it all culminated in healing many old wounds.

While focusing on second chakra issues I also began to address the relationship of my internal male and female energies, attempting to bring my yin and yang energy into balance. I traditionally had difficulty in being productive, often feeling like I wanted to *do* something, but lacking the drive or ambition to get whatever it might be done. This left me feeling impotent. I was great at being passive, but taking an active role was a challenge. I could come up with plenty of ideas for things that I would like to do, but could rarely get myself around to actually carrying the idea to fruition. It was clear that my female or yin energies (receptive, passive, submissive, etc.) were dominant, and that my male or yang (active, assertive, driven, etc.) side was in hiding. I recall during this period having a dream in which I was in the bedroom of the house I lived in as a child, when a slender, tall, gentle man walked out of my closet. He was not the least bit threatening, but I was terrified of him all the same, running out of my room as the dream ended, awakening with my heart pounding out of my chest. I interpreted this dream to mean that there was a part of me that was terrified of my own male energy, so much so that I kept it in the closet. This dream inspired me to work on confronting my fears about expressing male energy, bringing these energies into balance, and allowing my male side to fully emerge—a pursuit that I began back then and continue to work on to this day.

The solar plexus center or third chakra deals with issues related to personal power, will and energy. This center supplies vital energy to the abdomen, stomach, pancreas, gallbladder, liver, kidneys, spleen, adrenal glands, lumbar vertebrae, and the upper intestine. Malfunctions brought about by a deficient solar plexus chakra include: timidity, low energy or chronic fatigue, submissive approach to life and digestive troubles. Lack of self-worth or a hidden sense of shame are typically root causes for third chakra blockages.[7]

These all sounded quite familiar, describing me to a tee. If my symptoms of chronic fatigue, digestive troubles, low-self esteem, and submissiveness were indeed an indicator of an imbalance in my third chakra, then my work in bringing this center into balance was clearly spelled out for me. It was a time when my focus was on personal empowerment.

I traditionally avoided conflict at all costs. I was terrified of it and did my utmost to back out of a fray whenever possible. This fear of confrontation left me feeling intimidated by others and prevented me from entering into relationships based on equality, rather than the one-up, one-down dynamic that I was accustomed to. I went through life trying not to make any waves. My father had always given me the admonition, "Keep the peace." I did my best to follow his bidding, even if keeping the peace meant being submissive, unassertive, timid and ineffective.

During the last year of therapy, early 1991 to March of 1992, I began to make some changes in this area. As a result of the gains I had achieved in therapy, I was feeling better and better about myself. My self-esteem, self-confidence and sense of self-worth were definitely on the upswing and it was beginning to show in my relationships and interactions with people. This new sense of power, reflecting an energetic opening of my solar plexus, came out most strongly in my relationship with my therapist.

Richard Gerber, in his book, *Vibrational Medicine*, makes the point that "persons who become preoccupied or 'stuck' in the lessons of the solar-plexus center may either be tyrannical in their outward aggressiveness and assertiveness, or just the opposite—they may be cowardly, meek and submissive."[8] I believe that my therapist fit the first description and I fit the second. This combination worked well until I began to come more into balance within myself, inadvertently throwing our relationship out of balance. I no longer wanted to play the role of the timed and submissive client in a child-parent, one-up, one-down relationship. I wanted to claim my power. As a result, we began a period of entering into one power struggle after another—a battle of the solar plexus. This situation afforded me the opportunity to practice my newfound skills of standing up for myself without fear and feelings of intimidation, but it also sounded the death knell of our therapeutic relationship. Although painful at the time, it was a valuable and essential part of my healing process. It was the healing of this aspect of my life that empowered me enough to "make some waves" in the relationship and stand up for myself, even if it meant leaving therapy after more than three years. I had gained much from our work together, but I felt the time had come for me to move on and to continue my journey unaided by anything other than my inner guidance.

As a result of this experience I was beginning to question whether my father's advice about keeping the peace was useful. It had helped me survive the challenges of childhood, but as an adult, did it still serve me? Would it have served me to "keep the peace" and not stand up to my therapist when that would have meant retarding my growth? Richard Gerber, in a discussion of third chakra issues speaks to this notion:

> Many illnesses, which are manifestations of chakra imbal-
> ances, are the results of faulty data on old memory tapes,
> which have been recorded and programmed into the
> unconscious mind during early portions of the individual's
> life. These tapes have been unconsciously playing back
> messages told to them by others or falsely thought by
> themselves, which are no longer appropriate to present-
> day circumstances. Regardless of their inappropriate
> content, these inner tapes are used as reference material
> by the unconscious mind to formulate each person's phys-
> ical self-image and sense of self-worth. In order to change

the blockage and imbalances in the chakras, it is necessary to recognize the bad messages we may be sending our-selves and to change the inner programming.[9]

My father's message of keeping the peace was on one of my old memory tapes. Though well intended, it was clearly disempowering. It instilled in me a sense of fear and unrealistic responsibility, setting up a situation that put me in an untenable position. Sometimes it is wise to keep the peace, but it hasn't always served me to do so, and I needed to change the old programming that was causing a block-age in my third chakra. I struggled with this issue my entire life. Even on his deathbed, in March of 1994, one of the last things my father said to me, just hours before his passing was, "Keep the peace." I loved my father dearly and always wanted to honor him, so I found myself in a double bind. How could I honor my father's admonition and honor myself at the same time?

This matter has since been resolved. During a psychic-awakening workshop that I attended in October of 1995, I participated in an experiential exercise of communicating with the deceased. Each participant wrote the name of the deceased loved one they wanted another participant to communicate with on a piece of paper, and the names were placed in a bowl for members of the group to draw from. I put in my father's name, and when it came my turn to draw a name, it was his name that I drew. I don't believe in accidents, and I think he had a burning need to get a message to me directly, for as the message was coming through I couldn't write fast enough. Following is the complete, unedited text of the communication I received:

> Hello, babe. It has been a long time since we talked. I am doing quite well here. I have learned so much since I departed and there is still so much more to learn. I am finally at peace and, although you all are not so happy that I left, it was the best thing for me. I needed to move on. I

was wearing thin. My heart ached, not with the disease, but with the pain of living a life filled with chaos and disharmony. I did not learn while on earth how to find peace and harmony with your mother. That is my one regret. I was not open to learning it. I did not believe that it was possible. Now I know that it is. You helped me right before I left to find peace. The gift you gave to me is eternal. I don't think that you fully comprehend the enormity of it, but without your loving words and send-off I might still not have found the peace I have always sought.

"Peace—keep the peace," I have always admonished you. I have since learned that peace must be an inner peace and that sometimes keeping the external peace prohibits the inner peace. I want you to understand this, as I have come to on this side. I release you from this admonition. The only peace you need to keep is your inner peace. You do not need to be the family peacemaker, as was your assigned role. I see that your calling takes you far beyond this role. You are a child of light and you must live your calling. Let go of fear and doubt that inhibits you. Be free, my dear child. Know that I am on your side. I love you, Margie. Daddy

Such healing words I have never heard before. What a gift my father gave to me that day, a year and a half after his death. He released me from an outdated maxim, and empowered me with a new freedom to honor my needs, my convictions, and to stand up for myself when the situation called for it, rather than always remaining silent in the name of "peace." His words resolved a lifelong conflict, releasing blocked emotional energy. Even more importantly, his words provided an affirmation of who I am and what I am doing, thus encouraging and empowering me to do what I am called to do. I will always be grateful for this precious gift from my father.

The fourth chakra, the heart center, is associated with issues of love, compassion, forgiveness and healing. The emotions of both joy and grief reside in the heart center. The heart chakra provides nutritive energy to the lungs, heart, arms, hands and the entire circulatory system, and is related to the thymus gland, which is an important component of the body's immune system. A deficiency of vital energy to any of these areas can cause dysfunction. When the deficiency is in the thymus gland this may contribute to a variety of diseases, including adrenal failure and diseases of the "autoimmune" type in which the body's defense system actually begins to attack its own cells. An open heart chakra is integral to a person's ability to express love, both self-love and love for another. According to Gerber, "Blockages in the heart chakra may arise from an inability to express love; but even more importantly, dysfunction frequently arises from a lack of self-love."[10]

It would appear, given the nature of my symptoms (depression, chronic fatigue—which may be a result of adrenal failure—and Raynaud's Phenomenon—an autoimmune condition affecting the circulation in the hands) that my heart chakra was not functioning optimally. Moreover, the opening of my heart chakra has been primarily related to issues of the expression and reception of love, including self-love. This issue is of such magnitude that I have devoted an entire chapter to it, Chapter Nine: "Love As Healer." Suffice it to say here that during the time period following termination of therapy in 1992, my focus shifted to clearing blockages in the heart center, and I achieved a measure of success. What I would like to discuss at this point has to do with what occurred as a result of this opening.

Throughout the entire year of 1992, I had been working furiously to open my heart chakra. I believed that there was a connection between the Raynaud's disorder in my hands and a blockage in my heart center. Hoping to eliminate the Raynaud's by opening my heart center, I employed a variety of techniques—physical exercises, visualizations, affirmations, shamanic journeys, crystal healing, energy work, meditation, and prayer. I had hoped that once opened, the energy from the heart would travel down my arms to my hands thereby healing the coldness caused by the Raynaud's condition. I also knew deep inside that I was a healer, and I believed that I would not be able to do hands-on energy healing as long as this condition persisted.

One day early in 1993, after a very deep meditation, I began to feel an intense heat in my chest as if I had rubbed it with menthol and a tingling in the palms of my hands. The next time I meditated, the same thing happened. I felt heat in my chest and a tingling sensation in the palms of my hands. At first I didn't think too much of it, but when it continued each time I meditated, I began to think that maybe something was happening. Then it occurred to me that this tingling that I was feeling was energy, vital energy or chi. Moving down through my heart center and into my hands, this energy could be used in hands-on healing. The Raynaud's in my hands was still present, but that did not affect the energy emitted from them. They could be ice-cold, but heat would emanate from them regardless. I was delighted! Perhaps I was to be a healer after all—the wounded healer yes, but a healer all the same. I began to try my new abilities out on my family and friends. Tom was quite impressed when, during a vacation in Hawaii in April of that year, my hands-on energy healing resulted in relieving the chronic pain he was experiencing in his knee from running. I used the hands-on technique with several of my friends, with positive results as well. I was excited about the possibilities, about what this might lead to, and looked for a system of hands-on energy healing that would teach me more. It was then that I became acquainted with Reiki.

The word Reiki means universal life energy, defined as being that power which acts and lives in all created matter. When performing Reiki, the healer is channeling this energy, a spiritual, sacred light energy capable of raising consciousness and promoting healing.

Essentially Reiki energy is Love. The Reiki system of healing is a simple, natural method of transferring this universal life energy for healing others as well as for self-healing. Treating with Reiki brings a person back into harmony with self and the Universe by bringing into balance aspects of the four levels of being—physical, mental, emotional and spiritual.

I was attuned to First Degree Reiki in March of 1994 and Second Degree in September of that same year. The following November I had an opportunity to put the self-healing component of Reiki to the test. By this time my lower back problems were a thing of the past. I had not been to the chiropractor for over a year and I was doing just fine. One Sunday afternoon I noticed some pain in my lower back, an old, familiar pain that usually meant trouble. The next morning when I got out of bed, I knew I was in trouble. I could not stand up straight; my spine was out of alignment with one shoulder higher than the other—a familiar stance I had experienced before. I knew exactly what I had, as it had happened so many times in the past. My sacrum was sprained and my pelvis was rotated out of position. Typically, this particular ailment would require at least three or four chiropractic adjustments, wearing a special brace, and a good four to eight weeks to heal completely. I was beside myself with disappointment, as I had thought that I had healed to a point that this serious of a sprain was no longer an issue. I became discouraged and immediately called the chiropractor's office to make an appointment, hoping to get in that day (Monday). The chiropractor was ill and would not be in the office that day. The next available appointment was on Friday. In the past, I would have toughed it out until seeing the chiropractor, believing that only she could "fix" me. I made the appointment, but, this time, decided that I would have to take action myself. I could not wait until Friday to stand up straight or be rid of the pain.

I rolled up my sleeves and went to work. I lit candles and turned on my meditation music. I spent the entire morning lying on my family room floor, meditating and giving myself Reiki, feeling very connected to Spirit. As I lay there with my hands on my body, I could feel the energy moving through my hands and coursing through my entire body, bringing with it the healing power of Reiki energy. By afternoon I began to notice a difference. The pain had lessened and I could stand a bit straighter. I continued to give myself Reiki treatments over the next few days. By Thursday I was not bent over at all, and by the time I went to the chiropractor's on Friday, there was no trace of the sprain.

What I gained from this experience was a deep, first-hand realization that, for me, self-healing involves a connection to Spirit, and being with Spirit in the presence of the Reiki energy proved to be a genuinely effective self-healing technique. This certainly sold me on the power of Reiki and the following February I became attuned as a Reiki Master-Teacher. Today I share this healing energy with others, incorporating Reiki healing sessions into my clinical practice.

The fifth chakra, the throat center, is related to issues of communication, creativity and self-expression. It is the center associated with higher creativity involved in writing, art, composing music and other forms of artistic expression. At the physical level, it supplies energy to the thyroid gland, the neck, shoulders, arms and hands. At a psychic level, it is related to clairaudience, or inner hearing. When an individual's throat chakra is blocked, the person may experience such malfunctions as an inability to communicate or express oneself, blocked creativity, sore throats, stiff neck and shoulders, thyroid problems, or hearing problems.

Perhaps the major indicator that my throat chakra was not in balance was that I had difficulty writing. I have always had good writing skills, but I have also always felt blocked when it came to writing. I especially had difficulty writing in a journal. The journaling that I have done over the years has been sketchy at best. A past-life memory that surfaced in 1993 just prior to being accepted into my doctoral program (which would necessitate a good deal of writing) shed some light as to why this was so. Healing this situation went a long way toward opening my throat chakra. Following is a journal entry dated August 12, 1993, which explains the situation:

> Last June, during the psychic-awakening workshop, when asked to go to a past life that related to blocks of spirituality in this life I saw myself waiting to be burned at the stake. I knew that I was a young girl of only 16 and that I was about to be executed for having written something about Jesus that was out of line for the time. I was being held, waiting my turn to be burned at the stake. I could see that three or four others were presently being burned. I could hear their cries of agony and smell the smoke and burning flesh. I was terrified. I knew that I had awareness in that lifetime that the current religion had Jesus, his life, his purpose and his message all wrong.
>
> During the workshop exercise, as a way of healing the past trauma, I had been given the directive to redo the scene the way I would have liked it to happen. In the replay, I saw Jesus come down and appear to the crowd in the courtyard. Jesus told them that what I said was true, that they had missed his message and were way off course. Then I was released and went off with Jesus.
>
> Last Saturday while watching the movie, "1492," there was a scene very similar to the one I had seen in my past life exercise [at the workshop]. It was all I could do to refrain from screaming in my living room as I watched the video. The courtyard was as I had experienced it and there were three or four persons being burned at the same time. One of them was a nun, who, unlike the other women, had her head covered. A priest handed her a cross to kiss before they started the fire beneath her.

The next day, still quite upset by the scene, more of my own story came to me as I was meditating. I remembered that I too had been a young nun in that lifetime. I had entered the convent at age 13, very devoted to Christ. When I was almost 17, I wrote in my personal journal that I believed that the Church had Jesus' teachings and message distorted, along with my personal feeling of frustration and sadness. Another nun found my journal and reported me. I was promptly taken away and sentenced to being burned at the stake for heresy. The year was about 1500.

This past-life memory certainly explained my reluctance to write, especially to write in a journal, as I had been burned at the stake for something I had written in a journal. I evidently carried the fear of writing from that life into this one. No wonder my throat chakra was blocked. According to Gerber, past-life experiences can affect an individual's chakra system in a current lifetime:

> Interestingly, the unlearned lesson may not originate within the present lifetime. Disease may also be related to past-life carryovers. These include both physical and mental disorders. Hypnotic past-life regressions of individuals with unusual phobias have helped them unlock the real traumatizing emotional events, which caused the phobias. When the individual remembers the traumatizing incident from the past life, the phobia usually disappears. In the case of physical illnesses relating to past-life difficulties, there are different energetic pathways involved. The chakras are also an important mechanism behind the karmic expression of illness. For instance, an individual who has not yet learned the important life lessons of the heart chakra in one lifetime will carry over these unbalanced energies into future lives.[11]

It appears that I may have carried over the fear of expressing my thoughts and feelings in writing from that lifetime almost five hundred years ago as a result of the traumatic experience of being burned at the stake. Gaining this awareness, together with healing the trauma from the past, has helped to release that fear and to free blocked energy in my throat chakra. At least this was a beginning.

The realization that my throat chakra was still in need of some major work came to me while at Spirit Camp in Montana during the summer of 1994 (as discussed in Chapter Three). One afternoon, we were all together in the large group singing. I was admiring how beautifully Brooke Medicine Eagle sang, wishing I had a voice and singing ability equal to hers, when I noticed that my throat was hurting from singing. This was nothing new. My throat always hurt when I sang. What was new was the realization, which came to me for the first time at that moment—the name I had been given by Spirit was "Thunder Song", and it hurt me to sing! When given the name, I had been told by Spirit that I "was to sing Great Spirit's song," but my throat hurt when I sang. Something wasn't right here. Why did my throat hurt when I sang? I know that I don't have an especially good singing voice and that carrying a tune is not one of my gifts, but it still shouldn't hurt me to sing. What was the metaphor in this situation? What was my throat saying to me? Later that day I made this journal entry:

> I can't sing because my throat hurts; yet my name is Thunder Song. No wonder I feel so stuck as far as my career, service and educational issues go! How can I sing my Thunder Song [the message from Great Spirit that I need to convey to others] when it hurts to sing? I believe that I must have a power [energy] leak. I need to "get my voice."

While on my vision quest several days later I was told by spirit that I was to write this book (*Inner Shaman*) telling the story of my personal healing journey and that this book would be how I was to sing my "Thunder Song." I accepted the challenge Spirit presented to me and agreed to write the book, but I knew that I had some work ahead of me, and that in order to write a book I would need to find my voice. This marked the beginning of a determined quest dedicated to that end. The way I believed this could be accomplished was by opening my throat chakra. Since that time to the present, the focus of my healing intentionality has been on this goal. I have done just about everything imaginable—vocal emotional release work, drumming and chanting, singing solo in front of others (something I generally have avoided at all costs), poetry writing, journaling, etc. —in an effort to free up this blocked creative energy. The sore throat was merely a metaphor for a closed throat chakra, not the problem. What needed healing was my blocked creative self-expression. I believe I have come a long way in healing this impediment. The writing of this book—the singing of my Thunder Song—is testimony to my achievements, for, to be sure, I could not have accomplished this work otherwise.

The sixth chakra, the brow center, is the seat of intuitive perception, psychic as well as conscious awareness, imagination and inner vision. Known as the "third eye," it is the internal visual screen upon which we project images from imagination, dreams, memory or clairvoyance. This chakra is the center of "seeing," related to the vibration of light. It is developed by various types of meditative practices, which enable the practitioner to introspect or see within. The brow chakra is associated with the pineal gland, the pituitary gland, the spinal cord, the eyes, ears, nose and sinuses. Disorders related to dysfunction of this center may indicate an individual's reluctance to look within and to "see" their inner or spiritual truth. Energy blockages at the level of the sixth chakra often manifest as sinus problems, visual problems, headaches, nightmares or hallucinations.

Although, as already discussed my ability for inner vision was present in childhood, it needed to be more finely developed during my

adulthood. Throughout the past fifteen years of my spiritual awakening, my meditative practices have been continuously working
toward this end by clearing energy blockages in my sixth chakra.
What I have come to realize recently, however, is that I didn't need
to work so much on opening my sixth chakra as I needed simply to
recognize and claim my intuitive abilities. I have always denied or
minimized my intuitive or psychic abilities, which disempowered
and denied my experiences. I was both afraid of the power and
doubtful of it at the same time. What I needed to do was to let go of
my fear and to simply validate my visions, my inner voice, my intuitive impressions, etc. I needed to refrain from devaluing or
ignoring them as I so often did.

My experience at Spirit Camp while on my vision quest brought
this to my attention. I had gone to Montana that year to participate
in a vision quest hoping that I would have "the Mother of all
visions." I was hoping that I would see something with my physical
eyes, not just with my inner eyes as I always did. I wanted this so
badly that I was willing to risk the dangers of the wild and go without food for two days to get it. I did not get what I wanted, but I got
what I needed—a realization of the importance of my spiritual
experiences, whatever they may be. Following is an excerpt of what
I wrote in my journal describing my experience the second day of
the quest:

> I felt really disappointed that I had not had any major
> VISIONS. I had hoped for some magical vision of Jesus or
> Buffalo Woman that I could see with my eyes, but all that I
> had was my ordinary, everyday inner visions that I get at
> home. I didn't need to go off alone into the wilderness and
> starve myself for two days for that!
>
> But as I watched the stars later that night I realized that I
> was always connected to Spirit. How many times during the

course of a day do I communicate with Spirit? I am so gifted in this regard. Maybe this is the major learning. Spirit is
in *all* things; all things can be our teachers. I truly am connected to Spirit. I realized the importance of this
connection. I need to stop devaluing my spiritual experiences and making them so ordinary and to celebrate my
special gifts.

Since then I have refrained from underrating my experiences. I
have learned to stop doubting, criticizing, judging, censoring and
ignoring them as well. I now simply take them at face value.
Whether they are *true* is not an issue. Whether my past life memories are *real* is not an issue. Whether I *really* travel to the upper world
or the lower world during a shamanic journey is not an issue.
Whether I *really* see Sky Hawk is not an issue. Whether it is *really*
White Buffalo Woman that speaks to me is not an issue. None of this
*really* matters. What matters is that I receive the message that I need
to receive, learn what I need to learn and grow where I need to
grow. What matters is that in appreciating the value of my experiences, I allow healing to occur. And what matters most is that I
honor my experience, whatever it may be. In so doing, I allow the
energy to flow and open the gateway for more of the same.

The seventh chakra, the crown center, is the highest vibrational
center. It is associated with thought, expanded consciousness,
understanding and spiritual or inner searching. It is the point of
entry for the higher life force energies that continuously flow into
the body, nourishing all aspects of our being. For this center to be
fully awakened there must be a balancing of body, mind, heart and
spirit. The opening of the crown center allows one to experience
expanded or higher states of consciousness. At the physical level,
this center is linked to the pineal gland, cerebral cortex and general central nervous system functioning. It also plays a role in the
synchronization of the right and left brain. Abnormalities in energy

flow at this level can manifest as various types of cerebral dysfunction, psychosis, depression, confusion, apathy, boredom and inability to learn.

As I discussed earlier, I have spent my life looking for ecstasy, that wonderful expanded state of consciousness characteristic of a profound spiritual experience. This experience of ecstasy or bliss is associated with an open crown chakra, which can be triggered by the rising of Kundalini energy. I was gifted with such an experience several years ago during my first encounter with Kundalini.

In the Hindu tradition the goddess Kundalini is believed to be a sleeping serpent, lying dormant, coiled around the first chakra at the base of the spine. When awakened, this healing energy moves upward, chakra by chakra, until it reaches the crown center at the top of the head, bringing with it awakening and a "higher" state of consciousness. The upward movement of Kundalini, often triggered by undulations of the spine, may be accompanied by shaking spasms or feelings of intense heat, with the wavelike rhythm activating pleasure centers in the brain, resulting in feelings of bliss. Kundalini rising is often a unique, intense and powerful experience capable of bringing about a profound consciousness change.[12]

My experience with Kundalini, the serpent goddess, proved to be similar to this description. It took place in May of 1990 during a Jean Houston Mystery School weekend. This particular session was devoted to exploring archetypal energy. Participants were asked to choose an archetype with which they resonated most strongly as their personal archetype for the weekend. I chose to spend the weekend with Jesus. Late in the afternoon on Saturday, Jean led us through a process intended to activate the Kundalini energy as a way of making contact with our archetype. We were led through a series of psychophysical movements to free the spine and open the energetic pathway. Then she led a guided imagery moving the energy from the base of the spine out the top of the head into a realm of light, where we were to meet the "Beloved," and back down again.

Sitting on the floor undulating my spine, as Jean was leading the guided meditation, I could feel the energy moving slowly up each chakra, bringing with it an intense feeling of pleasure. "Orgasmic" is the best way to describe what I was feeling. It was not a sexual orgasm limited to the genital region, but more of a total body orgasmic sensation, both as the energy moved up and as it descended, resulting in the most intense experience of ecstasy and bliss that I have ever experienced. Words cannot accurately describe what I experienced, but it was profound. And, I met the Beloved. I felt as if I had an intimate encounter with Jesus, a communion that goes beyond any frame of reference that I could use to describe it. My journal entry for that day reads:

> I have just had the most profoundly wonderful experience of my life—the Kundalini rising. My consciousness went up into a golden, white light and when it came back down I experienced intense feelings of union with the Beloved, a sensation of being "filled." As the Kundalini began rising I had an intense feeling of having an orgasm, without muscle contractions, in total ecstasy. I cried and moaned during the entire experience. I am so filled! The experience of ecstasy lasted for about a half an hour after the process ended. I kept thinking, "I have waited all my life for this day. He has always been with me and now we are finally united! I will never be the same after this."

This was, without question, the most powerful, profound, healing and wonderful experience in my life. It reminds me of the ecstasy I experienced as a youth while sitting in the Church on Holy Saturday, which I described in Chapter Two, only a much, much grander version. I have since attempted on a number of occasions to replicate it, but to no avail. I have had numerous experiences with Kundalini rising, but none so grand as that. I believe it was a gift, for which I am forever grateful, and it may have been a once in a lifetime experience. I hope not, but that remains to be seen. In any case, it represents a significant step in my healing journey, as it was a true experience of Oneness, serving to accelerate and deepen my process of reconnecting to Spirit, of moving into the light.

## HEALING JOURNEY:
### Activities for Going Inward

JOURNAL EXERCISE: Assessing the Chakras

After reading Chapter Six, you should have a basic idea of the Chakra system and its role in your health and healing. Using the "Rambling Writing" technique, assess the health-related issues for each of your seven chakras. Beginning at the First Chakra and working your way on up, write about the issues in your life in need of healing which relate to that particular chakra. For the first chakra, for example, you might write about your dislike of being in your body and for the second chakra about a relationship in your life that is out of balance, and so on for the rest of the chakras. Remember that these issues could be on any of the four levels of being—physical, mental, emotional or spiritual.

GUIDED MEDITATION: Visiting the Control Centers

Sitting in a comfortable position with your back straight and your eyes closed, begin to pay attention to your breathing. Resting your hands on your abdomen, begin to take in long, deep breaths that go all the way down to your belly. Breathing in a comfortable, relaxed manner, allow your breath to fill your abdominal area. Feel your abdomen rise as you inhale and fall as you exhale—rising as you inhale, falling as you exhale. Rising and falling, rising and falling, feeling more and more relaxed and peaceful with each breath that you take. Rising and falling, rising and falling, feeling so very peaceful.

Continuing to breathe in any way that feels comfortable and relaxed, shift your attention now to the inner world of your imagination. Imagine that you are becoming very, very tiny and that you are going to take a journey through your body's energy centers. Imagine now that you are on the ground floor and that there is an elevator right in front of you. As you stand there looking at the elevator, you notice that the doors are beginning to open. You step inside the elevator. You look at the numbers above the door and you can see that the elevator stops at seven floors. On the wall to your right you see a control panel with seven differently colored buttons numbered from one to seven. You press the red button marked "1" and wait. The doors begin to close and you feel the elevator move slowly upward.

When the elevator comes to a stop, the door opens and you step out into a small room. It is the control center for your body's first energy center—the Root Chakra. This center is located right at the base of your spine. It supplies energy to the feet, legs, lower spine, hips and pelvic region. It is related to issues of fear, survival, being grounded and connected to the earth and safety in the physical world.

Look around the room now and notice what the energy is like. The energy should be free flowing and balanced, with neither too much nor too little energy moving through the center. The color of the energy in the room should be red. Looking over at the wall on your right you will find a large control panel. It has a variety of different instruments that can make adjustments to the flow, intensity and color of energy moving through this control center. Take a moment now to make whatever adjustments are needed to assure that the energy in the room is balanced and flowing with just the right amount of energy moving through it. Adjust the lighting so that the entire room is a vibrant color of true red. [Allow a short pause.] When you feel that you have made all of the necessary adjustments to this energy control center, affirm to yourself, "My root chakra is functioning optimally and I am harmonized and aligned with physical reality." Now walk over to the elevator. As the door opens, step inside. Press the orange button, marked "2" on the panel to the right and wait as the elevator begins to ascend.

When the elevator comes to a stop and the door opens, step out into another small room. This is the second control center for your body's energy system. It is the Spleen Chakra, located just below the navel. It supplies energy to the spleen, urinary bladder, large and small intestines and sacrum. This energy is related to the expression of sensual emotion and sexuality and issues of relationship. Taking a look around this control room, notice what the energy is like here. Is there a balanced flow of just the right amount of energy? Is the color a brilliant shade of orange? Does the energy feel harmonious? Walking over to the control panel in this room, make whatever adjustments are necessary to this energy center so that the energy is a brilliant shade of orange and just the right amount of energy is moving through it. [Allow a short pause.] When you have completed making your improvements to the energy in this center, affirm to yourself, "My second chakra is functioning optimally and I have satisfying and loving relationships with other people." Now walk over to the elevator once again and go inside. Press the yellow button marked "3" and wait as the elevator takes you up another level.

Once again, as the elevator comes to a stop, step out into a small room, the control room for the third energy center—the Solar Plexus Chakra. This center, located just below the rib cage, deals with issues related to personal power, will and energy. It supplies vital energy to the abdomen, stomach, pancreas, gallbladder, liver, kidneys, adrenal glands, lumbar spine and the upper intestines. Notice what the energy in this center feels and looks like. Going over to the control panel, adjust the instruments so that the energy is moving through this center perfectly, with just the right amount coming in and going out. Make the lighting also perfect, so that the color in the control center is a magnificent shade of bright yellow. [Allow a short pause.] Do not leave until you are satisfied that you have made the color, frequency and intensity of the energy in the room as beautiful, harmonious and balanced as possible. When you feel complete with the adjustments, affirm to yourself, "My solar plexus chakra is functioning optimally and my inner strength and power is awakening." Now walk over to the elevator and step inside. As the elevator doors close behind you, press the green button marked "4" and wait as the elevator rises to the fourth level.

The elevator stops, the doors open and you walk out into another small room. This is the control center for the fourth energy center—the Heart Chakra. Located between the breasts, the heart center provides nutritive energy to the lungs, heart, arms, hands and the entire circulatory system. It is associated with issues of love, compassion, forgiveness, joy, grief and healing. Quickly assess the energy in this center and going to the control panel, make whatever adjustments are necessary to assure its optimal functioning. Be sure that the energy is flowing in the perfect intensity and rhythm, and that the color is a clear, vivid shade of emerald green. [Allow a sort pause.] When you are certain that the energy in this center is perfectly balanced and harmonious, reflecting its beautiful shade of green, affirm to yourself, "My heart center is functioning optimally and the giving and receiving of love in my life is in perfect balance." Now walk over to the elevator and step inside. Press the blue button marked "5" and wait as the elevator begins to move upward.

When the doors open, step out into the control room for the fifth center—the Throat Chakra. This center, located at the throat, is related to issues of communication, inner hearing, creativity and self-expression. It supplies nutritive energy to the thyroid gland, the neck, shoulders, arms and hands. Looking around this room, sense the energy. Using the instrumentation on your control panel, adjust the energy in this center so that it is flowing smoothly and freely, in just the perfect intensity and frequency. Adjust the lighting controls to make the color of the light in the room a heavenly shade of sky blue. [Allow a short pause.] Do not stop until you are satisfied that the energy is flowing in perfect harmony and balance. Affirm to yourself,

"My throat chakra is functioning optimally and I express myself to the world with love, truth and light." Then, walk over to the elevator and step inside. Press the dark blue button marked "6" and wait as the elevator ascends to the next level.

As the doors open, step out into the control room for the sixth energy center—the Third Eye or Brow Chakra. This center, located slightly above and between the eyebrows, is the seat of intuitive perception, psychic as well as conscious awareness, imagination and inner vision. It is related to issues dealing with "seeing" at any level. Once again, sense the energy in the room and notice how it is flowing, its intensity and color. Make whatever adjustments are necessary to make sure that the energy is moving perfectly with just the right amount of deep, indigo blue light flowing through the center. [Allow a short pause.] As you complete making the adjustments, affirm to yourself, "My brow center is functioning optimally—my vision is clear and I see the truth easily." Then, walk to the elevator, go inside and press the violet button marked "7."

As the elevator doors open, step into the control room for the final energy center—the Crown Chakra. This is the highest vibrational center and it is the point of entry for the higher life force energies that nourish the entire body. It is associated with thought, expanded consciousness, understanding and spiritual or inner searching. Assess the energy in this center and use the instruments on your control panel to make whatever adjustments are needed. Be sure that the energy flows freely and smoothly, in a balanced and harmonious way. Make the lighting in the room as beautiful a color of radiant violet as you can possibly imagine. [Allow a short pause.] When you feel satisfied with the adjustments to your crown center, affirm "My crown center is functioning optimally and I am open to expanded awareness and connection to a higher reality." Now, walking back to the elevator, step inside and press the button marked "G" for ground floor.

As you slowly make your descent back down through your body, imagine that there is a beam of white light that fills the entire elevator shaft. As you descend back down through all of the chakras, the white light balances and aligns all of your energy centers so that they function together optimally and in complete harmony, with just the right amount of energy moving through all of them. When you reach the ground floor, step outside of the elevator and allow yourself to return to your normal size. Then begin to return to normal, everyday consciousness. Allow your body to begin to move and open your eyes, feeling completely alert and fully awake.


### RITUAL: Crystal Rainbow

This ritual will help you to become mindful of your different energy centers by focusing your attention on each center, one at a time. Find seven crystals or healing stones (they may or may not be in jewelry) that correspond to the colors related to each of the chakras—red for the root chakra, orange for the second chakra, yellow for the solar plexus, green for the heart center, blue (turquoise will work) for the throat center, indigo (dark blue) for the third eye, and violet for the crown chakra. (If you can't find crystals or healing stones, different colored marbles or cut glass will work as well.

The color and intention is what is most important.) Put the crystals or stones in a place of honor on your altar.

Each day for seven days, focus on one particular chakra at a time by wearing or carrying the crystal or stone that corresponds in color as a reminder. You might also wear clothes and eat food of that particular color, and pay attention to the issues of that chakra. For example, on the first day (Root Chakra), red is the color of the day. You might wear a garnet and a red sweater and eat red food—beets, marinara sauce, etc. Be mindful all day of your connectedness to the earth, taking time to feel your feet on the ground beneath you. On day two, remind yourself of the Second Chakra by thinking orange. You might carry a piece of coral, wear an orange sweatshirt, eat carrots and oranges and pay special attention to your sexuality and relationship issues. Continue each day in this manner until you have acknowledged each of the seven chakras. If you have issues related to one of your chakras that you would like to focus on for a longer period of time, you can stay on one chakra longer, carrying the stone for days or even weeks at a time, until you feel complete. (I remember wearing a hunk of dioptase—a dark green healing stone—almost every day for months when I was working on heart chakra issues.)

You can embellish this in any way that you choose. Be creative with it. As always, there is no right or wrong; it is the intention that counts. A wonderful book to refer to for this ritual is *The Sevenfold Journey: Reclaiming Mind, Body & Spirit Through the Chakras* by Anodea Judith and Selene Vega.[13]

# WHITE BUFFALO

Alone she stands.
In radiance she shows herself to me.
The glory of her whiteness she unfolds for me to see.
I watch as she looks toward me,
her eyes aglow with the light of forever.
She seems to look within my soul,
to know exactly who is there.
She sends her love with her eyes,
her strength comes forth in her stare.
I know from afar that she has come to gift me with her presence.
I can hear her speak with my heart;
I can see her smile with my soul.
She tells me of my task, of what I am called to do.
She speaks of energy that I must hold,
of many things that I must learn to do.
I do not know how long we gazed into each other's eyes,
but I know that her gaze was a gift of love.
Oh, White Buffalo, you have come to me.
You have shown me the purity of your essence.
I am in awe as you whisper with your eyes,
as you speak with your stare.

— M. S.

*April 26, 1995*

## CHAPTER SEVEN

# The Search for Meaning

*IN THE SHAMANIC WORLD VIEW, everything that exists, as you know, is part of the great Web of Life, and as such is considered to be alive, to have its own spirit. Starting from the lowest forms of life to the highest, everything is one and everything is alive. Shamans view a rock as being every bit as alive as a turtle, or a tree as much alive as a bear. There is no hierarchy here; nothing is better than or more important than anything else. Each part of the Web is equally important, serving its own vital and useful function.*

*Because shamans view the world in this way, it follows that they would assign a definite meaning to everything that happens in light of this understanding. So, when a shaman, while on a journey, sees a group of stones, for example, that remind him or her of an ear of corn, then corn must be a significant piece of the puzzle. It would then be the shaman's job to ascertain exactly how corn might enter into the picture or how it might be useful to the patient in answer to whatever the question at hand might be.*

*The shaman operates within the world of symbolism and metaphor, where one thing represents or stands for another. This opens up a whole new and completely unlimited world of possibility to the shaman in performing his or her healing role. The benefits of this are many, as the shaman while operating in this paradigm, has absolutely no barriers, no restrictions as to what the meaning of the illness or the problem might be. Finding the meaning is, of course, essential, as this is where the awareness that the patient needs to know lies. Here is where that connection to the spiritual level is most likely to be found. And, as you know, it is what is going on at the spiritual level that is ultimately what needs to be addressed, what needs to be healed.*

*Using this system gives the shaman a valuable tool that others in the tribal community do not have. Assigning meaning in this way is one of the things that sets the shaman apart from the others who look to him or her to find the hidden meaning in whatever the problem is to be healed. The shaman is the master at this because he or she has the assistance from the spirit world in achieving this goal. It is generally Spirit, during the shamanic journey, that will give the shaman the insight that is required. This is truly the essence of the shamanic journey—finding the meaning in the illness or dis-ease so that the patient can gain an awareness and deeper understanding of the underlying nature of the dis-ease and then do something about it. Finding meaning at the symbolic, mythic, or metaphorical level is one of the most important roles of the shaman, and it is the role that opens the door to all healing. Once the meaning has been discovered, the patient has the awareness that will enable him or her to make the necessary changes that are required for the healing to be complete.*

*It is the shaman's role, once the meaning has been discovered, to help the person to shift his or her perspective in a way that is consistent with this meaning. This often takes some doing on the part of the shaman-healer, but it is a most necessary part of the process. Unless the person to be healed makes a shift in consciousness, healing will not occur. To reiterate, this shift in consciousness is essential for healing to take place.*

*This ancient technique, employed by shamans for thousands of years, is currently enjoying popularity among many within both your New Age communities and the Holistic Health field. Finding the metaphor, or deeper meaning, or psychospiritual connection in the illness or symptoms is a very important aspect of holistic medicine. These practitioners know that there is much more to the dis-ease than meets the eye, and that finding this meaning is truly essential for the healing to occur, for it is at the heart of the matter.*

*Until this underlying meaning, this connection to the spiritual level is found, the shaman-healer is powerless to help the patient. This is essentially what the shamanic journey is all about. It is the search for meaning, the quest for the answers that will shed light on the underlying cause of the dis-ease— the answers that will inform the patient as to why he or she lost power, so much so that dis-ease occurred.*

*Dis-ease, as you know, is the great wake-up call. It is how our higher self, through our body, communicates to us to inform us that something is not right. It is how the spiritual self communicates to the personality self that there exists an imbalance at some level causing a loss of power, or that the conscious self is not in synchrony with the higher self, is not living a life in alignment with the soul's spiritual purpose.*

*Here is another important notion that enters into the picture. Within the shamanic world view, the purpose of life is a spiritual one, not a physical or materialistic one. It is believed that life is about spiritual growth and evolvement, so that when this is not occurring as it should, when one is not following his or her soul's agenda, then dis-ease is the wake-up call that is meant to present the opportunity to turn this around. There are no accidents or random occurrences within the shamanic world view. Virtually everything has meaning, purpose, and relevancy. Every illness, every apparent "accident," every "chance encounter," every situation that comes our way has a meaning and purpose that is in one way or another related, at some level, to spiritual growth and development. Nothing happens that is not within the context of a greater schema or a divine plan. Everything that happens to us is meant to be an opportunity, that when realized, will propel us along on our spiritual journey of growth and development.*

*Illness or dis-ease, then, is truly an opportunity. It is not a punishment or a disaster, when taken in this sense. It is an opportunity presented by the soul for the growth and evolvement of the person. When viewed in this light, as an opportunity rather than a punishment, dis-ease, at whatever level, becomes a totally new experience. Dis-ease is the opportunity that our soul presents us with to learn how to heal. Dis-ease is the opportunity that the soul presents for the person to learn and grow, eventually evolving to a higher state of being, a higher level of consciousness. Dis-ease, in other words, can thus provide the opportunity for initiation and the transformation that is inherent in this process.*

WHEN I PONDER THESE TEACHINGS of Inner Shaman on the search for meaning, the first thing that comes to mind in my life is the meaning that I have assigned to life itself and how that has shifted dramatically over the years, bringing with it healing and renewal.

I spent the greater part of my life, the first thirty-five years anyway, operating within a paradigm based on fear and predicated on the notion that there is absolutely no rhyme or reason to life. The primary assumption was that things just happen because they happen, not for any special reason or purpose. There was one exception to this rule, however. If bad things happened, that could possibly mean that God was punishing you for your former misdoings. I recall as a small child falling and skinning my knee, and Mother saying to me, "Good for you, that's God punishing you for all the times you were bad!" Living life from this perspective makes the path one walks a bit scary. The old, tried and true sayings, "Shit happens," and "Life's a bitch and then you die," described my perspective to a tee. The modus operandi of this world view went something like this:

> Things simply happen by chance, and chances are that bad things will come your way more often than not, so you'd better be on your guard at all times 'cause you just never know when life, or God, is going to zap you next. The best way to be on your guard is to arm yourself with lots and lots of worry and anxiety, along with a touch of paranoia, and chronic depression. This will help prepare you for the worst, as it's bound to happen sooner or later, most likely sooner. Being on your guard also requires that you be always completely in control, keeping things as structured and ordered as possible, following an obsessive-compulsive regimen, whenever and wherever possible. This will help to minimize the negative impact of whatever bad thing you happen to be zapped with next. Of course, the upside to all of this is when you finally do get zapped, you get to be a victim-martyr and whine and cry a lot and, maybe, just maybe,

if you're lucky, you'll get some attention and sympathy. The downside is that there is always that chance that no matter what you do to be on your guard, that your worst fears will come true and you will get sick and die and end up in hell for all eternity.

This was essentially the way that I lived my life for a very long time. It was a lifestyle marked by negative thinking and plagued by worry and its sidekick, anxiety. Mild chronic depression and the obsessive-compulsive need to always be in control of things, always on top of things, were a way of life for me as well. And all of these responses were based on one common denominator—fear in all of its radiant glory. Fear provided the infrastructure upon which I based my world view and, consequently, my life.

Even in childhood I was anxious, prone to worry and depression. If today, as a psychotherapeutic clinician, I were to diagnose myself back then, it would have to be Generalized Anxiety Order of Childhood. I was in a constant state of nervous upset with one symptom after another indicative of anxiety—asthma, allergies, eczema, nervous fidgeting and frequent upset stomach and headache. I recall as a young child, feeling sick to my stomach each morning, and literally having to force myself to eat breakfast and to get myself off to school. One time in third grade, in response to a stressful situation at school, I broke out in a rash that covered my entire body. The dermatologist didn't have a clue what it was, but gave me lots and lots of cortisone to eradicate my symptoms. I was always worried or anxious about something, and my body reflected this vividly.

This pattern went on well into my adulthood, and in my mid-twenties I went through a period, once again, which I would now diagnose as a full-blown anxiety disorder of some type. It was a stressful time in my life. Debbie was then three years old and Sherri was just about a year old. My relationship with Tom was at one of its low points. He was traveling for work, spending weeks at a time away from home. I felt abandoned, left totally alone with two small children to tend to with no help from him. I also resented the fact that he got to travel and I was stuck at home with the kids. Needless to say, we were having some rather animated arguments and conflicts at the time, one of which ended up with some physical blows coming my way. And, to top things off, my uncle, my father's brother, was dying of cancer. My victim-martyr was operating on overload, and I felt overwhelmed.

On the evening of Sherri's first birthday, September 21st, we had invited my family and our neighbors over for birthday cake. In those days, I needed to have everything just perfect. I had been cleaning house and baking all day (a banana chiffon cake, layered with whipped cream and sliced bananas) and had worked myself into a typical frenzy by the time the guests arrived. In the hectic moments right before serving, I noticed that the cake, which I had worked on all morning, was lopsided—the whipped cream didn't hold up. Then I noticed that the refrigerator wasn't cold. After a quick inspection Tom determined that the compressor on the thirteen-year-old refrigerator wasn't working. The immediate impact of a lopsided cake was one thing, but the long-term impact was another. This development meant that we would be without a refrigerator until we could get the old one repaired or buy a new one. I saw that as a major disaster and I got extremely upset. My upset, as typically was the case, got Tom upset as well. Quite a commotion ensued that I responded to with my usual anxiety, tension and turmoil. In the grand scheme of things, this is a relatively minor upset, but I was living right on the edge most of the time, maintaining a tenuous balance. This little thing was enough to throw me completely off balance, and it sent me over the edge. It might as well have been the end of the world! I felt completely overwhelmed and I simply broke down. I developed a feeling of tightness or closing in my throat. It felt as though I actually had a lump in my throat. This sensation began that night and remained for the next eight months. I was, although I didn't know it at the time, in the middle of a full-blown anxiety disorder with a condition known as "globus hystericus" (the lump in the throat) as an accompanying feature.

During those next eight months, I never told a soul what I was experiencing. I kept it all inside. I did go to see a doctor who looked in my throat and told me it was fine and sent me on my way. I didn't see a therapist or receive any medication. I was on my own. Of course, I didn't know what it was, and the notion that it was cancer or something of a more serious nature haunted me everyday, but I still said not a word to anyone. I kept it all inside. This went on and on, every night I would go to bed with a lump in my throat and every morning I would wake-up with the same lump in my throat. Day after day, week after week, month after month this went on. It affected my appetite, as it became increasingly difficult to swallow. I quickly went down from 112 pounds to about 106. But I still told no one, and kept it all inside. I was a nervous wreck, terrified that I was dying of cancer and too paralyzed in fear to do anything about it but continue to respond with fear and anxiety, which was like adding fuel to the fire. I was caught in a vicious circle and I saw no way out.

This went on for about eight months, until finally one evening, as I lay in bed, it occurred to me that I had never once prayed and asked for help for this problem. I had always been one to pray. I owned, and still do to this day, a set of very well worn rosary beads that attest to this fact. So, I don't know why I hadn't prayed before this time, why I had gone so long without asking for help, but I hadn't. I began to pray. I prayed like I had never prayed before, calling out to God, crying for help, for an end to this pain. I had had enough; I couldn't take anymore. The next morning, when I awoke the lump in my throat was gone and it never returned.

This story demonstrates Inner Shaman's claim that healing, even at this superficial level, results from a connection to Spirit. I was not, by any stretch of the imagination, healed at this point, but I believe that the message that Spirit was giving me was clear, "We're here when you need us, and when you call on us, help will be there." In looking back, I see this incident as a wake-up call inviting me to begin my healing journey with Spirit. Unfortunately, it was much, much later, after many more wake-up calls, that I finally began to awaken.

I tell you this story to demonstrate how deeply caught up I was in the world view that I described earlier which ruled my life. I was trapped in a self-made prison of fear and anxiety, which was supported by a belief that the universe operated by chance and randomness. Within this belief system, I was a helpless, powerless victim being tossed about by life's fury, with absolutely no resources with which to respond. At the time I had no understanding of the bigger picture, or the grander scheme of life. I didn't have a clue about my higher self and it's lesson plan for me. I didn't know the reason we are on earth is to learn and grow, and that sometimes we need to be challenged in order for that to happen. I had no idea that life is a process of becoming, of blossoming and flowering, and that stretching ourselves beyond our comfort zone is one way that this occurs.

Instead of looking for a meaning and purpose to it all, I felt like I was in the middle of a combat zone, being attacked from all directions. Instead of looking at my symptom, a closed throat, and listening to the rather evident message that I needed to "speak my truth," I kept things locked up inside even more. I had no deeper understanding to assist me in facing the challenges and to move through them. Rather, I became consumed with the fear of it all. I became taken up in the conflict, hopelessly losing the battle, until, in complete desperation, after suffering in silence for eight months, I finally called upon Spirit for help. But even then, I didn't understand what was happening. I had a severe case of tunnel vision and myopia, and was unable to see the bigger picture, the larger drama called Life, that was unfolding in perfect divine order around me.

I continued to live my life this way, day after day, year after year, every step I took rooted in fear and marked by anxiety, conflict and inner turmoil. It was as if I had nothing to hold onto, nothing to provide grounding or anchoring for me. The Catholic religion—or at least my interpretation of it—only fed into the belief system that was contributing to my problems and offered no help for me. I felt so alone, so isolated, so completely disconnected, as if I were set a sail, alone, in a stormy sea with no understanding of how to navigate or sail the ship. Totally unassisted, I was being tossed about by the wind and water and all I could do was to stand there frozen in fear, not having the faintest idea of what to do. It was I, alone, against the world.

And so, I waged a continuous struggle with one anxiety and stress-related symptom after another, my body trying desperately to awaken me to fact that something was not right. Unrelenting migraine headache, stomach problems, cardiac palpitations, fatigue, nervous fidgeting, tightness in the chest (all anxiety related symptoms) were part of my daily routine. This went on and on, until that fateful day, in the summer of 1981, when just by "chance" (and I don't think for a minute that it was chance at all) I picked-up that book from K-Mart, *What Dreams May Come*, that I described in Chapter Two. It was then that I began to read about what life is really about. This marked the beginning of my awakening, and the dramatic shift in consciousness that has accompanied it.

Although I formulated this new world view seemingly on my own, before Inner Shaman spelled it out for me, it is essentially the same perspective, encompassing all of the same elements. It is the shamanic consciousness that I now espouse as my world view, my modus operandi. Actually, I believe that this last statement needs further clarification, for it truly is at the heart of the matter. In my unrelenting quest for truth, wisdom, understanding and awareness, as I moved along my spiritual path, I collected the thoughts and ideas that resonated within me at very deep levels (from both external and internal sources). I put together an ideology or belief system that "felt right" to me, one that, to this day, is continually evolving right along with me. But, although I was not aware of it as I was going along, I now believe that it was Inner Shaman who led the way, directing and guiding me along the path of awakening. Perhaps more accurately stated, Inner Shaman was pointing the way and I was responding by allowing the shamanic consciousness to awaken within me. I am uncertain about the exact way that it happened, but the fact remains that it did happen, and that because of it, my life has been forever changed.

During the past fifteen years, I have gradually come to view and experience life in a dramatically different way. Moving into this new and different world view has made my experience of virtually all of life, with its ups and downs, challenges and adventures, much more palatable. It has helped me to move from the victim consciousness into a consciousness of empowerment and responsibility. It has helped me to face hard times, illness, pain and loss with a new understanding that provides me with the strength to go on, even in the darkest of times. And when I begin to fall back into some of the old thinking patterns, as I occasionally do when things get tough, I can count on getting a gentle nudge from Spirit to get me back on the right track.

I no longer live my life consumed by fear, worry and anxiety because I trust that "everything happens in perfect divine order," and when challenges come, they serve a vital purpose in giving me the awareness or experience that I need to learn and grow. In other words, I now see challenge as an opportunity for transformation, a means of moving to a higher level of being, and I look for the "gift" inherent in any challenge that comes my way. I now have much more confidence in both myself and life in general, and adhere to a much more positive outlook on life. I now feel supported by the Universe and connected to something greater than myself. I now am aware that there is a grander scheme involved in my life and believe that everything happens according to a plan that is moving in the direction of my highest purpose or good, whether I understand it or not.

My life now has meaning and purpose and I can see how the pieces of life's puzzle fit together. Life is much, much better.

My modus operandi, these days, is quite a bit different from the old one. It is much less complicated, requiring a lot less effort to live by, as well. It now goes something like this:

> You are alive on earth to experience all that you can experience to help you to learn and to grow, as evolvement is your soul's ultimate purpose for inhabiting a body. Everything that happens occurs for a reason. Everything happens in perfect, divine order. That means that there are no mistakes or accidents in the universe. Whatever occurs happens exactly as it is meant to happen, without exception. You, along with your higher self, are co-creator of your life's situation, having the ability at some level to create your reality with the thoughts that you think. There is always a greater plan that is being played out, so even when you don't understand what is happening, you can trust that whatever is happening is happening for your highest good. When challenges come into your life, they are meant to be your teachers, providing you with the opportunity to transcend them and move to a higher state of being according to the Divine Plan of life. There is no need to fear, since you are always connected to Spirit and to the Greater Circle of Life and have access to the power and assistance available there. In any given situation, letting go of fear and coming to a place of surrender and trust is the course of action that is most effective, as it is what makes your connection to Spirit possible, and it is here that wonderful things can happen.

Living my life according to this new modus operandi has been, without a doubt, a much more pleasurable experience. This new set of guidelines offers a much more efficacious way of moving through life, one that allows for a greater degree of inner peace and harmony. One of the major aspects of this new set of rules that I find most useful relates to the notion that there is a grander scheme or bigger picture to be considered in any situation. When things simply don't seem to be going the way I think they should be going, I have a tendency to get ruffled feathers. In the past I would pout and carry on with a temper tantrum and get myself all worked up over something that was completely out of my control, blaming everyone and everything for my disappointment. Now, when things don't go my way, I am able to assign a different, more positive meaning to the situation, and, in so doing, unruffle my feathers. I find it comforting to be able to stand back and tell myself that even though I don't understand what's happening or why it's happening, I can trust that it is part of a Divine Plan for the unfoldment of a higher good. Let me give you an example.

Several years ago Tom and I had made plans to take our next vacation to Sedona in March (1994), leaving on the 18th and returning on the 29th. I had just started my doctoral program and I had a very heavy schedule of weekend classes, so it wasn't too easy to squeeze a block of time in that we could go. In early January I received a notification that one of my weekend classes had been changed to the weekend of March 18th, 19th and 20th, right during the time that we had planned our vacation. The next block of time that I would have available wasn't until the end of May. Well, my initial reaction was the old ruffled feathers routine, wondering why this was happening and why they had to change the class dates and spoil my plans. I quickly calmed myself down, however, by shifting into the perspective that everything happens for a reason, and told myself that maybe we weren't supposed to go to Sedona in March that maybe May would be much better. I quickly stopped resisting the whole thing, accepted the situation and made our travel arrangements for May. I didn't give the situation another thought.

On March 21st, my father, who had been struggling with congestive heart failure for a number of years, had a heart attack. On March 22nd, I visited him in the ICU and we talked and cried together for an hour, sharing one of the most precious moments I ever had with him, a moment of healing for both of us. That evening my mother told me that my dad was the most peaceful and happy she had seen him in a long, long time. She wanted to know what I had done when I was with him because he seemed to be a changed person. On March 23rd, my father made his transition into his new life as I held his hand. As he was passing, I could see a white mist billowing out the crown of his head and I knew that that was his spirit leaving his tired body to begin its journey home. What a profoundly precious moment that was! How grateful I am that I could have been with him in those last moments, midwiving him into his new life. It was a moment and an experience that I shall never forget, one that will remain with me always.

While on my morning walk one day the following June, an awareness hit me like a lightening bolt. I hadn't realized it before that moment, but if that class hadn't been canceled and rescheduled Tom and I would have gone to Arizona on March 18th, as originally planned, and we would have been in Sedona, almost two thousand miles away, when my father had his heart attack. The doctors were saying that he was going to make it. Would we have come home? Would I have made it home in time to be with him when he passed on? I really don't know the answer to these questions. But, what I do know, as certain as the sun rises in the East, is that there is a Divine master plan, and someone out there (although I'm not sure who it is or how it works) is looking out for my best interest and taking care of me. It was no accident or coincidence that that class was rescheduled and we postponed our trip. Things happened exactly as they were meant to happen because I was supposed to be there with my dad at that moment in time—and it was so.

Another dramatic example of the healing power of shifting perspective and assigning a more positive meaning to an experience
occurred in the summer of 1994. A week after returning from my
wilderness adventure in Montana (Deepening of Spirit Camp), I
returned home in the early afternoon after running a few errands. I
entered the house through the garage door that leads into the laundry room. The moment I opened the door, I noticed the front
doorbell was ringing and reasoned that someone must have tried to
ring the doorbell and it had stuck, as it often did. So, I thought nothing of it until I walked into the front foyer several minutes later to
find that the front door was ajar and there was a pile of things strewn
all over the foyer and adjacent dinning room. I stood in disbelief,
not comprehending what I was seeing, feeling like I was in the middle of a bad dream. It took me several moments to come to the
realization of what had occurred. Someone had forcibly entered
through the front door and vandalized our home. When I finally got
over my state of complete shock, I noticed that the pile on the floor
was the contents of my drawers and jewelry boxes. I ran into my bedroom to find the same thing in there. The drawers in my bedroom
and bathroom were also strewn about. I felt such a sense of violation.
Someone had gone through my personal belongings. Then I realized what was missing—all of my jewelry. Every last piece of it had
been taken, except for what I was wearing at the time—my wedding
ring and the diamond tennis bracelet Tom had given me for our
twenty-fifth wedding anniversary. Every pair of earrings, every gold
charm, every necklace and chain, every ring, everything was gone.
When I recovered enough to begin to think clearly, I ran to the
phone and called 911. I was told to go outside and get in my car (in
case there was still someone in the house) and wait for an officer to
arrive. I grabbed Brittany, ran outside and got into my car. I called
Tom at work from my cellular phone. About three minutes later a
squad car pulled into my driveway. The police officer, with pistol
drawn, checked every square inch of my house for the intruder, dis-

covered that the back patio doors were ajar and assumed that he or she must have left through those doors. The police enlisted the aid of a dog, but the thief was never found and my jewelry was never returned.

After all of the commotion settled down, the police officer asked me to make a list of what was missing. As I sat there writing one thing after another that had been taken, I began to feel a deep sense of loss. Every piece of jewelry that Tom, my children, or my parents had ever given me was gone forever. I felt so angry at having been violated, and I felt grief over the loss of my jewelry. The loss of the gold jewelry was difficult, but the loss of my crystals and healing stones was the most difficult for me. I was especially attached to a quartz crystal that I had worn almost everyday for the past three years, which had been through some very special times with me. For the next three days, I cried and grieved over the loss of the quartz crystal and my healing stones. The loss of the expensive gold jewelry was insignificant in comparison. These stones had been a part of my healing journey for the past few years. They were so special, so sacred. I kept asking, "Why? Why did my sacred objects have to be stolen?" In my anger and grief I simply couldn't come up with an answer. It seemed meaningless, such a waste. I was stuck in anger and grief for three days. On the fourth day, I prayed for help in moving through these feelings. I needed to get over it but didn't know how. As I prayed, I asked that my healing stones end up in the hands of someone who would benefit from their healing power as much as I had, that my stones would be a gift of love to someone who needed them more than I did. At that moment, I was filled with a sense of peace. The anger and outrage was somehow miraculously gone, and I was able to let go of my attachment to my crystals. After moving out of the anger and grief in which I had been stuck, I soon came to believe that the letting go was another important element of this experience. I needed to learn to let go of my attachment to material things, and this experience provided me with that opportunity.

In assigning a more positive meaning to what had happened I shifted my perspective. This changed the entire experience for me. I no longer felt like a victim who had been violated. Rather than feeling like something had been taken from me, I felt as if I had given a gift to someone in need. This was truly a moment of profound healing for me, one that I will always remember.

As I continue to ponder the teachings of Inner Shaman on these issues, and as I continue to reflect on how they fit into my personal healing story, I believe that there is another element that comes into the picture. Believing in the logic of this world view and giving "lip service" to it is one thing. But, in order for it to change my life I needed to begin to live it day by day, allowing it to play itself out in my life—I needed to "walk my talk." I realized that I needed to be open, to let go of my fear and to surrender and trust, so that the Universe can do what it does best—to support and protect me and to look out for my best interest. I believe that this will occur no matter what, but if I allow fear, doubt or mistrust to interfere, things will be more difficult. What I have found is that when I am truly open and in tune with this process, wonderful things happen, and they happen very easily.

One of these wonderful things happened to me in the acquisition of my drum. Let me tell the story. It was Christmas week, 1994. Tom and I had spent the holidays at our townhouse in Sedona. During one of my meditations while sitting on one of the red rocks, I had a vision of the White Buffalo. At the end of the vision, I saw the White Buffalo pictured in a circle, in what looked like a round drum. I was then told that I needed to buy a drum, and that the drum must have the picture of the White Buffalo on it. I was further instructed to begin searching for it that very afternoon, and that I would find one that cost about $250. Well, in recent years I have made a habit of listening to the guidance of Spirit, and, following its bidding. I have found that not doing so usually gets me into trouble, but this one seemed a bit far-fetched. Where was I going to find a drum with a white buffalo on it? Miracle, the white buffalo calf, had just been born in August. I seriously doubted that she would have made it onto a drum by that time, just four months later. But, following the surrender and trust format, I gave it a try all the same.

That afternoon Tom and I went all over Sedona searching every nook and cranny for a drum with a white buffalo on it. We didn't have much luck. At the last store that we scoured, there were a number of drums, but none with a white buffalo. I asked the saleswoman if she had ever seen one. She responded, "Oh, I wouldn't buy a drum in Sedona. I just got back from Taos and I bought one there. That's the place to buy a drum." I thanked the woman, and as I walked out of the store a light bulb went on in my head—my good friend, Magee, had just moved to Santa Fe. Maybe she could, by some slim possibility, find a drum with a white buffalo on it. We suspended our search in Sedona, and upon returning home, several days later, I gave Magee a call.

When I told Magee of my situation and my special need, she responded, "A drum with a white buffalo on it? Fat chance! But I'm going skiing in Taos tomorrow and on the way home, I'll see what I can do." I thanked my friend and said good-bye. I hadn't heard from her for a few days, so I had given up, assuming that she didn't have any luck.

About a week later the phone rang and Magee's cheery voice was at the other end. She told me that on her way back from Taos she was driving past a store, and although she had no intention of stopping there, she felt a strong attraction to turn into the parking lot. Without thinking, she made a quick turn off the road at the last minute—so quick that her dog had been thrown off the back seat as she made the turn—and walked into the store. It was a store owned and operated by Native American people. She went right up to the saleswoman and told her about her friend (me) and her friend's strange request for a drum with a white buffalo on it. The woman very animatedly told her that this was such a coincidence. She had just sold a drum fitting that description earlier that morning. Although she didn't have another like it, she would be glad to special order one that would be painted by a Lakota Sioux artist who lived in Taos. And the price of the drum? $256! I immediately gave Magee the go-ahead to order the drum, thanked my friend for her part in the miracle and waited for my drum to come home.

My drum arrived two days after my birthday. It was more than I expected. It was beautiful. In the center was a picture of White Buffalo Woman holding a pipe and surrounding her were four white buffaloes. What a gift from the Universe! My birthday gift from Spirit! I was instructed by Spirit to ritually play the drum everyday, and was told that when I drummed, I would be calling upon the energy of White Buffalo Woman. I was to keep the drum sacred, never beating on it just for fun, only in a sacred ritual or ceremony. Nor was I to allow anyone else to beat the drum—it was for my use alone. Since that time I have drummed everyday, whenever possible. Every time I sit down to record the words of Inner Shaman, White Buffalo Woman, I beat my drum to prepare myself and to call up her energy. Was this a coincidence? Did this drum come to me merely by chance? I think not. I believe that this happened because I both cooperated with Spirit and got out of its way. I trusted my inner guidance even when it seemed absurd. I was meant to have that drum, and it was so.

In researching for this book, I happened to run across an interesting tidbit of information on how an Ojibway shaman acquires his or her drum:

> ...it is not the shaman himself but the ancestral-spirit who chooses the kind of drum that the shaman will use. In addition, the ancestral-spirit also determines its size, the kind of wood used in its construction, the animal skin stretched across it, and the designs painted on it. These instructions are pronounced by elder tribal shamans.[1]

This description sounds remarkably similar to what happened to me. The selection of my drum was totally out of my hands. It was handled, as I see it, entirely by Spirit. Is this coincidence or is there more here than meets the eye, a grander scheme being played out or higher drama being enacted? I believe the latter to be true and agree with Inner Shaman when she says, "...*every situation that comes our way has a meaning and a purpose that is in one way or another related, at some level, to spiritual growth and development. Nothing happens that is not within the context of a greater schema or a divine plan.*"

## HEALING JOURNEY:
### Activities for Going Inward

JOURNAL EXERCISE: "Modus Operandi"

"Modus operandi" is defined in the *Webster's II New Riverside University Dictionary* as "a method of operating." I see it as a way of navigating through life, a set of beliefs and operating principles that determines our behavior. Our "modus operandi," typically formed very early in childhood, is a product of the programming that we received as children. This programming is a combination of what we were directly and indirectly taught by our parents, teachers and social institutions, our personal experiences, and our response to them. It is generally a very adaptive tool that helps us to get through the challenges of childhood as best we can. The problem is that it was formulated by an immature mind, with insufficient—and sometimes inaccurate—data based on very limited experience in a very limited world. We often run into trouble as adults if we continue to follow the "modus operandi" we developed as a child. Although it was very useful as a guideline in the world we lived in as children, it is no longer applicable to the world we live in today—we have changed and so has the world around us.

In your journal write what you believe to be the modus operandi that you had as a young adult (similar to the one I wrote early in Chapter Seven which reflects the world view I held when I was about twenty-five.) After you have written it, examine it and decide if it represents the world view that you hold today. Or, does it need to be brought up to date, revised for a new you and a new situation? If so, rewrite it so that it is more in keeping with the world view you hold today. (You might then want to begin to mindfully live your life in accordance with this new modus operandi.)

GUIDED MEDITATION: Healing A Challenging Situation

With your eyes closed, sit quietly in a comfortable position and begin to focus on your breathing. Allow your breath to be deep, long and rhythmic. As you breathe in, imagine that a white light is entering through the top of your head, bringing with it a sensation of inner peace and calm. As you breathe out imagine that you are letting go of any thoughts that might distract you—just let them all go. As you let each thought go, feel your mind emptying of all of its clutter, so that it becomes like any empty wicker basket. With each breath in, see the basket becoming filled with light, more and more light with each breath that you take.

Find yourself now becoming very tiny and going into that light-filled empty basket. See yourself resting on a large, billowy soft pillow that lines the bottom of the basket. This is a very special basket. While you are in this basket, your thinking is sharp and clear. Insight and awareness come easily. You have a deep level of understanding and clarity of inner vision. As you rest on your pillow, you feel very comfortable, calm and relaxed. You know intuitively that this is the place where you can go to work on healing a challenging situation. You know that healing involves a shift in consciousness or perspective, so you have come to this place to get more clarity and understanding, a different viewpoint, a change in attitude. It is a place where you can get a different outlook on any situation in your life that is challenging, troubling or that needs healing so that you might experience it differently. Now think for a moment and identify a challenging situation that you want to heal. [Allow a minute or so for this.] Good.

Imagine now that someone joins you as you are reclining on the soft pillow in your empty basket pondering your situation. You notice that it is a familiar face, your Inner Shaman. He or she comes close and sits down next to you on the pillow. You tell him or her about the challenging situation that you would like a different perspective on, and your Inner Shaman listens intently as you explain in detail exactly what your challenge is. When you have finished speaking, your inner teacher hands you a beautiful golden box and tells you to open it. You accept the gift with an acknowledgment of gratitude and quickly open it to see what is inside. As you open the lid, you see within a curious tubular object. At one end of the tube is a translucent disk through which you can see what appear to be some small, ordinary pebbles. At the other end, is a small lens. After examining the object, you realize that it is a kaleidoscope, something that you may have not seen since you were a child. Your Inner Shaman nudges you and tells you to peer through the lens and look inside. You do as he or she bids and quickly become mesmerized by the beauty of what you see. You recall that when you turn a kaleidoscope slightly, the image inside changes. So you begin to slowly rotate it, with each turn finding another exquisitely beautiful image appearing before you. You know that what you are viewing is only a collection of common, ordinary pebbles, but when viewed through this object they take on a magical beauty.

Then your Inner Shaman whispers to you, "You must see your challenging situation through the lens of a kaleido-scope. You must change your perspective on it, with each shift in perspective looking for its hidden beauty, its secret gift. This new way of viewing your situation will help you to experience it differently and to heal it." Now, for a few moments as you gaze into the magic kaleidoscope, with your Inner Shaman assisting you, allow yourself to see your challenging situation from a more positive perspective, one that will enable you to experience it differently, to heal it, to let it go and move on. [Allow two or three minutes of clock time for this.]

Remembering all of the insights and understanding that you have received, thank your Inner Shaman for the gift of the magic kaleidoscope and begin to say good-bye. Know that anytime you want to find a different way of viewing and experiencing a challenging situation you can return to your empty basket. Your kaleidoscope will be there waiting for you to assist you to see things differently. Now, leaving the basket behind, you return to your normal size and begin to come back to ordinary, waking consciousness. Begin to move your hands and feet and feel your body on the chair you are sitting upon. As you open your eyes, you feel wonderful, wide-awake, alert, and refreshed.

### RITUAL: Shifting Your Perspective

Inner Shaman tells us that a shift in perspective or consciousness is necessary for healing to occur. This ritual is designed to help you make such a shift. It is very simple—rearrange or shift things in your physical environment to create a shift in perspective at the physical level. The idea is to create a new and different visual experience— seeing things differently—to symbolize or represent a shift in perspective at other levels. Change as many things in your environment as possible. Move furniture around in your bedroom. Put a new picture on the wall in the living room. Sit in a different chair at the dinner table (if you usually sit in the same one). Rearrange your kitchen cabinets. Put new wallpaper in the bathroom. Drive to work following a different route. Move your desk at the office. Etc. It doesn't matter what you do or how many things you do. What matters is your intention—to mindfully make a shift in your visual perspective to signify making a shift in consciousness.

Each time that you make a shift in your environment, affirm to yourself that you are willing to see things differently. (If you are working on healing a particular situation, specify that you are willing to change your perspective in that situation—"I am willing to see_____situation differently.") By doing this, you are not only reprogramming yourself, but you are also demonstrating your willingness to be open to seeing things differently—at all levels.

# FLOWERS AT MY FEET

Before me she stands, with flowers in hand.
White radiance surrounds her; it reaches out to me.
Looking deep within my soul, she places flowers at my feet.
Vibrant flowers of purple hue, she puts before me.
I feel the drums; I hear the chanting.
I feel the power, the power of the sound, the power of the words.
I am surrounded by the grandmothers, the grandfathers,
all there to gift me with their love,
all there to place the flowers, the beauteous flowers, at my feet.
Surrounded by the sweetness, I stand, accepting the gifts they bring,
knowing in my depths that I am the flower,
I am the blossom that is unfolding, opening to be the me that I can be.

He comes, sits before me.
He gives me the sweet medicine, the power of opening.
I see the color and hear the sounds.
I feel the energy of a world unknown.
With a clarity and brilliance I explore this new world,
a world alive with images of color, sight and sound,
with words swirling all around,
knowing, in my soul, that I am being gifted with the gift of words,
opened to a new place, a fresh space.
I stand in the circle, flowers at my feet,
feeling the power of this new blossoming,
giving thanks for these sweet, oh so sweet, flowers at my feet.

— M. S.

*May 4, 1995*

# CHAPTER EIGHT

---

# Co-Creation

*WE, AS INTEGRAL PARTS OF THE GREAT CIRCLE of life, have the power of creation. We are all one with that which you would call the "creator" and, as such, have within us the power to create. This is not in the biblical sense of the word, but true all the same. Creative power lies in the realm of thought, in the mental realm. All of creation first existed as consciousness, as a thought, as a word. The "logos"—"In the Beginning was the word ... And the word became flesh."*

*This is the essence of creation. This is what it means to create. This is how we, and the Creator God, create. First is the thought, the consciousness. Then, and only then, can it be brought into manifestation on whatever level we are speaking of. Manifesting on the physical level is, of course, the most difficult, but it is what we tend to think of when we think of creation—making something take on a physical form or structure. But there is so much more to creation than this. We create on all four levels—physical, mental, emotional and spiritual. Creation begins, once again, on the mental level, in the realm of thought. This is the first stepping stone in the creative process.*

*Shamans have always known the importance of the power of thought, of the power of the imagination to create, for it is within the realm of the imagination that the shamanic journey takes place. It is within the world of thought, the mental realm, that the shaman does his or her healing work. A shaman knows how important the meaning that one assigns to something is, or the beliefs that one holds or the perspective that one comes from. Working within this realm is where the shaman is most at home. The shift in perspective or consciousness that is essential for healing to take place is within the realm of thought. This is vitally important for you to understand. Thought precedes feeling and it precedes manifestation at the physical level. This is the way things are. It is that simple. Without thought there would be nothing. Consciousness is the primordial sea from which has sprung all of creation, all of it.*

*I hope I have made my point?*

*Your society has somewhere along the line lost this notion. It has lived according to a belief system that says that only God can create, and **he** did that a long, long time ago. Well this cannot be further from the truth. We, everyday of our lives, co-create with the creator. We create in some way, at some level our entire reality. We create our emotional, physical, mental and spiritual reality. This is not to be disputed. What needs to be pointed out here, however, is that we are multidimensional beings existing on more than one level of realty, or in more than one dimension at a time. We have other "parts" of ourselves that we are not aware of that are co-creating with us. Our higher self, for example is one of those unseen, unaware parts that acts in this capacity. There are others, but we will not go into them at this time.*

*What is important to remember is that we are constantly creating on all levels of our being, each day, each hour, each minute, each second of our lives. Hawaiian shamanism, the Huna philosophy, terms this "Ike"—the world is what you think it is. "You think" things into existence, "you think" your life situation into existence, "you think" things into physical form. This is the first step in the creative process. This is the intuitive, feminine aspect, the yin element, of creation—the Conception of the idea, of the thought that leads to its creation.*

*The second part of the process is in the taking of action, based on the thought or idea that has been conceived. This is the male or yang aspect. This is doing what needs to be done, at whatever level it needs to be done. It is that simple. The creative process, thus, is an interactive process between male and female, between the yin and the yang. That is why those who view the creator as male are sadly mistaken—it takes male and female to create. The male, which is the one that takes the action, has traditionally been the one to get* the credit, but it takes male and female. Do not forget that, as it is a vital concept to the notion of creation.

The creative process, then, becomes this interaction between the male and female energy that is present within each of you. When we speak of creativity, we are referring to this process, this dance between male and female energy, between structure and movement, between stillness and form. This is what creativity is. It becomes a rhythmic dance, a cycle that alternates back and forth between the two—stillness, followed by movement, intuition, followed by action. This is the way it works.

The most important thing to remember about creativity is that it is how we connect to our divinity. The creative energy is the divine energy. It is the sexual energy—they are one and the same. It is our birthright to be creative beings, to create on all levels, whether it is art, cooking, child bearing or whatever. It is part of the human nature to be creative. When this creative energy is blocked, it causes dis-ease at some level. This energy must be allowed to flow and it must be encouraged to do so. The creative process is not automatic. It requires nurturance and participation, once again, the male and female aspects. Creativity is nothing more than allowing the divine, creative energy to flow through you, allowing the energy to move through you. It is that simple.

*"CREATIVE POWER lies in the realm of thought."* I knew this statement was true, from a very early age. I didn't know that I knew, but I behaved as if I did. I daydreamed quite a bit and spent a good deal of time in the realm of thought, imagining over and over all the things that I wanted life to bring me—the man of my dreams, children, lots of money and a big house. And for the most part, the dreams of my childhood came true, in one way or another, in my adulthood. In reflecting upon this pattern of daydreaming during my childhood, it occurred to me why I may have come to believe that if I wished and dreamed hard enough, my dreams would come true.

When I was very little, the Walt Disney production of Cinderella was popular. It was, by far, my favorite fairy tale. I saw it at the movies several times, and I had a 45 RPM record set, which gave a condensed version of the story on record with a picture book to accompany the vocals (those were the days before the videotape had become a household word). I listened to this record over and over again, living and reliving the story in my imagination. I remember that I especially liked Cinderella's Fairy Godmother and the magical ability she had to create with a word (sounds a bit like the "word", the "logos", that Inner Shaman speaks about). All it took was one word, "Bibbidi-Bobbidi-Boo," and she created a miracle, a "dream come true." I liked that and I believed, at some deep level, that it was possible.

But, of course, Cinderella was my favorite character, and I think that what I liked about her was that she was a dreamer, just like me. I identified with her completely. The words from the song, from her song, which I used to sing along with her, seem to tell it all:

A dream is a wish your heart makes,
when you're fast asleep.
In dreams you will loose your heartaches.
Whatever you wish for you keep.
Have faith in your dreams and someday
your rainbow will come smiling through.
No matter how your heart is grieving,
If you keep on believing,
the dreams that you wish will come true.

The words of this song spoke to me and inspired me. I didn't have the conscious awareness way back then that *"creative power lies in the realm of thought,"* but I surely believed that dreams could come true. I developed a pattern of creating my reality by thinking it into existence, a pattern that began in childhood and that has stayed with me to this day. Today, I have come to realize that dreaming the dream, as Cinderella did, is how we co-create. It is our participation in the creative process that paves the way for the dream to come into our lives, into our reality.

In reflecting upon the story of Cinderella, I can see how that fairy tale helped to lay a foundation for the awakening of the shamanic consciousness within me many years later. It quite literally created a model or patterning within me, programming me at a very tender age to think in a way that is consistent with the shamanic consciousness. If our thoughts do truly create our experience, as Inner Shaman maintains, then the Cinderella fairy tale was influential in creating an inner environment that was receptive to the shamanic consciousness.

The similarities between Cinderella's world and the world of a shaman are quite pronounced. Cinderella, like the shaman, lived in a world in which animism existed. The mice and birds could talk, and anything was possible. She was at home in this world and one with it, living the dictum of "WE ARE ALL RELATED" that defines the shamanic consciousness. She lived a life that demonstrated this oneness with nature, and one that showed that she knew the importance of being in right relationship, living in balance and harmony, with everyone and everything, even her mean stepmother and step-sisters. Cinderella, like the shaman, lived in two worlds, the world of ordinary reality and the world of non-ordinary reality or dreams. She journeyed nightly, moving easily between the two worlds to find her "medicine"—the hope and faith that kept her going—in the world of dreams, the world of Spirit to the shaman. The story even portrays the importance of meaning and the notion that everything happens for a reason that Inner Shaman emphasizes. There was a grander scheme at work here, for if her stepsisters had not ruined the dress the mice and birds made for her, there would have been no need for Fairy Godmother's intervention. Cinderella, then, would not have worn such an exquisite dress to the ball, and may not have been found so attractive by the Prince. There was a gift to be found in the pain of the loss of the first dress. Finally, Cinderella's healing came when she opened to Spirit. It was her connection to Spirit (her Fairy Godmother) that restored her power and ultimately led to her healing, a healing defined by allow-ing love into her life.

After making this connection between the Cinderella story and shamanism I can't help but think of Inner Shaman as my Fairy Godmother! Perhaps there may be more to this fairy tale thing than I fully comprehend. In any case, there is undoubtedly a reason why Cinderella was my favorite childhood story, why I grew up believing that dreams could come true, and why I was open and receptive to the awakening of the shamanic consciousness in my adulthood. The significance is really quite profound. I believe that by entering into the world of the imagination and vicariously living the life of Cinderella, I found a measure of healing in my childhood (one marked by a host of physical symptoms as well as depression, anxi-ety, poor self-esteem and lack of self-love). This identification with Cinderella unquestionably helped set the stage for the resonance that I have felt with the shamanic consciousness in my adulthood.

It appears that I somehow always knew, at some deep level, about the potentials of daydreaming, but I never realized how extensive and powerful it really was until I began to investigate the area of the mind-body connection. It was during the early 1980's, when I had just begun my quest for an understanding of what life was all about, that I happened across a book entitled *The Power of Your Subconscious Mind,* written by Joseph Murphy. It was my first formal introduction into the cognitive aspects of the workings of the mind and its relationship to co-creation. Prior to this time I had an intuitive knowing that I could think things into existence, as I had seemed to be doing that for years, but I never had any cognitive structure or form to plug this into.

Dr. Murphy pointed out the difference between the conscious and subconscious minds and how they work together to create our experience. The conscious mind is the rational, thinking mind, while the subconscious is the irrational, receptive aspect. The subconscious does not discriminate or evaluate what it is told; it merely accepts what is impressed upon it or what one consciously believes as truth and acts accordingly. It proceeds on the information that it has been given, like a computer that has been programmed with a certain type of information, and works to validate this truth. What we habitually think establishes deep grooves in the subconscious, which can be favorable if your habitual thoughts are positive, and not so favorable if they are not. The subconscious mind, in other words, is the creative mind and it creates according to the nature of your thoughts, managing to find a way to create in your life what you believe to be true.[1] If you believe that you are unlucky in love, for example, your subconscious mind will find a way to create that situation in your experience, setting you up over and over for unsuccessful relationships.

Not long after reading Murphy, I came upon a book by Shakti Gawain, *Creative Visualization.* Her ideas were similar, and she also explained the mechanism, in energetic terms, of how this process worked. Everything is energy, and we all exist in one large energy field. Thought is a relatively light, fine form of energy, while matter is relatively more dense and compact. Energy is magnetic, and energy which holds a certain quality or vibration attracts energy of a similar nature. In other words, thoughts and feelings are capable of attracting energy—in the form of people, situations, material objects, etc.—of a similar vibration or quality to them. That is why our thoughts have the ability to create. We literally energetically attract to us what we are thinking about. The more that you think about or focus on a thought the more energy you put out and the greater the possibility of attracting a similar energy. Gawain points out, " …We always attract into our lives whatever we think about the most, believe in most strongly, expect on the deepest levels, and/or imagine most vividly."[2]

Reading these books opened up for me a new way of experiencing life, a way in which conscious, mindful and intentional thinking became vitally important. What this meant was that as I day-dreamed, I was programming my subconscious, seeding it to create that which I was so vividly imagining. Unfortunately, it also meant that the litany of negative things that I used to say to myself had also programmed my subconscious computer for negative things to happen in my life. I was a chronic worrier, a grand pessimist, tending to always look on the negative side. The words that I spoke, and thought, were extremely negative, critical and non-affirming. I was a master at negative, limited thinking. This generally worked against me.

I recall one situation that stands out vividly in my mind as a perfect example of the power of negative thinking. It was sometime in the mid '70's. Debbie and Sherri were quite young—third and first grade. Tom needed to go to California in late February for a trade show that he went to each year for his company. We decided to take the kids out of school and make it a family vacation. We would be staying at the Disneyland Hotel in Anaheim, and it promised to be a wonderful opportunity. We had an abundance of snow in Chicago that year, so the thought of Southern California sounded just great. I was excited about the vacation. My excitement, however, was completely overshadowed by my worry and anxiety.

There were two things I was worried about—that one of the girls would get sick and that the weather would be bad. I recall that when I was picking up the airline tickets from the travel agent I asked about refunds in the event that someone should get sick. Of course, the tickets were non-refundable. Right then and there I began to obsess about one of the girls getting sick. My limited thinking also made it unquestionable to even think about going on a vacation with a sick child, so I worried and fretted, and prayed that neither one of them would get sick. I was also concerned about the weather. It had been raining quite a bit that winter in California and I was convinced that it would be the end of the world if it rained during our vacation, so I worried and obsessed about that too.

Two days before we were to depart, Debbie came down with some sort of flu, accompanied by a sore throat and fever. I rushed her to the pediatrician in an effort to get her well as quickly as possible, but I was mostly concerned that Sherri would also get sick. I remember asking the doctor to prescribe medication for both of them in the event that Sherri should come down with whatever Debbie had. He went along with my paranoia and gave me two prescriptions for antibiotics. Debbie seemed to be getting better quickly, but I was holding my breath, just waiting for the bug to hit Sherri—which it did the night before we left! I was beside myself, afraid to take two sick kids on a trip, but Tom told me in no uncertain terms that we were going, sick or not. So off we went. Sherri was really quite ill on the plane, and when we got to the hotel she had a fever of 104 degrees! Fortunately, she bounced back rather quickly and by the next day was able to be out and about. And, as you might suspect, the weather was lousy. It rained and rained the entire week. We never saw the sun. We walked around Disneyland in pouring rain, with raincoats and umbrellas, and water squishing in our shoes as we walked.

It wasn't exactly the dream vacation, but it was the vacation that I dreamed would occur. This time the daydreaming worked in reverse. My worry, fear and negative thinking attracted to me the very things that I was most afraid would happen. This worked exactly as Shakti Gawain claims—"...We always attract into our lives whatever we think about the most, believe in most strongly, expect on the deepest levels, and/or imagine most vividly." Instead of visualizing and imagining beautiful weather and two healthy kids basking in the sunshine, I spent my time and energy focusing on what it was that I didn't want. This negative thinking attracted that very thing to me. Did I cause that stormy weather system to stall over Southern California? Did I cause both of the kids to get sick? Did I create these things by my negative thinking? I don't think that there is a simple cause and effect relationship here. But, I do think that it's possible that in some way I attracted this situation to me, and that at some level I was co-creating this experience. What I do know for certain is that my chances for creating the vacation that I would have liked would have been much greater if I had dreamed a more positive dream.

Here, then, was where my challenge existed. I needed to begin to reprogram my inner computer, to reeducate it. I needed to stop my incessant negative, limiting thinking and speaking and abandon my skepticism and cynicism. I needed to let go of my undying belief in Murphy's Law, "What can go wrong, will go wrong," and begin to see the water glass as being half-full, rather than half-empty. I had spent a lifetime viewing the world through a pair of dark colored glasses; it was now time to change the color of my lens to a lighter, brighter shade, one that lets in more light.

This has not been easy and it still presents a challenge to this day. The knee-jerk reaction to think negatively still crops up occasionally and I have to mindfully and consciously shift my thinking and language into a positive framework. Today, when approaching a parking lot that I anticipate might be crowded I see myself pulling into a space easily, and I surprise myself at how often this really works in getting a parking space. When I'm beginning to feel anxiety cropping up, I imagine the best possible scenario for whatever the situation is (instead of the worst one as had been my pattern in the past). This goes a long way in alleviating my fear and anxiety. I am also conscious of the language that I use, avoiding words that have negative connotations, and saying positive affirmations when appropriate. I have found that these simple techniques have helped me to create a life that is much easier to live than the old one.

I have taken this pattern of creating with thought to the level of mind-body healing as well, and have found it to be useful for self-healing purposes. The basic premise of mind-body healing, very simply stated, is that the subconscious mind controls the body, and when we make suggestions to the subconscious while in a relaxed state, through words or imagery, it responds and makes physical changes in the body accordingly. I have used this technique successfully on several occasions.

One of two occasions that stands out for me as remarkable, occurred while I was taking a self-hypnosis class early in my doctoral program. Several days after receiving the notification that I had been accepted into my Ph.D. program, I began to experience heart palpitations. (I thought I had everything under control, but my body wasn't so sure, and it was speaking to me about its concern.) The palpitations began in August and went on for months. I had unsuccessfully tried visualization and herbal remedies. It was now January and I was still lying awake at night listening to my heart go "thump, thump, thumpity, thump," wondering why the noise wasn't waking my husband, who was lying next to me. One of the assignments for the class included recording a self-hypnotic induction and autosuggestion on an audiotape. We could suggest whatever we chose, so I chose to focus on my heart palpitations. In the tape, following a lengthy progressive relaxation induction, I simply suggested that "my heart beats smoothly, rhythmically, and perfectly at all times." After making the tape, I listened to it one time at home before the class. Much to my surprise, the palpitations stopped that very night. I was able to sleep without the "thump, thump, thumpity, thump" that night for the first time in months after listening to the tape just one time. I thought that was remarkable. I continued to repeat the suggestion on a regular basis and managed to eventually completely eliminate the palpitations.

Another noteworthy, mind-body healing experience occurred on a hiking trail in Sedona the following May. It was our first day there and Tom and I had done a rather long, hard, four-hour hike into Long Canyon. During the trek back out of the canyon, my right knee began to hurt, getting worse and worse with each step I took until I could barely walk. This was the first day of ten that we planned to stay in Sedona, with nothing on the agenda but hiking, hiking and more hiking. My motivation for a self-healing success was quite high. That evening I iced my knee and had Tom massage it. I also gave it a Reiki energy treatment in an attempt to get it to heal as quickly as possible.

My knee felt much better the next day, but still not 100%, so we took a very short walk to some Indian ruins instead of a long hike into a canyon. It felt fine the first hour or so, but as we were walking back it began to hurt again, worse than ever. I was beginning to be concerned that Tom would be dragging me back to the car on some tree branches, as it became harder and harder to walk with each step that I took. I quickly decided that I would give it my best shot with some on-the-spot mind-body healing, as I had nothing to lose at that point, and everything to gain. I recalled that the body has its own natural painkillers, known as endorphins, and I kept repeating to myself, "I am now releasing endorphins that will ease my pain." I said that over and over, along with some visual imagery of little "endorphin creatures" running through my blood stream bringing tiny ice packs to relieve my hurting knee. Within less than five minutes, the pain began to subside and was soon completely gone, and it never returned for the rest of the trip, even with some fairly difficult hiking. Once again, the power of the mind to create worked to effect a mind-body healing, just when I needed it most.

The power of the mind to create, as Inner Shaman attests, occurs on all levels of being, including the physical. Here is where the realm of creativity is to be found. Here is where we can take a thought or idea and bring it into manifestation on the physical level. Here is where we can embody the non-physical, the unseen, in the physical and give it shape, form and structure. Here is where creativity and art forms of all kinds interface. To be creative is our birthright, an inherent feature of what it means to be human. We need to create! Norman Shealy and Carolyn Myss, in their book, *The Creation of Health,* attest to this: " ...what is deeply ingrained into human nature is the need to create, the need to contribute something physical to this life that is a validation of our being alive. We are born—and designed—to create."[3]

Although I never thought of myself as being artistic and would never presume to describe myself as being creative, in looking back, as long as I can remember I have had a need to create things, to take a pile of materials and make something out of them. As a child, most of my favorite play activities involved making something out of some sort of material, be it sand, clay, tinker toys, blocks, miniature building bricks or what have you. Even though I had been told at school that I wasn't much of an artist, I loved to make things; it gave me a great sense of satisfaction.

This pattern was carried into my adulthood. One of the first things I did after Debbie was born when I was a full-time, stay-at-home mom, was to get a sewing machine and learn to sew. I loved to be able to take a pile of material, some thread, a zipper and some buttons and make an article of clothing. During those homemaker days, I spent most of my spare time sewing or doing needlework.

Shortly after Sherri was born I became involved in making Raggedy Ann and Andy dolls, which I sold. Over the next five or six years, I made over two hundred dolls, embroidering each face by hand, stuffing each body, making all the clothes and pulling the yarn through the little heads to create the hair. I spent hours and hours in this enterprise, loving every minute. As I embroidered the little I-Love-You hearts on each little chest, I infused my love into the doll. I hoped that the child whose hands would hold it would feel the love and care that I put into each one of my precious creations, and that my creation would bring that child happiness. This was a truly satisfying creative endeavor for me.

This all came to a sudden halt when, at age 35, I returned to graduate school. I gave up sewing, crafts and needlework and devoted my energy to schoolwork. Of course, there was opportunity for my creative outpouring to continue in the way of writing papers and assignments. The problem was I didn't view this activity as creative at all; I viewed it as a drudgery, a huge, undesirable chore I forced myself to do, and so my creative life was stifled. The majority of the creative endeavors that I undertook—writing assignments for school—were thus forced, performed without joy, passion or vitality. What a difference it was from the joy and satisfaction that I used to get from sewing. I wrote well. I even won a writing award while doing my undergraduate work, but I hated writing with an intense passion. I hated every minute of it. Because of the way that I viewed writing, because of the belief I held that writing was painful, I created a situation in which my experience of writing became excruciatingly painful indeed. It was more like pulling teeth, without Novocaine, than effortlessly opening the faucet and letting the water flow, as it might have been. After receiving my master's degree I made a firm pledge that I would *never* go back to school, that I did *not* need a Ph.D., and that I would *never* write another paper as long as I lived.

210

Today, I am once again back in school nearing the end of my doctoral program and at the moment find myself sitting at a computer writing a book. What has happened between now and then to bring about this turn of events? The most important change is that I have consciously and mindfully shifted my thinking about writing. I have totally reframed my experience of writing, and with a bit of work, I have come to believe the new context that I have created. I have begun to view writing as an art form, as a creative expression of who I am, rather than a chore that I force myself to do. I tell myself that I am a "great" writer and that writing comes easily to me. I often remind myself of the writing award I received in 1984. I have changed the words I use to describe writing from "painful" to "tedious," and tell myself that I love to write and that writing is an enjoyable experience. In so doing, I have completely shifted my experience of writing from a painful drudgery to an enjoyable, satisfying undertaking. Changing my thoughts has changed my experience, creating a whole new one that feels so much better. I have thus healed this aspect of my life by changing my thinking. This is the shift in consciousness that Inner Shaman maintains is essential for healing.

Exploring the creative process, of which Inner Shaman speaks, and how that works for me is another thing I have done that has shifted my experience of writing. Inner Shaman has long been instructing me about the notion of the creative process. "Let the energy move through you" is perhaps her most favorite statement. I've felt a lot of resistance to this concept. I found it hard to believe that being creative was as easy as "letting the energy run through me." I have always believed that writing, art or any creative endeavor has to be work, hard, painful work not a rhythmic dance of male and female energies. What I am learning of late is that this is not the case at all, and I have a better understanding of what Inner Shaman has been telling me all along—creativity is more about allowing and less about doing.

Clarissa Pinkola Estes, in a set of audiotapes entitled "The Creative Fire,"[4] presents the same message. Describing creativity as "the nutritive mother of the soul," she maintains that creativity is the bridge between the inner world and the outer world and that "all that you need to do to create is to stand out of the way." It is not so much the end result, as the process, as the movement, passion and meaning of the expression of one's inner reality that matters. She also points out that this process is cyclical in nature, alternating between rising and falling energy. The energy rises to a quickening, a birth, a zenith, only to be followed by a decline, entropy, death, which is followed by a period of incubation and then another rising and falling. This is the cycle of creativity. This is the dance between male and female energies that Inner Shaman mentions. Coming to an understanding of this dance, from the inside out, has been an important aspect in healing the creative part of my life.

In the spring of 1995 I attended a seminar entitled "Faraway/ Nearby: The Intersection of the Inner Creative Expression and the Outer Exploration of Place." One of the requirements for the seminar was to choose an area of art or creative expression as a focus. I chose poetry writing. I had never seriously written poetry in my life, but always felt that there may be a poet inside just waiting to get out, and I wanted to give that poet a chance. In the weeks prior to the seminar I wrote about twelve poems, all of which seemed to pour out of me, effortlessly. During the seminar, while sitting alone on a hillside in the magnificent splendor of the mountainous terrain of the Ghost Ranch in New Mexico where we were staying, I let another poem spill forth. It was a poem that, unbeknownst to be at the time I wrote it, is a clear expression of the creative process in general, but more importantly, an expression of my inner experience of the creative process:

## THE DANCE OF STILLNESS

Beauty exquisite I find in the stillness,
but the wind whispers to me and invites me to the dance.
The sacred dance calls me with crystalline clarity,
and beckons me to enter into its lyrical flow.
As I answer the call that sweeps through my heart,
creative forces stir in my soul.
I move with the grace of the stillness within,
choreographed by a bright inner light.
The energy takes me to luminous places,
wondrous ecstasy to know.
Who can believe that the two become one,
that the stillness becomes the dance,
and within the dance is found the stillness?

*"The creative process, then, becomes this interaction between the male and female energy that is present within each of you. When we speak of creativity, we are referring to this process, this dance between male and female energy, between structure and movement, between stillness and form. This is what creativity is. It becomes a rhythmic dance, a cycle that alternates back and forth between the two—stillness, followed by movement, intuition, followed by action. This is the way it works."* (Inner Shaman)

The notion of the creative process being a dance between male and female energies took on deep significance during the writing of this book. Early in the summer of 1996, I took three weeks off from my practice and went alone to Sedona to work on this book. The night before I left I had a dream of giving birth. In the dream, I was somewhere in a group of people. I left the group and went off by myself looking for a bathroom, as I felt the need to have a bowel movement. When I sat down, however, I realized that I was not having a bowel movement at all. I was having a baby. I sat there and watched this tiny, but perfect, little baby girl move out of my body into my hands. As I held her in my hands, I realized that her delivery had been painless, swift and easy. I had felt the pressure and the effort to push her out, but there was no pain. I had given birth without pain. The next day as I sat alone on the airplane, alone with my thoughts, the profound meaning of this dream hit me. Just as in my dream, I was going off by myself to give birth to my book, to participate in the great creative process of giving birth (which is the culmination of the dance between the male and female) and it would be painless!

During the next three weeks, I allowed the creative process to unfold around me, as I had never done before. I stayed with it and felt the rhythmic rising and falling, periods of intense activity when the words flowed endlessly from deep within me, followed by periods of frustration when virtually nothing would come out, no matter how hard I tried. But it wasn't until I had been in the middle of this dance for a while that I finally realized what was happening. During a telephone conversation with my husband after the first week, I recall telling him that things were going okay, but also complaining that I was either "hot or cold," and that I felt really frustrated when I was cold. As I was speaking those words, I had the sudden awareness that I was squarely in the middle of the creative process. I was truly dancing the "dance of stillness." The periods of "cold" that I was experiencing were the feminine aspects of stillness and intuition during which the ideas germinated and incubated. The periods of "hot" activity were the masculine aspects of movement and action when the energy spilled forth with fervor. Together, they constituted the creative process, that magnificent dance between the male and female energies within. When I finally came to realize this, that the periods of stillness were not "bad" but were a necessary part of the process, I was able to move even more deeply into the rhythm of the process and to allow it to take on a life of its own. It must have worked, because I completed more than six chapters in less than three weeks.

But more importantly, I realized the pain I had previously experienced in writing had been a result of not being in sync with this process. It was the periods of stillness that I had labeled bad, that I had felt so much frustration with that caused my experience of writing to be painful. I had put too much emphasis on the male, yang aspect, on producing a product, on achieving a goal, and failed to appreciate the necessity and power of the feminine, yin aspect, the stillness of generativity. Once I learned, experientially, about the rhythm of this stillness and movement, I was able to do the dance with joy, ease and delight, letting go of the pain and giving birth to my own creativity. This was a profoundly healing experience for me, one that can be expanded to my entire creative life, not just writing. I learned, at a very deep level, how to dance the "dance of stillness," and, in so doing, to participate in the divine creative process that is my birthright, to be a co-creator with the divine in a mindful, intentional and conscious way. And this, I believe, is what we are all called to do.

## HEALING JOURNEY:
### Activities for Going Inward

JOURNAL EXERCISE: Writing a Poem

"A *dream* is a *wish* your heart makes when you're fast asleep."

Identify one of your *dreams*, waking or sleeping, that you *wish* to bring into existence—making a career change, starting a business, getting a college degree, writing a book, having a baby, building a new house, taking a "dream vacation," etc. Then simply write a poem about your dream. Before starting, sit in stillness for a short time, calling upon the assistance of your Inner Shaman. Then listen and write down the words that come into your head, letting yourself co-create a poem that reflects your innermost dream. Remember, all you need do is to get out of the way and let the energy flow.

If you have never written poetry before, or believe that you "can't" write poetry, don't be intimidated by this exercise. Just let the words come out, without censorship, letting go of any attachment to the final results. There is no right or wrong to this. There will be no one to critique your work but you, so let go of any fear of "not doing it right," and simply write. Long or short, free verse or iambic pentameter, it doesn't matter what the structure is. This exercise is not about creating prize-winning poetry—although that certainly is within the realm of possibility. The purpose is simply to stretch you just a little to help you to explore your creative potential. Let go and have fun with it!

## GUIDED MEDITATION: Creating Your Dream

(Before starting the meditation, if you have not already done so in the journal exercise, identify a dream or wish that you want to bring into existence in your life. Remember that within this inner world, the realm of the imagination, there are no limitations—anything is possible.)

> Allow yourself to be in a comfortable position and begin to take long, deep breaths. With each breath in, feel a sensation of peace and relaxation wash over you. With each breath out, let go of all tension and every day concerns. Breathing in peace and breathing out tension. Letting go at a very deep level, feel yourself go deeper and deeper into a state of total relaxation. Allow your breath to take you to a place of complete peace deep within yourself, to a

safe, warm, comfortable spot inside where your mind is unclouded and your thoughts are clear.

Imagine now that it is a glorious day. The sun is shining brightly overhead, the birds are singing in the trees, and it seems as if the entire earth smells sweet and fresh, like the scent that follows a cool, refreshing summer rain. See yourself walking down a path through a wooded area. The path is a familiar one that you have taken many times before. It leads to your secret retreat—a little cabin in a secluded spot in the woods where you go when you want to be alone. It is your studio, your artist's studio—the place where you can create anything you wish, where you can make dreams come alive on canvas, in clay, in woodworking or whatever medium you desire.

See yourself approaching the door to the cabin. Open the door and walk in. Once inside, you look around and see that your studio is equipped with just about every tool, material, and art supply that you could imagine. There is an easel with a palette of oil paints, a table with a supply of clay for sculpting, a workbench with a tiny saw and chisel for wood working, a desk with a sketch pad for charcoal, pencils or oil pastels. There is even a computer with an elaborate drawing program. There are any art mediums that you could possibly want available here in your artist's studio. It is a place where you can be an achieved artist and create anything that you want to create.

Looking around again, you notice that someone is sitting quietly in the corner. It is your Inner Shaman who has been sitting patiently waiting for your arrival. You walk over and greet him or her, saying "Thank you for coming."

He or she is in your artist's studio to assist you. Together you will co-create a work of art that represents the dream that you want to bring into existence in your life.

Now, sitting down next to your Inner Shaman, with the eyes of an artist about to create a work of art, visualize the dream or wish that you want to bring into existence in your life. See it—with all of your senses—with the eyes of an artist. In your artist's imagination, allow yourself to experience the situation that you want to manifest. Envision it in elaborate detail. Experience it fully, feeling what it will be like, seeing yourself as you want to be, doing what you want to do, hearing yourself saying what you need to say. See the sights, hear the sounds, smell the smells, allowing the fullest sensory experience possible. See your dream happening exactly the way you would like it to happen. You have total control over this. [Allow a minute or two for this.] Good. Now that you have a sense of what you want to create, commit your artist's vision to canvas or clay, or whatever feels appropriate. Choose any art medium that you would like and create a representation of your dream in a work of art. [Allow another pause.] Know that as you create your work of art, you are embodying your dream in an art form and helping to bring it into manifestation in your life.

After you have completed your artwork, stand back and admire it, affirming to yourself that you have created this situation in your life. As you prepare to leave your studio, you say good-bye and thank your Inner Shaman for his or her presence and assistance. As you leave and walk back down the path through the woods, you know that you can return to your artist's studio anytime that you want to create something in your life, in any way, shape or form.

Take long, full breaths and become aware of your body. Move your hands and feet and open your eyes, coming back into full awareness of this time and place, feeling wide-awake and alert.

(Be sure to make some notes in your journal about what you experienced and created in your artist's studio.)

## RITUAL: Calling in Your Dream

Whenever I want to bring something into existence in my life, the first thing that I do is drum. I use drumming as a way to call in whatever I want to happen—getting new clients, finishing a project, going on a vacation, etc. As I drum, I pray, asking for what it is I want and visualizing my prayers and intentions going out into the Universe on the sound vibration. I believe wholeheartedly in the power of prayer, and see the drumming as enhancing my prayers. In addition, I see it as following the same principle of that old saying, "The squeaky wheel gets the oil." The more noise I make the more likely I am to attract the attention of Spirit and get their assistance. I'm not sure exactly how it works, but it seems to work for me.

Think of a situation that you would like to bring into existence in your life, a dream that you want to create for yourself. Then combine prayer and drumming to help you to call whatever it is into being. If you don't have a drum, rattling or beating two sticks together can work just as well. Any form of sound can be equally effective—chanting or singing can produce the same effect. You might, for example, create a song or chant that calls in your dream. (If you do, you could use the poem you wrote in the *Journal Exercise* for the lyrics of your song.) Once again, what is most important is your intention—to use sound to call to you or attract to you the situation that you want to manifest in your life.

Set aside a time each day to call in your dream by using sound. Continue your daily ritual until you get results. Have fun!

# AWAKEN

Awaken, awaken, awaken, oh, my soul.
Open to the truth existing within your depths.
Hold onto the ancient wisdom; do not let go,
but open to the new that comes from the Sacred Oneness.

Awaken, awaken, awaken, oh, my heart.
Listen to the truth that echoes in your depths.
Do not be afraid, as you are not alone.
Listen to the truth as it stirs within your soul.

Awaken, awaken, awaken, oh, my love.
Allow your beauty to simply shine forth.
Allow the light to penetrate deep within your essence,
radiating to all around as it permeates your being.

— M. S.

*July 10, 1995*

# CHAPTER NINE

# Love as Healer

*THE ROLE THAT LOVE PLAYS IN HEALING is a most vital and essential part. Without the opening to the power and the energy of love, no healing will occur. It is as if love holds the key to healing, both at the individual and the collective levels. The vibration of love is, as you know, the highest vibration in the universe. It is the Essential Self of the universe, the God Self of ALL THAT IS. Without this energy nothing would exist. It is the creative force of the universe. It is the divine breath of life that invigorates and vitalizes all living things. Without love, once again, nothing would exist. This, then, is the reason for love being essential to healing. It is the way that one finds his or her way back to the Source, to the Essential Self, to Spirit, to the Divine Oneness that is the ultimate source of all creation. It is the power that energizes the entire universe. Without love there would be no life. Love is life. Love is the very substance of life. It is the primordial sea into which one must plunge to open to the Divine. It is the wellspring of all of life and the source of all of creation. It is the energy that holds everything in place. It gives form and structure to all of creation.*

*Love is the great healer. It is the cleanser of the impurities of the world. It is the fountain from which all life spurts forth. As such, it is also the source of all renewal, rejuvenation, and rebirth. It is the emanation of the Godhead as it manifests into the physical dimension. It is the key to finding harmony both within oneself and within the larger circle of life. It is love that shines forth when humankind walks in balance with the earth and all of creation. It is the essence of the concept of all my relations. It is the circle of life. It is the Oneness that we have spoken of.*

In shamanic terms, love is seen as being essential, first of all, at the individual level in the form of self-love. If the patient does not truly love him or herself, at least in some small way, healing will not occur. This is well understood by shaman healers. Love between the healer and the patient is also necessary. If it is not a relationship marked by love the healing cannot take place within the context of that relationship. This is one reason why native healers never took money for their services—it was intended to be an act of love, not a thing to be bought or measured with a price. This love that I speak of is not as you would think of it today in your society. It is more of the universal love that is present in a flower, or a rainstorm, or a rushing river. It is the same love that sweeps across your face as the gentle wind blows. It is found in a dewdrop, the sunshine, in a cocoon, in a spider's web. It is not romantic love or an emotion. It is an energy, one that emanates from the heart. It may, of course, be accompanied by a warm feeling of happiness or peace, but it is more than that. It is the energy that vibrates the same as that of the heart. It is not necessary for the healer to feel love for his or her patients, but it is necessary to have the intention of working within the vibratory rate that is love.

More on self-love. This is perhaps the most difficult of any step in the healing process, coming to a place of full, unconditional acceptance of oneself as a person. You have been taught by your Western society, erroneously to be sure, that it is bad to love the self. Selflessness has been the order of the day for many centuries. There is some merit to this concept at certain times and in certain circumstances, but not as a matter of course. It is necessary to come to a realization that selfishness is essential. This is not to be taken to the opposite extreme either, but a balance must be attained. Your culture is currently out of balance in this area. You have raised a collective consciousness that is into self-denigration, self-hatred and self-abuse. This is widespread and insidious throughout your society. Most people do not have the foggiest notion what self-love is all about and to even suggest it makes them highly uncomfortable. This is one of the banes of your time. This is indicative of the fact that your people have lost hold of the idea that we are all one, that to love God or the other, as you have been told is what you must do to be "saved," is really to love the self. There is no separation; we are all one. We are all related, one to the other. Within this context, if you love yourself, there is no question that you will love all of creation. You would not even consider doing the things that you are doing, both individually and collectively, to yourselves and to your environment.

The healing that we are striving for is not merely individual healing; we have much too much at stake here. There really is no such thing as individual within this context. Everything is related. It is like saying that you as a person have a sore throat and that having that sore throat does not affect or involve any other parts of your body. The pain may be localized, but the problem is system wide and affects each and every cell in your body in one way or another. Just the fact that your immune system is working overtime to handle the situation gives proof to this, as it is connected to each and every cell in your body. It is not your throat that needs healing. It is you. Perhaps the sore throat is accompanied by a fever, or tiredness, or a cough or what have you. Your entire system is affected by the sore throat. Even something so remotely localized as a hangnail also affects the larger system in very subtle ways. Nothing is separate; nothing is totally in isolation. This is not the way of the universe. Everything is related, each to the other. This is the way that the Creator ordained it, and this is the way that it is.

The secret to all healing that you are searching for is to be found deep within your heart. It is about the openness to love. This is the key to all healing. Love is what, in the end, always heals in one way or another. Only those who are open to taking in love are capable of healing in the fullest sense of the word. The vibration of love is the highest and finest vibration that exists. It is the one that is capable of reversing the lower vibratory rates that keep a person stuck in illness, dis-ease or depression. Only the vibration of love is able to propel a person beyond the deadening lower frequencies that hold them to their pain and dis-ease, of whatever type. At the spiritual level, this involves opening first to the love of the self and then to the love of the Source. Unless one loves the self first, even the divine love cannot penetrate. That is to say that the Great Spirit could send all the love in the universe to you to do the healing, but unless you love yourself, you will not be open to accept this love *and the healing changes that it will bring. It is as if a channel is either open or closed depending on whether you love yourself or not. If you do, the channel is open; if you don't, the channel is closed. Partially opened channels allow only for partial healing.*

*You know when you love yourself when you first and foremost count yourself. "This above all else, to thine own self be true." These words could not be more true and more beneficial. This is the essence of self-love. If everyone were true to themselves, honoring and respecting their deepest wants, needs and wishes at all times, there would be no illness, no dis-ease in the world. It is when we get out of touch with who we are, what we need and want and the true purpose of the self, when we're not true to the self, that we find ourselves in a state of dis-ease. Without the component of self-love, healing is not possible. This is ultimately what healing is—coming to a place of utter acceptance and love of the self. This will lead one to do all of the things necessary to come into balance and harmony in relationship with self, others, Spirit, and the natural environment. When this takes place, healing is imminent. When this is out of balance and harmony, dis-ease at some level will persist.*

MY JOURNEY INTO SELF-LOVE has been the longest and most difficult of all, presenting, by far, the most challenges. You see, there was a time when I hated myself. I'm not sure when the self-hatred started, but I believe that it was very early. If I had to make a guess, I would think it started when I started hating my body, which happened when my body began to get out of control around six or seven as I entered a premature puberty. The first parts of my body that I remember really hating were my breasts. As they began to blossom, when I was just six, I used to walk around with my arms crossed in front of my chest. I felt so ashamed and embarrassed about what was happening to my body. I hated it, especially those bumps that were appearing on my chest. I remember one time playing with a little girl friend of mine who was a year older than me, but still completely flat chested. In the middle of our play, she suddenly poked my breast with her hand and said, "What's this?" I was totally taken back and excruciatingly embarrassed. How could I answer her question? I didn't know the answer myself. The training bra came sometime during first grade, amid an ocean of pain and silent tears. I hated that bra, but most of all I hated that part of my body that went in it.

It was around this time that my eczema began to get out of control as well. I had a severe case of it on both my hands and feet, which caused itching, swelling, and very painful cracked and dry skin. I remember that when I was learning how to write I had a lot of difficulty. Because of the swelling and pain, I couldn't hold the pencil correctly, and I still don't to this day. I also remember having to soak my hands and feet in a purple solution that actually stained my skin. So not only did I have itchy painful hands and feet, but they were purple as well. I hated the eczema and I hated my hands and feet because of it.

I was a big child, at least a head taller than all of my peers and chubby as well. In the third grade, I was 5'1" tall and weighed 125 pounds. I looked about five years older than I was. At the end of third grade, one month after my ninth birthday, I remember coming home for lunch one day and not feeling well. I found blood on my underwear and went into a panic thinking I was surely about to die. When I told my mother, after assuring me that I was not dying, she handed me a sanitary napkin and told me that this would happen to me every month from now on, and that I needed to wear one of these napkins—and that was that. I found myself amid another ocean of silent tears, feeling so betrayed by my body. I absolutely did not understand what was happening to me, nor did I like it. I simply hated my body, especially that part of it that was now hurting and bleeding.

It was three or four years before the rest of my peers caught up to me, and during that time my body image and sense of self-esteem went from bad to worse. I seldom felt as if I fit in, and I always felt uncomfortable in my body. It wasn't until seventh or eighth grade, after having lost about thirty pounds, that I began to feel somewhat comfortable. By that time, the other girls were all wearing bras and having periods too, and I began to feel a bit better. But that was when the acne started and went totally out of control—big-time, ugly, awful acne. I used to buy Clearasil cover up cream by the case-load. I hated those pimples. I hated that acne. I hated my face. I hated having to go to the dermatologist (but at least he helped to get the acne under control).

I remember somewhere around the age of fifteen, suddenly noticing one day that I had crooked teeth, not crooked enough in those days to warrant braces, but crooked all the same. My two upper lateral incisors were twisted, and I hated them. I remember becoming almost obsessed with just how much I hated them. The alternative to crooked teeth—braces—didn't sound too appealing either. I prayed for a miracle. I prayed that I would wake up one morning and have straight teeth and a beautiful smile, but that never happened. I went on hating my teeth and feeling extremely self-conscious about my smile, until I was nineteen. It was then that

I finally asked my mother if I could see an orthodontist. She agreed and I wore a retainer for about a year, which helped a little. After I was married, I had crowns put on which eliminated the twisted teeth altogether.

Right about the same time that I noticed that my teeth were crooked, I looked in the mirror one day and it was as though I was seeing my nose for the first time—and I didn't like what I was seeing. I was Italian, and I had an Italian nose. I hated that nose. It was too big, and it was crooked. I hated it! Not only did I notice it but others did as well, and would make fun of its size. Being so sensitive about my nose, and my entire body image, I was crushed by the kidding. Sometimes I would burst into tears if someone began poking fun at my nose. I prayed for a nose miracle! I prayed that I would wake up one day with a straight, small nose, but that never happened either. I remember thinking that we all had our "crosses to bear in life," and that I carried mine in the middle of my face. I definitely hated my nose.

There certainly wasn't too much about my body that I liked. But, after all, I was too busy focusing on what I hated about it to even consider what I may have liked, or maybe even loved.

It wasn't just my body that I hated either. It was the rest of me too. As a child, I never felt loved or lovable. That's why I felt that I had to work so hard to get people to love me, and developed the co-dependent pattern. If I was operating under the assumption that I was unlovable, then how could I possibly love myself? In addition, the message that I got from my religion indicated that it was better to love others than yourself, so the notion of self-love wasn't even a consideration. With the words said during the Mass, "Lord, I am not worthy to receive you ..." echoing in my head, I also got the message that I was not worthy, not deserving, not worthwhile. I was certainly not connected to the Divine, but separate and, more over, not even worthy to be one with it. So, with this type of programming, it was a natural conclusion for me to draw that it was much better to put myself down. After all, Pride was one of the seven capital sins and it was better for me to hate myself than it was to love and accept myself. Self-hatred and self-denigration, then, became the rule of the day. Self-love and self-acceptance was a foreign concept. Somewhere along the line, I also began silently saying "I hate myself!" on a regular basis. I said it so much that it became my mantra.

This pattern that had developed in my childhood carried over into my adulthood—low-self esteem, poor body image, self-hatred, self-denigration. The first ray of light, however, began to shine when I was in my early thirties. I believe I was thirty-two. I had been going through one of my periods of obsessing about how much I hated my nose, following an episode of some neighbor children making fun of it, and I was getting myself depressed about it. I told Tom, as tears rolled down my face, how badly I felt about my nose. Several days later he told me that he had made an appointment at a plastic surgeon's for a consultation for cosmetic surgery for my nose. He said we could sell some stock to pay for it. I was delighted and we kept the appointment. The surgeon told me that I had a deviated septum and, yes, I was a good candidate for "rhinoplasty." He then proceeded to tell me what "rhinoplasty" would involve—local anesthetic, sawing the bone, six weeks of headaches, swelling and discoloration, and one year for total recovery. I thanked him and went home with a lot to consider.

The "miracle" that I had prayed for as a teenager was being handed to me on a platter, but now that it was within reach, I wasn't all that sure that I really wanted to go through with it. After some serious soul-searching, I made a decision not to have the surgery. My decision was based on two considerations (other than the fact that I didn't at all like the word, "rhinoplasty"). The first was that a good friend of mine at the time was about to undergo surgery for a double mastectomy, to be followed by reconstructive surgery. Her surgery was necessary for her health, mine wasn't. I asked myself if I really wanted to put myself, my body, through all of that pain and trauma voluntarily. The answer that quickly came was "no."

In looking back, although I wasn't consciously aware of it at the time, this was truly an indictor of self-love, at least in its early stages. I loved and cared about myself enough not to put myself through that ordeal. The second consideration that helped me form my decision was based on a process of coming to a place of self-acceptance. I genuinely accepted my nose, telling myself that it was the one God gave me and he must have given it to me for a good reason. I decided, at that moment, to finally accept this part of my body that I had scorned for so long. This decision was, as I see it today, a milestone in my journey into self-love. It definitely reflected a good measure of self-love and acceptance, something that had previously been foreign to me. (Today when I look in the mirror I can't even imagine what all the fuss over my nose was all about. It's really not that bad! As a matter of fact, I kind of like it—it gives me a Roman goddess look.)

This was a beginning, but only a beginning. I still needed to walk many more miles along the path that leads to self-love. The next ten years brought with them a gradual increase in self-awareness and some personal growth, but the pattern of self-denigration supported by self-hatred still persisted. The silent mantra, "I hate myself!" never let up. Finally, at age forty-two, feeling as if I couldn't bear to hear myself say, "I hate myself!" one more time, I began individual therapy. The very first thing that the therapist said to me was, "So what do you hope to accomplish by coming to therapy?" Without a moment's hesitation, I responded, "I want to learn how to love myself." And so the pace of my journey into self-love accelerated.

One of the first topics we addressed early in therapy was my incessant inner critic, that inner voice that never let up about what a "shit-head" I was. I had always set an exacting set of standards for myself and if I fell short in any one, I became the butt of this inner criticism. No matter what I did, it wasn't quite good enough, and when I did happen to make a big mistake, my inner critic went out of control. This little guy needed to be tamed and taught some manners, and that's what happened. It took a while, but I soon learned to recognize when the little fellow was just beginning to act-up and I learned how to calm him down, and get him to support me rather than criticize me.

Learning how to do this helped heal the chronic depression that I had struggled with virtually all of my life. Depression is often defined as anger directed toward the self. Well, it was my inner critic who was angry with me most of the time, causing my depression. Once I got him to settle down and begin to work with me instead of against me, the depression started to ease up.

Another important lesson that I was learning, which helped me to move toward my goal of self-love, was that my feelings are always okay, no matter what they are. I had always spent a great deal of time and energy either denying and stuffing my feelings, or beating myself up for having them because I had judged them in one way or another as "bad." This, of course, was another contributing factor in my depression, but even more importantly, I realized that by ignoring my feelings, I was discounting and dishonoring myself. I learned to stop my inner critic from judging my feelings and to merely acknowledge and accept them, allowing myself to experience them. Then, I was able to choose what I was going to do with them. It was quite an earth shattering awakening to realize that I really had a choice about how long I wanted to remain angry, or if I even wanted to get angry in the first place. As I learned to accept my feelings without judging them, I was able to listen and to hear the messages that they were giving me, messages that indicate what I want and what I need. I learned, in other words, that to be able to honor my wants and needs and to find a way to fulfill them, I needed first of

232

all to listen to my feelings, instead of disowning them as I always had in the past. This was a giant step in my journey into self-love.

It took some work, and a lot of conscious effort, but it wasn't long before I was able to change my mantra from "I hate myself" to "I love and accept myself exactly as I am." Saying that was one thing, believing it, really believing it, was another. I still had a long way to go.

One of the issues that still needed addressing was my physical condition. Although I had suffered from the condition for quite a while, the autoimmune disorder had just recently been diagnosed. What it is, essentially, is an immune system gone astray. Instead of fighting off only foreign invaders such as cancer cells, viruses or bacteria, the immune system, unable to distinguish between the so called enemies and the cells of the body for some reason, begins to attack the body's own cells. Depending on the specific disorder, this can lead to attacks on the joints, muscles, nervous system or internal organs and, in its most extreme cases, can even lead to death. In my case, the doctor's said that it was an "unspecified" autoimmune condition. I had a very high anti-nuclear antibody count, which meant that there were a lot more antibodies wandering around my body than there needed to be, with the potential of doing some damage.

The issue for me at this point was not so much the damage that might be done, as I was already on the mend, with my health having improved dramatically by the time the diagnosis was made. The issue was more the question of why had my body begun to attack itself in the first place? When I considered the metaphor in this, as Inner Shaman points out, it became clear to me that my autoimmune condition was a condition that merely reflected my persistent history of hating myself, hating myself so much that my body actually began to attack itself. When I came to this realization it was like an undeniable wake-up call that I best reconsider this life-long pattern of self-hatred, and make the necessary changes. This, of course, is the whole point of Inner Shaman's teachings on healing—we need to look for the underlying cause, the reason why we have lost our power. Very simply, I had lost my power because I gave it away by hating myself and thus disconnecting from my Self. It was the reconnection to Self, and subsequently to Spirit, that needed to be established. Love of self is the way this is accomplished.

It was at this point in my journey that my direction began to shift to a more spiritual level. I had worked through most of my wounded inner child and inner critic issues, and, quite frankly, I had had enough. I was now ready to go to the next level. This is just about the time when Sky Hawk showed up in my life. With his appearance, my meditations began to take on a new life. We began to journey. I began to have more and more visions. I began to accumulate more and more spirit guides and teachers and power animals. I began to feel comfortable and at home in the world of Spirit. I began to listen to what Spirit was telling me and to follow its bidding. Sky Hawk's presence in my visionary life helped me to reconnect to Spirit and to my Self and, in so doing, I opened up to a whole new world in which self-love was a major element.

My goal of healing my physical condition was ever present. I focused quite a bit of energy in this endeavor, in prayer, meditation, visualization, and journeying. Each time I would ask Spirit, "What is it that I need to do to be healed? When would I be healed?" the answer always came back: "You will be healed when you *truly* love yourself." If I asked that question once, I asked it a thousand times, and a thousand times I got that same answer, "You will be healed when you *truly* love yourself." As a matter of fact, I still get that very same answer today when I ask that question. I've stopped asking it.

In my zealous search for healing at the spiritual level, I found myself attending the 1992 Jean Houston Mystery School. I recall one experiential process that I did with a partner (a shamanic soul retrieval) which proved to be another very important step in my healing journey. After the process was over, I was overwhelmed with an awareness that brought with it a rush of pain and emotion. Amid my sobs and tears, I realized at a very deep level that I was unable to take in love. I couldn't let others love me. I just didn't know how. I knew how to give love but I didn't know how to receive it. What a sad, but profound, awakening this was.

It was that same weekend, during another Mystery School process in which Jean was leading us in a guided imagery, that I received another awakening. I was deep into an altered state. I was flying high, so to speak, but all of a sudden I felt a tap on my shoulder. I was annoyed that someone would tap me on the shoulder during the process, but too far gone to give more attention to it than that. I stayed with the process and remained in the altered state. After it was over and my feet were back on the ground, I remembered the tap and wondered who might have done that. I asked the people who were sitting around me if anyone tapped them or if they felt anyone moving about. No one had felt a thing. I was really puzzled. I was absolutely certain I had felt a tap on my left shoulder, although I hadn't sensed another person moving about either.

Several days later while meditating at home I had a vision. It was a vision of the Blessed Mother Mary. She was radiantly beautiful, dressed in white, trimmed in gold, with a golden aura surrounding her. As she stood before me I could see a beam of white light going from her heart to mine. She told me that I needed to learn to open my heart to receive love, her love, Divine love. During the vision I asked her about that tap on my shoulder. The answer that came was direct and clear. It was Spirit who had tapped me, calling me to awaken. As the tears streamed down my face, things began to come into focus for me. I realized that it was not just the love from humans in physical bodies that I was unable to take in, but it was also the love that emanated from the world of Spirit, Divine love, that I could not accept. I had shut myself off to love on one level, and it was occurring at all levels.

One of the reasons I had blocked the intake of love was because, on a very deep level, I still had that old belief from my childhood that I was unlovable. I was still operating under the illusion of separation, feeling alone and disconnected. What I needed, then, was to open to love and, in so doing, I would also open to loving myself. The two go hand-in-hand, love of the self and love of the other. You really can't have one without the other, at least on a genuine, authentic level.

My next step was to focus my energy on allowing love to enter my life and on opening my heart chakra. I set that intention and allowed it to happen. Shortly after the experience at Mystery School, while having a massage, I told my massage therapist that I wanted to focus on taking in love during the massage and asked it that was all right with her. She was fine with it and, instead of experiencing the massage on a physical level only, I imagined that love was flowing from her hands into my body and I visualized breathing it in through every pore. I felt a bit uncomfortable at first, but then I noticed a deep sense of warmth and relaxation moving throughout my body. It was a wonderful massage. This experience was at once a metaphor and embodiment of what I needed to be doing on a larger scale and, as such, helped me to reprogram myself to begin to open to love on a conscious level.

Opening to love, both love of the self and of the other, has been an integral part of my healing journey. This is precisely what Inner Shaman teaches us, is it not? *"The secret to all healing that you are searching for is found deep within your heart. It is about the openness to love. This is what always heals in one way or another. Only those who are open to taking in love are capable of healing, in the fullest sense of the word. Unless one loves the self first, even divine love cannot penetrate. That is to say that the Great Spirit could send all the love in the universe to you to do the healing, but unless you love yourself you will not be open to accept this love and the healing changes that it will bring."* This has been, and remains, my challenge.

Although I make no claims whatsoever, of being anywhere remotely close to having achieved "enlightenment," I must credit myself for having come a long way since the days when "I hate myself" was my incessant chant. Have I come to the point of *truly* loving myself yet? I think not, but I'm on my way. Today, although I must still consciously work at loving myself, things are quite a bit different.

When I think in terms of self-love and how it plays itself out in my life, I can see that a shift has taken place since my journey began. Perhaps the primary indicator of how I love myself is that I make a point of counting myself, at all times, no longer making a habit of discounting myself. I truly live by the "I count me, I count you" guideline. Living by the dictum of being true to myself is another way that my self-love is manifested. I adhere to my principles and convictions without question and sometimes that's not easy to do. And most of all, I listen to my inner voice and I am true to it—even when it tells me to do things like write a book! I have found that my life now vividly reflects the words of Inner Shaman: *"You know when you love yourself when you first and foremost count yourself. 'This above all else, to thine own self be true.' These words could not be more true and beneficial. This is the essence of self-love."* This is also the essence of healing as Inner Shaman describes it, for coming into synchrony with our Self, with our soul's purpose, is essential for restoring our power and, ultimately, our health.

I know that I love myself when I consider my wants and needs and do whatever it takes to take care of myself. I love myself when I respect, celebrate and honor myself and all of whom I am. I love myself when I allow myself to have fun and pleasure. I love myself when I stay in my power and walk in integrity. I know that I love myself when I can accept myself without condition and laugh at myself without judgment. And most of all, I love myself when I am open to being loved and when I give love to others, for we are all one, connected in love.

When I probe even deeper into what the essence of self-love means to me and ask myself the question, "What is self-love all about for me?" the following words come forth:

Self-love is about going into my depths and loving and accepting what I find there; it's about getting to know myself, really know myself, and still loving me anyway.

It's about embracing my shadow, the dark side of me, as well as the me that I like and approve of; it's about accepting the good with the bad.

It's about being able to gaze in a mirror and, looking deeply into my eyes, to be able to say, and mean, "I love you."

It's about opening my heart to give and to receive, and it's about feeling worthy to receive when I do.

It's about not preventing or blocking the flow of Divine energy and allowing its beauty, love and goodness into my life. It's about feeling worthy to be one with the Divine.

It's about appreciating and valuing all that I am, all that I am becoming.

It's about giving myself a break, going easy on myself. It's about talking to myself in a way that is nurturing, loving and supportive.

It's about allowing myself to have my feelings, without judgment or self-criticism, and listening to them and honoring them.

It's about loving myself so much that I will follow my heart, my inner voice, no matter how difficult that may be.

It's about thinking enough of myself to share myself with others.

It's about seeking and allowing pleasure into my life.

It's about challenging myself when I need to be challenged and letting up on myself when I need to let up.

It's about being in synchrony with myself, of dancing in rhythm to the beat of my heart.

It's about taking care of myself by honoring my wants and needs in a way that is good for me.

It's about not being afraid to be who I am and to let my light shine for others to see.

It's about walking my path, owning my power and accepting the responsibility that accompanies it.

It's about loving myself, even when I make a mistake, and it's about giving myself the freedom to not always be perfect.

It's about facing, accepting and living my truth, living always in the integrity that comes from so doing.

It's about having the courage to stand up for what I believe in, no matter what others think, to speak out, to sing my Thunder Song for all to hear.

It's about being patient with myself, letting myself be where I need to be and do what I need to do.

It's about living my life with a sense of wonder, suspending judgment of myself.

It's about letting myself live. It's about letting life flow without trying to control, surrendering and trusting in the process of life, confident that the river of life will take me exactly where I need to go.

It's about not scaring myself and letting myself be in the moment without fear, worry or anxiety.

It's about being there for myself when no other is there, with compassionate understanding and love.

It's about all of this and so much more ...

## HEALING JOURNEY:
### Activities for Going Inward

JOURNAL EXERCISE: Love Letter to the Self

This suggestion for a journal exercise is quite simple—write a love letter to yourself. Write it as if you were writing to a lover, opening your heart, telling your innermost feelings and stating how much you love and care for him or her.

When writing your letter, consider focusing on both your positive characteristics (your "Sunny Side") and your less desirable qualities (your "Shadow Side"). You might address your "Sunny Side" by starting with the statement, "I love you because..." and your "Shadow Side" with "I love you even when you..." For example, a "Sunny

Side" statement might look like this: "I love you because you are honest and sincere." A "Shadow Side" statement might look like this: "I love you even when you are not on time."

Spend some time with this, owning and embracing all of you and telling yourself that you love and accept yourself exactly as you are. You might not be able to complete this in one sitting. Perhaps making this an ongoing process over a period of days or weeks would be a good idea.

## GUIDED MEDITATION: Self-Love

Put yourself in a comfortable position right now. Allow your mind to empty itself of all thoughts or concerns and your heart to fill with feelings of peace and contentment. With each breath that you take, feel your body becoming more and more relaxed, as if you were beginning to float. Allow this feeling of floating to move throughout your body as you move deeper and deeper into a state of peaceful relaxation. Breathing in peace and tranquillity and breathing out cares and tension. Going deeper and deeper into a place of peace, a place deep within yourself. Going deeper and deeper, until you come at last to the center of your being, the core of who you are.

Find yourself surrounded now by a mist of green light, emerald green, the color of the heart chakra. Allow this light to take you deeper still into a place of peace within yourself, coming to rest at last in your heart. Feel the energy of your heart. Feel its gentle warmth. Hear its rhythmic beating. See it as it pulsates with an energy of love. Know its essence as you go deeper and deeper into your heart. This is the place of love, compassion, forgiveness, healing and joy. Allow yourself to go into this place, into the stillness, and to feel its energy, to sense its essence. Imagine it as going home, home to a place of complete peace and love. Allow yourself to be at home in your own heart, to be at One with yourself. This is the place of unconditional, unqualified love. It is the place where you can love yourself completely, with compassion and understanding.

Imagine now that within your heart is a magnificent waterfall, with cascades of clear, emerald green water flowing down from a ledge overhead. See yourself standing under the green waterfall and feel yourself being bathed with its crystal clear essence of love, acceptance and forgiveness. As the water cascades over you, imagine that you are now letting go of any patterns of self-loathing, self-denigration, self-judgment, self-criticism, or self-blame that may be present, forgiving yourself at a very deep level for any mistakes that you have ever made. As these old patterns are being washed away you feel a new, vibrant energy of complete self-love and acceptance wash over you and you just let yourself soak it up.

Allow yourself now to feel this energy, the energy of love that is within your own heart. See it as a brilliant green light and feel its gentle warmth, its loving vibration. Imagine it as a wave of warmth radiating out from your heart center to your entire body, and feel your body warming with the glow of your own love for yourself. See your heart expanding and opening, unable to contain the energy of love and compassion within, unable to hold back the vast sea of love that is present. See your heart open and allow this light energy of love to emanate out from your heart, moving out in all directions so that it begins to permeate every cell in your body. Feel it moving throughout your entire body, bringing with it a healing glow of love. Then see it radiating out from your heart to everything around you. See it as a beam of emerald green light going out in all directions from your heart to your family and friends, to your neighbors and acquaintances, to all of humankind, to your pets and all animals, to the plants, flowers and trees, to the rocks, stones and mountains, to the air, to the lakes, streams and seas, to the entire earth, to the sun, stars and moon, to the Spirit world, to all of creation, to All That Is.

And now, imagine that the beam of emerald green light is coming back to you—coming full circle—for love is in both the giving and the receiving. Open your heart to receive the love of All That Is. Allow yourself to experience the love of the Creator and all of creation that is being mirrored back to you, that is radiating all about you. Feel it enfolding around you, surrounding you with a warm, gentle glow. See it, sense it, know it, experience it. Breathe it in; allow it to permeate your entire being, filling you with a feeling of blissful joy and peace. And in this moment, know that you are deeply loved and experience in your depths true love of the self. [Allow a short pause.]

And remembering this deep sense of peace and love for yourself and the feeling of profound joy in your heart, begin to leave your heart center and slowly come back to ordinary, waking awareness. Gently move your hands and feet and, when you're ready, open your eyes and return to everyday consciousness feeling revitalized, renewed, and reborn.

RITUAL: Marriage to the Self

For this ritual we are going to borrow from the work of Caroline Myss. In her book, *Anatomy of the Spirit,* Dr. Myss likens each of the seven chakras to one of the seven sacraments of the Christian tradition. She relates the fourth chakra, the heart center, to the sacrament of Marriage and identifies its symbolic purpose as: "to receive or bestow a blessing *making sacred a union with oneself,* symbolic of recognizing and honoring the essential need to love and care for oneself in order that one can fully love another."[1]

This is a ritual of Marriage to the Self—"making sacred a union with oneself." The essential elements of the ritual include entering into a loving partnership with yourself and blessing this "sacred union," making a commitment or vow to love and honor yourself, and marking the event with celebration. You can be as creative as you like with this, once again, making it as simple or elaborate as you desire. (This suggested ritual is based on the traditional Christian wedding ritual but you may alter it to fit into any religious tradition that you choose.)

Start by creating a sacred space by making an altar, with flowers, candles, and any sacred objects that you like. Add your favorite wedding music to complete the atmosphere and wear celebrational attire. Have your "marriage vows"—what you are promising as you enter into this loving partnership with yourself—written out ahead of time. Your marriage vows might go something like this:

> "From this day forward, I promise to be your loving partner. I promise to love, honor and cherish you and to accept you unconditionally, embracing all of whom you are. I promise to care for you and to count your wants and needs. I promise to honor your truth and live accordingly. I promise to be your friend and to be 'there for you when no other is there, with compassionate understanding and love.' "

Include a prayer for blessing your commitment of self-love and, if you like, have a ring to give to yourself to symbolize this commitment. Speaking into a full-length mirror when saying your marriage vows might heighten your experience. If it feels appropriate, you can even include another person to witness your "wedding ceremony." After you have completed your ceremony, have a grand celebration. You can include a symbolic—or real—meal, but be sure to include dancing as a way to celebrate the beginning of your new life with yourself. Congratulations and best wishes for a wonderful life together!

# THE SHAMAN'S DEATH

Shamans, they say, must die and be reborn.
They must be torn from limb to limb,
or eaten to the bone, with entrails strewn about,
or ashes cast to the four winds.
All this carnage, all this blood must be shed, so they say,
to initiate the novice into a higher state of being.
The shaman must die to the old way
only to be renewed once again, reborn into a new life.
The old way must go, so the new can commence.
Oh, how difficult to let the old go.
How scary to feel what once was real fall away as only a mist.
How can I get a grip?
There is nothing to grab onto, nothing of form or substance that remains,
only the silent, unfelt stillness in the empty void
of what once was real, but is no more.
Everything is falling away, structures crumbling all around.
They say it is all worth the pain, that in the end the reward will be great,
but as the shaman lies in the stillness of his mortal wounding,
I would think he wonders if this is really so.
Is it truly worth the pain, or was the old way good enough?
With only the promise of a brighter tomorrow to hold onto
I wait in the stillness for the glimmer of light that I trust will appear,
for I know in my depths that the new day will dawn in which
peace and renewal will come once again.
Oh, how bittersweet the shaman's death!

— M. S.

*December 2, 1995*

# CHAPTER TEN

# The Ritual of Initiation

*SHAMANS ARE CHOSEN TO FOLLOW their vocation either in a dream or by a physical teacher who knows that he or she is suited and has the calling to do the work. The shaman initiate must undergo a period of training, learning and intense preparation, adhering to a rigorous training regimen that teaches him or her how to perform the role of healer. The shamanic initiate may be in training for years, sometimes ten years or even more, before they are ready for the transformation into the role of shaman to occur. This process of transformation involves the death of the self. It is the loss of the old way of life to make way for the new. The death is often surrounded by pain. Cutting, burning of flesh and other forms of bodily mutilation may be involved. This is meant to symbolize the pain of letting go of the old and the death that one must go through in order to be transformed into a higher state of being.*

*The actual initiatory experience of the shaman involves three stages: separation, liminal period and reincorporation. The separation stage takes place when the initiate goes off by him or herself—actually cut off from the rest of the community or group—and enters into a dark night of the soul experience. This generally takes the form of a dream in which the initiate is somehow taken by a hostile force and devoured or ripped apart or otherwise destroyed. The shaman's death is a necessary part of the initiation. It demands the total annihilation of the old ways, of the old life style, the old physical body, the old way of thinking—a letting go, a releasing, a cleansing, a purging, and so on. It is the old dying so that the new can be born. The pain is not so much on a physical level as on a soul level. The shaman's soul is being reborn. Sometimes this is accompanied by actual physical pain or illness, but in all cases, there is a dramatic shift in the shaman's essential self that now emanates from the Essential Self. The old parts of self that are no longer useful or in service of the person that will be birthed are cast off. This occurs so that those parts of self that will be useful can be cultivated and allowed to flourish and grow in the new fertile soil that is now present. The initiate understands that the old must go so that the new can enter.*

*Once the shaman has died to the old ways, he or she then moves into the second stage, the liminal phase. This is when the initiate is in between the two worlds where the old ways have died or are dying, but the new ways have not yet matured or developed. It is a time of inner turmoil filled with confusion, questioning, challenge and awakening as the new life bursts forth. It is a time of awakening, of joyous rebirthing and renewal, yet somehow clouded with the pain of letting go, of grieving over what once was but is no more. The old life is cast aside, little by little, until there is hardly anything that remains of what used to be; the process is gradual, but noticeable. It is a transition stage from one state of being into another. The essential difference between the old and the new is that now the initiate must learn to walk in two worlds, the physical, material world and the world of spirit. He or she must let go of anything that remains that will prevent this from occurring, that will hinder this goal. The shaman must learn to bridge the gap between the two worlds; this is his or her primary role as shaman.*

*The third stage involves the initiate's reintegration into life as a shaman, as a person now reborn into a new life, somehow different yet still the same. The integration of the new ways of thinking, feeling and acting has occurred and now the shaman can fully perform the role he or she is called to do. This stage also involves challenges as it is like going into a foreign country in many respects, like entering into an unfamiliar territory. But, it does not take long to learn the ways and move into the new life unhampered by fear and the inhibitions of the old way of life. This is the stage in which the new shaman learns about his or her new life and how to live it effectively.*

*The notion of the shamanic initiation is one of great importance. It is the prototype for all of life's transformations and transitions. Just as the shaman dies and is reborn, so too each of you on your soul's journey must do the same, not just once, but many times. In many ways Jesus was a shaman. His death and rebirth also signified this transformation into a higher state of being, an initiation into the next level of awareness. Each of you is called to make the very same transformation that Jesus did, that the shaman must do. This is vitally important for people to understand at this point in history. Only those who make the transformation to a higher level of being will heal, and only those who heal will survive in the new energies of the world that will commence as the new millennia dawns. The Inner Shaman is, once again, the connection that you have to bridge the gap between the two worlds, as the shaman moves from one state of being to the next. All humankind right now is called to do just this—to move from one state of awareness to another higher, more alive state. The shaman is the prototype for how this is done. That is why the notion of the shaman's death is so important. It is the model for all transitions, all transformation, and so much of that will be occurring within the next few years as we approach the coming of the New Age.*

*You see, there is so much more here than meets the eye. The shaman and this shamanic consciousness is many faceted and holds the blueprint, the coding for what humankind needs to accomplish individually and collectively during the next several years. If one studies this blueprint, one will learn that life is filled with change and movement. The journey of the shaman is all about movement through darkness into the light. That is what is about to happen. This all must take place at both the micro and the macro levels, both internally and externally, both individually and collectively, both globally and universally. Humankind and the planet itself must take a quantum leap into a new dimension, must journey into an unknown realm like the shaman does. It must learn how to make the journey as the apprentice shaman does.*

*Humankind, as a whole, is collectively going through the shaman's death, the initiation into a higher state of consciousness. This has been going on for many years now and will continue for several more years to come. As the shaman sees all life being part of the bigger picture, so, too, humankind must see that life is hologramatic. What happens within happens without—so above, so below. Let me reiterate. The shaman as an archetypal figure symbolizes humankind at this point in time. As the shaman must go through an initiation, go through the throes of death and be reborn, so too the human species must go through the same type of thing in order to be reborn into a higher level of being. This is all going on at many levels, from the cellular level to the universal level, all creation is currently going through a shamanic initiation, a transformation from one state of being into another higher order. This is not limited to humans and the planet earth. The entire universe is making a quantum leap right along with the earth. Within each person, cellular structures are actually changing. People's lives are shifting faster than they can keep up with. Social, economic, political, religious structures are collapsing one by one—the shaman's death. This is happening across the planet to all that lives. The animal and plant life is affected as well. Species are dying off, one by one. This is not so much an ecological disaster as the shaman's death.*

*The role that healing plays in all of this is quite clear. Without healing at some level the transformation cannot occur. The transformation IS healing. Once one has healed, the transformation is automatic. Healing is the vehicle that gets you to the destination of transformation. The path of healing, once again, leads to transformation into the higher state of consciousness, a state that transcends all pain, illness and disease, one that leaves the bodily concerns behind. The physical body will be transformed right along with the mental, emotional and spiritual bodies. This is what will occur.*

*Once the transformation is complete humans will be as Jean Houston calls, "Godseeds," they will become as Jesus was—fully empowered beings, capable of utilizing all the God given abilities that have long been dormant. Jesus was the master shaman. All of his special powers were within the realm of what many shamans are known to do—heal the sick, control the weather, change water into wine, etc. These things have all been done by the great medicine men and women all over the globe. Jesus was able to do what he did not because he was a super human or a deity, but because he was living as the expanded human. He had achieved the desired state, the highest human potential that is your birthright. You are all meant to become this expanded being that Jesus was. Jesus, the Christed One, was the prototype for what all humans can become. It is only when people understand this that the healing of the human race will occur. Western people have been looking to external gods that they can worship and idolize. They are looking outside of themselves for God, when in reality they are the gods. Each person is a god in the fullest sense of the word. It is only when this godhood is accepted that the healing will occur. You see healing involves this acceptance of your birthright. Until you accept and wake-up to the fact that you are so much more than you think you are, this will not occur.*

*This is what is awakening at the moment. These abilities, most of which are utilized by shamans, will return and become commonplace. That is also why the shaman is the prototype for transformation. The shaman has the abilities that the transformed human will have, such as clairvoyance, psychic abilities, intuition, ability to astral project, control of the weather, etc.—all the things that Jesus and all shaman have been able to do as part of their healing vocation. This is what is about to happen.*

*So, we have the shaman as the prototype for this transformation, healing that comes through the initiatory process as the vehicle that takes one to the transformed state and Jesus as the model of what the transformed person will look like. Jesus and shamans both show us the way. Jesus said, "I am the way, the truth and the light. He that believeth in me shall find the way." If we only follow in the footsteps of Jesus and the great shaman, we will find our way to this transformed state. This is humankind's destiny; this is what the human race has been collectively moving toward, and evolving into since the beginning of human history. These are the times when humankind will make the quantum leap, individually and collectively, into this higher state of being. The shaman provides the model to follow for how to make this shift. The shamanic consciousness thus holds the key to the healing of humanity and, subsequently, the planet. If one looks into the depths of the shamanic culture and consciousness, one will find this key. It is necessary that this be understood so that there is a major shift in the consciousness, so that humankind changes its ways and moves in the direction of health and healing.*

ON A CHILLY AUTUMN DAY in 1993, long before I recorded these words of Inner Shaman, I had a vision. It was a vision that addressed an inner conflict that I had been dealing with for quite some time. How can I remain devoted to Jesus and live within the shamanic consciousness at the same time? My Catholic upbringing would certainly have scorned shamanism, yet it is every bit as much a part of me as Jesus is. How can I reconcile the two? I wrote of my vision in my journal:

> I was sitting around a fire with Sky Hawk. Drums were beating as the fire glowed in the darkness. Sitting in stillness with Sky Hawk, I saw the image of hands being pierced with nails. This immediately reminded me of Jesus being nailed to the cross, and it seemed to make the connection that I have been seeking. I hold the Christ within. I hold the Shaman, as well. What a strange combination, or is it? The shamanic initiation is strikingly similar to the passion, death and resurrection of Christ. Could it be that the two consciousnesses overlap? Or, are they in reality one and the same?

I concluded at that time that for me, at least, they were indeed one and the same. Coming to this realization was a healing experience for me as it allowed me to let go of that inner conflict that had haunted me since Sky Hawk first came into my life. I realized that there is no separation, that even at this level, we are all one, We Are All Related. Jesus was a master shaman and he modeled a life that pointed the way for transformation to take place, the transformation of the death and rebirth of the shamanic initiation, the path that allows one to move through the darkness into the light. Jesus' life was not about darkness, sin and death; it was about light, life and transformation. His journey, as the shaman's, is a prototype for all of us as we awaken, as we heal, as we move through the darkness into the light, and as we enter into the world of Spirit. When I view my own life through this lens, it takes on a whole new meaning, as it validates and affirms my process, making my journey somehow sacred.

*"The notion of the shamanic initiation is one of great importance. It is the prototype for all of life's transformations and transitions. Just as the shaman dies and is reborn, so too each of you on your soul's journey must do the same, not just once, but many times."* When I reflect on these words of Inner Shaman and how they relate to my journey, what comes to mind is how unquestionably valid this concept has been for me. As I look back on my life, I must have had dozens of deaths, some big, some little, but deaths just the same. Virtually all of them involved the process of letting go of the old so that the new can come in as Inner Shaman describes. Sometimes this dying and renewal process was easier to accomplish than at others, but the process always resulted in a significant transformation.

I have often heard that during life's journey we go through cycles of seven years. At the end of each cycle, we go through a transformation, moving out of one phase of our life and into another. (This can be viewed as the death and rebirth of which Inner Shaman speaks.) In reviewing my life in terms of these seven-year cycles, I found this truly to be the case for me, for at the end of each seven-year period there was a prominent transition that occurred. And when I look at the bigger picture, the seven cycles of seven that I have now lived through, I can see how dramatically my life's cycles have been, as Inner Shaman suggests, *"all about the movement through darkness into the light."*

The ending of the first cycle of my life at age seven was marked by a major rite of passage—First Holy Communion. Within the Catholic Church, when a child reached the age of seven years he or she was considered to have reached what was called "the age of reason." This meant that the child was no longer an innocent and incapable of committing sin, but was now able to make moral decisions about right and wrong behavior. Prior to this age, the child was not capable of understanding the concept of the Holy Eucharist and was not ready to partake of this sacrament. Along with attaining the age of reason, however, came the notion that now the child was responsible for his or her actions, and would need to confess his or her sins. Along with First Communion, then, came First Confession. For me, it came the day before. So, this rite of passage of First Holy Communion and First Confession, marked the ending of the innocent child stage and the beginning of the morally responsible stage. It was a death and rebirth in the shamanic sense, as it ritualized moving into a higher state of being, from the "age of innocence" to the "age of reason."

I also happened to have an extra-added attraction that went along with this passage. As mentioned earlier, I was a rather big child and entered puberty at an exceptionally early age. I began wearing a bra when I had just turned seven years old. This, perhaps more than the religious right of passage, presented the shaman's death for me. It was truly a difficult time, as I was the *only* one going through puberty at the end of first grade! I was physically ready for the changes it brought, yes, but certainly not mentally or emotionally ready. It was very difficult for me to let go of being a child at age seven and to begin to be "a young lady." At seven years old, this "old dying so that the new can be born" notion was not easy to take.

The ending of the next seven-year cycle, when I was fourteen, was not quite so tough, yet it had its own set of challenges. It was marked by the typical adolescent rite of passage—eighth grade graduation, followed by a host of graduation parties, a bad case of acne and my first date. It was the end of one phase of life, elementary school, and the beginning of another, high school. Moving out of childhood and into adolescence, I left the parish elementary school behind, and began a new life at an all-girls Catholic high school. The transition was difficult initially. I remember walking home from my first day of high school, carrying an armful of heavy books feeling overwhelmed, and thinking to myself that I would never survive the next four years. But, I soon adjusted to the new life, and, obviously, survived. All in all, it was one of the easier endings, and beginnings, of my seven-year cycles.

My twenty-first year, the ending of the third cycle, was a different story. It was a true death and rebirth, in the fullest sense of the word. I had been married to Tom after my second year of college, at age 20. I was going to college at the University of Illinois Chicago Circle, full-time, majoring in elementary education. It was 1968. The Viet Nam War was beginning to escalate and Tom was eligible for the draft. I was terrified that he would be drafted and leave me, so I prayed and prayed, saying three rosaries a day, that the war would end and he wouldn't be drafted. Well, my prayers were answered, only not as I expected. The war didn't end, but I got pregnant, unintentionally (thanks to the good old "rhythm method") and my pregnancy kept him out of the army. But, my pregnancy also was the reason that I quit school, with only one more year to go to get my degree. I was having some difficulty with spotting during the early weeks of the pregnancy, and the doctor advised me to stay off my feet. So, I even quit the part-time job that I had in retail sales at a large department store. Four months after my twenty-first birthday, I quit school and my job and became a stay-at-home housewife—a stay-at-home pregnant housewife, that is.

I must admit that I rather liked the idea of having an excuse to quit school, since I was feeling a bit anxious about teaching, and I was starting to think that I really didn't want to be a schoolteacher after all. But, with such an abrupt ending to my academic life and the goals that went along with it, there was a big empty hole in my life. If there was one place that I excelled, it was in the academic world. I was always a good student, right from the start. I graduated fifth in my high school class and, with the exception of one quarter, I maintained Dean's List standing during my three years of college. It was my lifelong goal to be a schoolteacher and now it all seemed to be gone before I knew what hit me. I had lost my personal identity of student, teacher-to-be, and salesperson, and now I was simply "Tom Schneider's pregnant wife."

It truly was a dying of the old way, but I'm not so sure, once again, that I was ready for the old to die so that the new could begin. Before too long, depression set in. I slept till 12:00 or 1:00 PM everyday, and then just sat around with nothing to do, waiting for Tom to come home. I just sat there. I didn't read; I didn't watch TV. I was bored, empty and depressed, and I suffered from severe backaches the entire pregnancy. I went through a period of mourning and grieving over the loss of the old life and the identity that went with it. This feeling lasted until the baby came. I didn't know at the time that I was mourning the loss of my old life; I simply thought life was pretty miserable.

Debbie was born one month before my twenty-second birthday, and my life was forever changed. She was two weeks early and weighed only 6 lbs. 6 ozs., but she was a perfect, healthy baby. The labor was tough, lasting eighteen hours, but the delivery was normal, without any problems. Ten days after her birth, however, I began to hemorrhage and had to be rushed to the hospital, with ambulance sirens blasting, for an emergency D&C. I was given two units of blood and remained in the hospital for three days. This was, without a doubt, the shaman's death, with the shedding of blood that both literally and metaphorically marked it. Physical death was at my doorstep, for without emergency medical attention, I surely would have died. This was also the metaphor for the other death that I had been going through—the passing from one stage in my life to the next, from one state of being into another, from childhood into adulthood and motherhood—a true shamanic initiation. I was still in the darkness, slowly making my way into the light without knowing it. This was part of my process, one of many steps in my life's journey into the light.

My twenty-eighth year, the ending of my fourth cycle of seven years, was not quite as momentous, but was marked by a letting go of the old and taking on of the new, as well. By that time, the girls were seven and four years old. After Debbie was born, it didn't take me long at all to get into the role of mother, and I simply loved it. I loved the baby stage and having little children. I wanted a third child, but that was not to be, as Tom was not of the same mind. I was beginning to accept the fact that there weren't going to be any more babies. That was the year that Debbie went to first grade. Sherri, at four, was not a baby anymore and would be starting kindergarten the following year. I recall going through a period of grief over the ending of the young mother stage, of having little ones around and all that that entails—bedtime stories, wiping running noses, cleaning up spilled milk, finding little fingerprints all over everything. But mostly, I think I was grieving the loss of the physical love and affection, the holding, touching, hugging, and cuddling, that went along with babies and little ones. I kept thinking that I have no baby anymore, no baby to hold, and felt such sadness and grief over that loss—the letting go of the old to make room for the new.

What came next was a whole new life, one that was centered outside of the home around school age children, rather than inside the home around little ones. As Debbie went off to school, life began to change as rapidly for me as for her. The first change occurred the September Debbie started first grade; I became a Brownie Girl Scout Leader. This was no little thing for me, the stay-at-home mom who spent her time cooking, cleaning and sewing, with bunco and bowling thrown in for fun. It was a major step for me to take on this role and all the responsibility that went along with it. This ushered in the beginning of a period in which I became extremely active volunteering outside the home—girl Scout leader, room mother, PTA vice president, church adult education committee member, church youth group leader. I did it all, and anything else that called to me along the way. It was a period of non-stop activity, life-in-the-fast-lane style. I loved every minute of it. It was during this time of going out into the world, that I began to open up more on a spiritual level. I became more involved with the church, which fostered the beginnings of the spiritual awakening that was just around the corner. I was still in the darkness at this point, but I was another step closer to my journey's destination, my life-long process of moving into the light.

The ending of the next seven-year cycle, at thirty-five years, marked a major transition for me. It was a time when my journey into the light began to pick up momentum. In the spring of 1981, Tom and I, once again, found ourselves in a marital crisis. In the heat of one of the animated arguments that we were known to have, Tom delivered a low blow, saying, "You're shit, nothing but shit! You may look good, but without me you're just shit!" I was completely devastated by his comment. I had long struggled with low self-esteem, but even so, I knew that this was not true. I was not shit! And it was there and then that I made up my mind to prove to him, to the world, and, most importantly, to myself that I was not shit. I did-n't quite know at that moment exactly how I would do it, but I knew that I would find a way.

And find a way I did. Several months later, I found that book from K-Mart in my hands—the one that triggered my spiritual awakening—and I embarked in earnest, and with consciousness, on my journey from the darkness into the light. One year later, in June of 1982, at age 35, I went back to college to complete the bachelor's degree that I had aborted fourteen years prior. I was going to show him that *I was not shit!* Two years later, I had a BA degree in Sociology and Family Studies, and five years later I had a Master's in Social Work degree. Today, when Tom and I talk about that time, I thank him for giving me that incredible gift. It was his words that echoed through my head during those five years that I was in school, spurring me onward to achieve my goals.

The return to school marked the ending of one way of life for me and the beginning of a new one. It was necessary to let go of many things that had been important parts of my life for the past seven years. I gave up just about all of my volunteer work, as well as sewing, bowling and television. There was less time to spend with the kids, and less time to spend with Tom. If I didn't have my head in a book, I was "chained" to the computer writing the seemingly unending papers and reports that were required. My identity as wife and mother was rapidly expanding. Now I was a student and soon-to-be professional. It was an exciting time for me. I felt as if I were beginning to come alive for the first time. It was a period of not only continued spiritual growth, but personal and professional openings as well. I was spreading my wings even further. I was not only going outside the home and the church-school community that I had been a part of for the past seven years, but I was now a part of the "real" world, the world beyond the little world with which I was so familiar. My world was expanding, my horizons were expanding, my life was expanding and I was expanding. I felt so good about myself, like I was important and able to make a difference in the world. It was an adventure and a true opening for me, a giant step in my journey from darkness into the light. I was now finally beginning to see the light.

On my forty-second birthday, the day that marked the closing of my sixth cycle of seven years, I picked up the keys to my new office in which I was to begin a private practice in clinical social work. It was another new beginning, preceded by another ending. The period that was ending was a seven-year education phase. It took me two years to get my bachelor's degree and three to get my graduate degree. Then I worked for two years in an inpatient psychiatric hospital, as I needed two years of supervised practice in order to be eligible for my clinical social worker license, a credential that was necessary to go into private practice. Once I received the license, I was out the psychiatric unit door and into private practice. A whole new era began.

That same year, Sherri graduated from high school and joined her sister away at college. The nest was finally empty. It was the ending of another era. I didn't spend a lot of time grieving and mourning; I really liked the nest being empty. Life was a lot less complicated and less stressful. It seemed that Tom and I got along much better when it was just the two of us. I didn't spend much time looking back. I was really focused on my new life as a psychotherapist. It was now time for me to begin to put into practice all that I had learned, not just during the past seven years, but the past forty-two. I loved my work. I loved being a psychotherapist, and I still do to this day. It was the beginning of an era in which I began to slow down. I worked, and still do, only fifteen to twenty hours a week. I had much more time to myself, more time to do the inner work that was now crying out to be done, more time to devote to my spiritual journey. So, at the beginning of this new beginning, I started individual therapy, a move that served to further accelerate my movement from the darkness into the light.

The ending of the seventh cycle of seven, at forty-nine years, brought with it a major initiation, a shaman's death in all of its glory. Menopause was no longer just a word that described what happened to other women. It was quickly becoming a word with which, at age forty-eight, I could strongly relate. About five months prior to my forty-ninth birthday I began to menstruate. The bleeding went on for three months, with only ten or twelve days during that time of which I was not bleeding. My blood count plummeted and I became anemic. Unlike the transition at age twenty-one in which bleeding was also a prominent factor, I was completely aware of what was happening. I knew that the bleeding was a metaphor for a deeper process that was going on inside me. There was a part of me that was dying so that a new part could be born. I knew that I was in the middle of a major initiation, a passage from one phase of my life to another, and I let myself be there.

During this time I experienced a deep sense of grief. I allowed myself to be in the stillness of it, to experience it fully. In the past, I would have fought the grief, labeling it depression, assigning a negative meaning to it, and making myself somehow "bad" for feeling that way. Of course, this would only make the depression worse. However, this time was different. I didn't fight it; I danced with it instead. I ritualized it. My life slowed down considerably. There were days when I would just lie on the couch for hours, simply staring into space. Sometimes I would sit in the bathtub for an hour at a time, crying, amid lit candles and soft music. I couldn't read. I couldn't write. I couldn't do work for my doctoral program. I could just be still. It was in the fall, a time in the past when I was always most vulnerable to depression, but it wasn't depression. It was grief, pure and simple.

As the blood flowed from my body, I allowed it to signify a cleansing, a purging, a releasing of the old. I wasn't even sure what "the old" was, but I knew that I needed to let go of whatever part of me that was dying, whatever it was that needed to be released. Perhaps it was the loss of my reproductive capacity as menopause drew nearer and nearer, or the loss of my youth. Debbie had been married the previous June, and Sherri had received her master's degree in May, moved back home again only to move back out, to be on her own, in October. The nest was empty for good this time. I'm sure I was grieving those losses as well. It clearly marked the ending of another era—it was the shaman's death. Yet with each death comes a rebirth, a new life follows the old. But what is the new life that follows this death? I wondered what the future held for me.

In her book, *Buffalo Woman Comes Singing,* Brooke Medicine Eagle points out that Native people believe that the nurturing and renewal of all life is the special charge given to women. It is during this time in a woman's life, the Moon pause (menopause), that she is able to shift her focus of attention from the concerns of raising and caring for her own family to the concerns of the Greater Circle of Life—to the nurturance and renewal of life at this expanded level. By not losing her blood every month, she has extra energy available to use for other things, to use in service of the Greater Circle. It is also a time when a woman comes into the fullness of her intuitive and visionary power and possesses the wisdom and experience to use in the guidance of others. Moon pause can, then, signify the beginning of a very powerful, productive and creative time in a woman's life.[1]

As I sit writing these words it is now six months past my forty-ninth birthday. I'm not certain what the new era that is just dawning will bring my way. But, as I look back over the seven major transitions in my life that correspond to the ending of a seven-year cycle, it seems that with each one came a broadening of my scope, an expanding of my horizon. It would follow that this pattern will continue—life, death, rebirth.

When I attended Brooke Medicine Eagle's Deepening of Spirit Camp in the summer of 1994, I was given the opportunity to enter the Grandmother's Lodge, which is traditionally a special ceremonial place for women in their Moon pause. At that time, it was expanded to include any woman nearing menopause who was willing to shift her focus of attention from her own smaller circle to the larger one. My initiation into the Lodge required that I make a firm commitment and pledge to direct all of my energy to the service of All My Relations for the nurturance and renewal of all life. I made that pledge, and perhaps that is what this new beginning is all about. Perhaps that is why I find myself writing this book at this moment in time. Perhaps that is why Inner Shaman's teachings are not merely about healing at the individual level, but at the collective level, at the level of the Greater Circle of Life as well. Perhaps this is the direction that my life's journey will take as this new day dawns.

I believe this is what is occurring, and my heart quickens at the thought of what the future holds for me.

Walking the shamanic path, then, involves a certain amount of responsibility. It is traditionally the shaman's role to serve the community in whatever capacity he or she is called; it is the shamanic vocation to bring healing to the community. In this spirit, taking what I have learned out into the community and sharing with others who are also on their healing path, is the next step for me. The words of Stephen Larsen, in his book, *The Shaman's Doorway* bear witness to this:

> The modern shamanic path consists in a creative and affir-mative relationship to life. It will be impossible to have true believers or card-carrying shamans because we are to be found among all arts and professions: therapists, artists, clergy, writers, poets, musicians, filmmakers. The creative shaman is the person who dedicates him/herself not only to visionary experience, but to *the revelation and sharing of the experience.* Thus our lives are made richer day by day, year by year, by an influx of creative works into them: the gifts of wonder. [2]

What exactly my "gifts of wonder" are only time will tell. I do know that as this new era in my life unfolds I am being called to serve the community, the larger circle of life, in one way or another—as ther-apist, teacher, writer, healer. I will find a way to answer the call and to share my experience with others.

In reflecting, once again, upon the words of Inner Shaman, "*The notion of the shamanic initiation is of great importance. It is the prototype for all of life's transformations and transitions. Just as the shaman dies and is reborn, so too each of you on your soul's journey must do the same, not just once, but many times,*" they now take on a deeper meaning for me. What I have learned is that when the initiations, the transitions, that we all go through in the course of our life's journey are taken to the level of ritual (as the prototype of the shamanic initiation models for us), these challenging times can be viewed and experienced much differently. Using the metaphor of initiation that Jesus and the Shaman model for us, helps us to look at life's challenges and major transitions in a new and different, more positive light. It helps us to make sense out of what might otherwise seem to be senseless. That is what I was able to do for my forty-nine year passage. In so doing, I experienced healing and transformation, rather than fear and despair. I entered into the darkness without fear and became one with it. I danced with the darkness and in so doing transformed it into the light. Being able to do this, I believe, is one of the ways in which I have been gifted by Inner Shaman and by living within the shamanic consciousness.

Joan Borysenko, in her book, *Fire in the Soul,* maintains that when crisis is viewed as an initiation and experienced as part of our psychological and spiritual growth rather than as a disaster, it can lead to healing and transformation, rather than pathology or stuckness. She points out that these experiences can then be a way to move from the darkness into the light:

> Dark nights of the soul are extended periods of dwelling at the threshold when it seems as if we can no longer trust the very ground we stand on, when there is nothing familiar left to hold onto that can give us comfort. If we have a strong belief that our suffering is in the service of growth, dark night experiences can lead us to depths of psychological and spiritual healing and revelation that we literally could not have dreamed of . . .[3]

I believe that this was undeniably the case for me as I moved through the passage of my forty-ninth year. It was a time of healing and transformation, a time of movement through the darkness into the light. As I was in the throes of the Shaman's Death, as the blood flowed from me, the words of this poem also flowed from me:

## CHILD OF THE SUN

Sing my soul; rejoice in the beauty of the dawn.
Let in the light as its radiance comes forth
in its magical splendor of vibrant hues of color.
Do not be afraid of the new day that dawns.
Do not shy away from the challenges it might hold.
Let in the light of the sun's golden rays
and let it across your heart dance and play.
Know in your depths that, at the end of the day,
you will be brought to rest filled with peace and tranquillity.
The struggles that face you as you move on your path
will seem small in the gentle warmth of the sun's golden rays.
Be open and free as you move on your way
and allow the sun's rays to help guide you along.

Sing my heart of a new life,
a life of beauty that unfolds before you.
Dance to the rhythm of the music within
and laugh and play in the delights of the day.
Do not give into fear and doubt,
rather trust in your heart and follow its lead.
You will always be guided, dear child of the sun,
as you move on your way, hand in hand with the One.
Remember to ask for the guidance you may need
and it will always be there to support and to lead.
Never allow the darkness to rule,
as you must walk forevermore in the light,
for you are called to the light, oh dear child of the sun.

Oh, sweet child of the sun, know in your heart
that you are the one who has been given the key.
Use the key wisely to open the door that stands closed before you,
and move through the portal of night into light.
Do not be afraid of the challenges that may appear,
simply follow the light and help will be there.
You are called to the light, oh dear child of the sun,
do not shy away, as you and I are One.

*November 6, 1995*

# HEALING JOURNEY:
## Activities for Going Inward


JOURNAL EXERCISE: "The Shaman's Death"


## THE SHAMAN'S DEATH

Shamans, they say, must die and be reborn.
They must be torn from limb to limb,
or eaten to the bone, with entrails strewn about,
or ashes cast to the four winds.
All this carnage, all this blood must be shed, so they say,
to initiate the novice into a higher state of being.
The shaman must die to the old way
only to be renewed once again, reborn into a new life.
The old way must go, so the new can commence.
Oh, how difficult to let the old go.
How scary to feel what once was real fall away as only a mist.
How can I get a grip?
There is nothing to grab onto, nothing of form or substance that remains,
only the silent, unfelt stillness in the empty void
of what once was real, but is no more.
Everything is falling away, structures crumbling all around.
They say it is all worth the pain, that in the end the reward will be great,
but as the shaman lies in the stillness of his mortal wounding,
I would think he wonders if this is really so.
Is it truly worth the pain, or was the old way good enough?
With only the promise of a brighter tomorrow to hold onto
I wait in the stillness for the glimmer of light that I trust will appear,

for I know in my depths that the new day will dawn in which
peace and renewal will come once again.
Oh, how bittersweet the shaman's death!

After rereading the poem, "The Shaman's Death," use the "Rambling Writing" method to express any thoughts and/or feelings that have been stirred up for you.

Here are some questions to help you if you are stuck:

- How does this poem relate to you and your life, both past and present?

- What memories does it elicit for you?

- What images, thoughts and feelings does it call up?

- Have you ever experienced the "Shaman's Death"? If so, what was your experience?

- Was it a "bittersweet experience"? If so, how?

GUIDED MEDITATION: Going Through the Doorway

Sitting with your eyes closed, adjust your body so that you are very comfortable and begin to pay attention to your breathing. With each breath you take you are beginning to feel more and more relaxed, more and more at peace. As you breath imagine that you are breathing in peace and breathing out white light-breathing in peace and breathing out white light, until you are filled with peace and surrounded by white light.

Now see yourself entering into a white mist, a dense fog that obscures your vision. Letting go of all fear and feeling a deep sense of trust, surrender to the mist. Allow yourself to go deeper into the mist and become completely surrounded by it. Become one with it. You look around and you can see nothing—nothing behind you, nothing in front of you, nothing on the side of you—only the white mist. See yourself beginning to walk through the mist. Although you're not able to see where your next step will take you, you walk undauntedly through the mist.

Continuing on, you notice that the fog seems to be lifting, the mist is getting lighter and lighter until eventually you can begin to see something before you, but you can't make out what it is. You continue to walk. With each step you are able to see better and better and soon you begin to make out what it is before you. It is an ancient stone wall. It seems to have no beginning or no end. It just goes on and on in all directions—up, down, left, right—all you can see is wall. In the middle of the wall is a huge ancient doorway, with a heavy wooden door centered in it. The door is closed and as you stand there looking at this endless wall with the huge closed door, you wonder what might be on the other side of the door.

You have an intuitive understanding that when you open the door and walk through the doorway and the door closes behind you, you will never be able to go back. Your life will be forever changed. You will be moving from one state of being into another, letting the old life die so that the new might begin—you must die to the old way so that you can be reborn into a new life.

As you stand there, looking at the ancient doorway in front of you, you notice that the mist has cleared. Looking behind you, you become aware of the setting sun on the horizon. You watch as it slowly sinks into the horizon, soon leaving you in total darkness. You stand alone in the darkness feeling a bit frightened, but knowing that it is now time to walk through the door, time to let go of your old way of life and begin a new way. In spite of your fear, you decide that you will go through the doorway that leads to your new life. As you begin to walk toward the doorway, still in total darkness, you notice the sound of the door beginning to open. As you approach, you see a hint of light in the doorway. You muster up all your strength and courage, take a deep breath and walk through it. The door begins to close behind you, and you are once again in total darkness. You stand there, still frightened, alone, not sure of what to do or where to go. Then, you begin to notice a faint glimmer of light on the horizon before you—it is the rising sun. It is the dawn of a new day. As the sun rises in the sky before you, a warm glow fills your being. You begin to feel an inner sense of peace and calm, a deep sense of hope and renewal. A growing feeling of excitement and exhilaration for the day that is now dawning wells up inside of you and, as you begin to walk in the light of the new day, you give thanks for the new life that is just now beginning.

Remembering all that you have experienced and feeling a deep sense of peace, renewal and hope, you begin to come back into waking consciousness. And, when you are ready, open your eyes and come back to the present moment feeling wide awake and alert.

RITUAL: Co-Create Your Own Ritual of Initiation

Rituals of initiation are often used to mark a transition from one state of being into the next higher level. In shamanic societies, the shaman's death is one such transition. Here the shamanic initiate undergoes some sort of symbolic death to the old way of life and rebirth into a new life. Some examples of rituals of initiation in modern day society would include graduation ceremonies, bachelor parties, wedding ceremonies, retirement parties, and funerals—all marking the ending of one way of life and the beginning of another.

Hopefully, during the course of reading this book and doing the suggested *Healing Journey* activities you have learned much about yourself and have grown considerably. You may have found, for example, that your perspective on life—and your response to it—has shifted dramatically. You may have noticed that you have changed as a result of this shift in consciousness, that you have moved from one level of being to another. Using the journaling and meditating skills that you have acquired to access your inner wisdom, engage the help of your Inner Shaman in co-creating your own ritual of initiation that marks your completion of this *Healing Journey* experience and movement into another level of consciousness. While journaling or meditating, ask your inner teacher to tell you (or show you) what to do for your ritual and trust in the answers that come to you.

Make your ritual sacred and celebrational, remembering to have fun with it as well.

# THE LIGHT

The light shone within the light,
bright, stunning, vibrant,
a veritable fountain of light and color
emanating out and out and out.
Open and charged, the fountain calls to me.
It beckons me go forth, go forth.
Be not afraid.
You are not alone.
Join with me.
Together we will make miracles happen.
Open, open,
go out, go out.
There is no end,
no beginning,
only NOW.
Now Is the essence,
the essence is now.
Hear the call!
Rejoice in the call!
Rejoice in the essence!

— M. S.

*November 6, 1993*

## CHAPTER ELEVEN

# The Essence of Healing: Journey Through Darkness Into Light

*THE NOTION OF THE INNER SHAMAN as the inner consciousness that is your connection to the spirit world, the divine source of all things, is the most important aspect of the message that I have been conveying. Healing comes from a reconnection to Spirit, just as illness comes from separation or disconnection. This is the way that it is. This reconnection to Spirit is the movement from the darkness into the light, the transformation that is the essence of the healing process.*

*It is so tremendously important at this time, as we approach the new millennium and the upheavals that will go along with it, that everyone move in the direction of reconnecting to Spirit, that each person awaken and move into the light of Spirit. Those who do not awaken will not survive. The New Age will be an age of Spirit. Those who remain stuck in the age of materialism will not last long. Everyone who will move into the New World will have to know how to connect to Spirit. It will be a prerequisite, so to say. Those who refuse to do this will not remain. Their vibration will not be in harmony or resonance with those of the New World and they will not even want to stay around, as they will feel very uncomfortable with these higher and more intense vibrations. This is not something to be treated lightly and cast aside. It is of the utmost importance that anyone who wishes to move into the New World be reconnected to Spirit. I repeat, those who do not will perish. The inner shaman is the prototype of this connection. It is the model upon which many who believe and who choose to enter into the New World depend. This is part of my message.*

*The other part is about healing more specifically, and that reconnection, moving into the light of Spirit, is the essence of healing. Dis-ease is being out of harmony because one has disconnected from Self, Source or Spirit. We must see to it that as many people as possible understand the basics of self-healing, because there will be a greater need for it during the upheavals that will accompany the dawning of the New World. This is true because medical care may not be as readily available then as it is now. This is also true because healing is what will open the doors for people to pass into the New World. Those who are not healed, in other words, will not have the key to open the door and will not be able to enter. Also, the planet will only heal when everything that lives on her has healed. This will occur after those who have chosen to leave do so, and all those remaining are healed. Then the Age of Aquarius will have come to its fruition. You have heard that the New Age will be a time of peace, love and harmony. This will only be possible if and when all creatures are healed, that is, when everyone is once again aware of the connection to Spirit and to each other, aware that everything is one, that everything is connected, that "We Are All Related", and live their lives accordingly.*

*This is the macro notion of "We Are All Related." There is also a micro notion that relates to healing. Healing involves an understanding and a respect for the idea that we exist on four levels, physical, mental, emotional and spiritual, and that all four are inseparably related. One cannot be well if the others are not. One cannot be healed unless the others are healed. The same holds true for the systems within the body. All systems within the body are interrelated and all of them have connections to the four levels as well. It is very important to remember that "We Are All Related" applies to the larger systems outside of self as well as those within. Here too, one level cannot be well if the others are. We must come into harmony with "all of our relations" on all levels for true healing to take place.*

*I would like to continue to talk to you about the nature of healing by reiterating what I have been saying all along. Healing is not necessarily about the eradication of symptoms or getting well from an illness, although it may involve that. Healing is about a return to integrity and synchrony with the self. It is about coming to a place of inner peace and acceptance of self, whatever that may mean. It is about knowing deep inside that all is well because we are all one. It is about understanding at a deep level that there is no separation. When one comes to this place, then the healing has occurred. Sometimes this is accomplished without the person's conscious awareness, but it always involves a sense of inner peace and acceptance of and love for the self. (Even if accepting the self means accepting that part of the self that is ill, deformed, handicapped, etc.) The sense of oneness involves a connection to Spirit and Nature. Once again, different people have different experiences of this, some on a conscious level and others on a more unconscious level. But always there is inner peace. This is the absence of conflict and tension. This is the place of integrity in relation to self and one's divine purpose. To be healed means to be whole. Wholeness means to acknowledge, accept and honor all of whom you are, at every level of your being.*

*All healing is self-healing. There is no other way for it to occur. Even the healings that appear to be miracles could not take place without the cooperation of the person's inner healer. This must be evoked, activated and open for healing to occur. Healing may, however, also involve grace. Grace is a divine gift that comes to one who is open to receive the gift. Many times we ask and ask for help or healing, but we are not open to receive the gift so the healing does not occur. Openness, with the addition of grace, is often what it takes to heal.*

*Self-healing is not just about the self. It is about the whole, about the entire planet and all of humanity, for to heal the self is to heal the other, to heal the other is to heal the self and together, to heal the whole. This is what is so important to remember. We each have a responsibility to ourselves and to each other to move in the direction of health and wholeness, to move into the light, not just for individual or personal reasons, but for the good of all, for the evolution of humankind. This is the only way that the transformation of the species will occur. Unless the focus is taken off of the self as distinct and separate from the other, this will not happen. The return to the concept of Oneness that is inherent to the shamanic consciousness is what is needed. This is the essential feature of healing. This is what must awaken within the hearts and minds of humankind in order to move to the next level of being that is its destiny.*

*Healing always involves a shift in consciousness, a change in beliefs, a paradigm shift. This is essential for the healing to impact at the spiritual, mental and emotional levels. Physical cures that take place are often illusory. They are only temporary remissions that will recur again and again unless this shift in consciousness occurs. Healing, then, is an ongoing, never ending process of self-growth and evolvement. It is not an event, nor is there really a goal or final state that one attains and then stops. It is a continuous, life-long way of being. It involves a shift of consciousness into this mind-set that looks for the healing in all things, all situations, and all relationships. When one assumes this mind-set of **healing intentionality**, one moves into a space of continued healing and will find themselves coming ever nearer to a state of wholeness and vibrant health at all levels of being.*

MY JOURNEY THROUGH THE DARKNESS of dis-ease, disconnection and fear into the light of Oneness in Spirit has been a
process of exploration, an adventure into the unknown. It has been
a process of trial and error characterized by both high times and low
times. Yet this self-healing experience has been rich in rewards, as I
have learned first-hand so much about the essence of healing.
Perhaps this can best be exemplified by exploring what I have
learned during a recent experience.

As mentioned earlier, within the past year my health challenges
have been primarily related to gynecological problems—repeated
abnormal Pap smear results, fibroid uterine tumors, menopausal
hormonal ups and downs, irregular menstrual cycles, excessive, and
often unrelenting, bleeding resulting in anemia. For a long time, it
seemed that this part of my body was simply out of control. I bled
almost continuously from mid-September until mid-December,
1995. I didn't have a period for almost five months and then the
unrelenting bleeding started again in late April, 1996. I do not
believe in taking synthetic medications and my preference is to utilize alternative healing modalities, taking only natural herbal or
homeopathic remedies. However, none of the remedies that I tried
seemed to stop the bleeding. I was faced with the choice of taking
the medication that the allopathic physician had to offer—Provera
(synthetic progesterone) or birth control pills—or continue to
bleed. My other options were surgery (a D&C) or, the most extreme
possibility, a hysterectomy. I chose the medication. I took Provera
for ten days on one occasion (November, 1995) and birth control
pills for three weeks on another (December, 1995). What I found,
however, was that although they stopped the bleeding temporarily,
they offered no long-term cure. I decided that I would not take synthetic hormones again.

The bleeding in April went on and on, and I was once again anemic. I insisted that the gynecologist prescribe natural progesterone
(instead of Provera) to stop the bleeding. She reluctantly agreed,

but it did nothing to halt the flow. After eighteen days of heavy bleeding, when the gynecologist prescribed birth control pills to be taken for six weeks, feeling desperate, I went against my earlier decision and took them. The bleeding stopped and all seemed just fine—until my next period, which came a few days after arriving in Sedona in June of 1996 to work on the writing of this book. By the second day of the period, the bleeding was heavier than it had ever been in my life (except for the time I hemorrhaged after Debbie was born). In addition, I was experiencing excruciating and debilitating cramps, the likes of which I have not experienced since I went through labor for my last child. I haven't had menstrual cramps since before my first pregnancy, so this was unusual and unexpected. I was so uncomfortable that sitting at a computer and writing wasn't a consideration. By mid-afternoon that day, I somehow managed to get myself to a nearby health food store and I purchased some homeopathic remedies for cramping. Within several hours the cramps were gone. I felt almost brand new, and I was able to get some writing accomplished that evening. I was elated. I was beginning to think that I had found the magic cure.

Upon awakening the next morning, the cramps hadn't returned, but I now had a severe pain in my lower right abdominal region. I was getting concerned and frustrated. I had only a limited amount of time in Sedona to get the writing done and time was wasting away as I lay around in pain. I called my gynecologist in Chicago, hoping that she could offer some insight. She basically told me that the cramping and pain were most likely related to taking the birth control pills and that all she could suggest was a painkiller. I felt so betrayed by the medical profession. How could they have given me something that would cause me this much pain? I became increasingly furious as I obsessed over this, and I began to beat-up on myself as well for having gone against my convictions and taken the pills in the first place. I remembered having heard somewhere that estrogen makes fibroid tumors grow and I became concerned that the estrogen in the birth control pills had caused mine to enlarge and that was the cause of both the excessive bleeding and the pain. I was feeling frightened, angry and becoming more and more desperate.

As I drummed later that morning (recalling Inner Shaman's teaching that every illness has a message or deeper meaning), I asked Spirit what it was that I needed to learn from this illness, hoping that once I learned the lesson the pain would dissipate. The answer was clear, direct and immediate. "You must stop fighting your illness and learn to dance with it" was the reply. This one was a challenge, indeed, as the pain got increasingly worse as the day progressed. Since I almost never take painkillers, I had none in the house, and the homeopathic remedies that worked so well the day before were not doing a thing at this point. I was in too much pain to leave the house to go to the pharmacy; I was becoming desperate. Try as I might to dance with the pain, by evening it was so bad that I broke down. I simply let go and plummeted into fear, anger, doubt and confusion and I cried and cried, calling out to Spirit for help. I asked over and over, amid my anger and fear, why Spirit had abandoned me when I was doing its work.

As I lay on the bed sobbing and calling to Spirit, I felt a familiar presence. It was my dear teacher, Sky Hawk. He had come to me in a vision to comfort me and to impart the wisdom that I needed at that moment. Responding to my question, he said:

> You ask why we have abandoned you when you are doing our work, but this is precisely it. This pain, bleeding and illness are about doing our work. They are meant to teach you all that you need to learn about healing in the only way that you could fully learn it—to experience it in the depths of your soul. As long as you stay in fear and anger, healing cannot occur, for it constricts the flow of energy. It causes you to lose power and as long as there is a power loss, there can be no healing. Pain, anger and fear cause constrictions

to occur at all four levels of being. At the physical level, muscles contract. At the mental level, you are kept in a place of very limited thinking where a vast array of possibilities is inaccessible to you. At the emotional level, the free flow of emotional energy is blocked, as you stay stuck in these same emotions. All of this closes the door to the spiritual, making it impossible to access. Please know that it is you who close the door to Spirit; it is not the other way around. The secret to healing is in embracing and then transcending the pain, leaving it behind with the fear and anger and completely surrendering to Spirit, trusting that all will be well."

He then took me on a journey out of my body, teaching me experientially how to transcend my pain, for when my consciousness returned to ordinary reality the pain had disappeared. After telling me that I was now healed, Sky Hawk left me. I felt wonderful, at peace for the first time in two days. I thought that my troubles were over, but I was wrong; my learning experience was not yet complete. I still needed to learn how to transfer what I had learned during my journey in the spiritual dimension with Sky Hawk into everyday, material reality. It was as if my experience in nonordinary reality with my inner teacher provided me with a template or a model of what to do in the "real" world. All I needed to do now was to find a way to embody it in ordinary reality.

The pain returned the next day, only this time by putting the awareness that Sky Hawk had gifted me with the night before into practice, I responded differently. I surrendered to the pain; I danced with it. Instead of fighting it, I listened to it and I went to the emergency room early that morning. After an examination revealed that there was nothing significantly wrong, I allowed myself to have a painkiller and the pain diminished in less than an hour and was entirely gone by that evening. The bleeding didn't completely stop for another three or four days, but my experience of it was different because I was at peace with it. And, herein lies the healing. Sky Hawk had taught me how to transcend my pain at the spiritual level, but I needed to find a way to do that at the physical level as well. I needed to stop fighting and fearing my condition and to accept it, to surrender to it, to dance with it. In this case, "dancing with it" meant that I accepted the fact that I had a potentially serious condition and I opened to the possibility that I needed medical attention. Once I allowed myself to have medical attention and I was told that "all is well," the fear abated and (with the help of a painkiller) my symptoms dissipated as well.

There can be no surrender as long as we refuse to accept, no trust as long as we fear, and no peace as long as we fight. My experience with Sky Hawk that night in Sedona helped me to put it all together, to complete the picture of the healing process. The notion that we need to let go of fear and anger and "dance" with our pain came to me at that time. I already knew about the necessity of achieving a shift in consciousness at the four levels of being and the need to surrender and trust and reconnect to Spirit. I learned that evening about the critical role that anger, fear and pain—energies associated with darkness—played in dis-ease.

Sky Hawk led me to this awareness and helped me achieve peace, surrender and trust. Once the fear has been transcended, surrender (letting go of the ego-self at a deep level and giving up the self to Spirit) and trust are possible. To surrender is to dance, to move in rhythm with the situation, rather than struggling and fighting with it. I learned that to heal is to come to a place of peace and surrender with the pain, the symptoms, the situation, or even with death itself. This is the essence of true healing, more so than the eradication of symptoms.

A number of months have passed since this experience. I have begun seeing a holistic physician who has treated me for the excessive bleeding with natural progesterone cream and herbal, homeopathic and vitamin remedies. These treatments have been moderately successful. My latest Pap smear is normal for the first time in two years. My last several periods have been routine, with normal-to-heavy bleeding lasting seven or eight days—also for the first time in over a year. But more importantly, I have come to accept the situation as a normal part of menopause, no longer fighting it. I have learned to dance with the bleeding rather than struggle with it.

It appears that what Sky Hawk told me may indeed be true and I have healed this situation. But was it because of the new remedies that I have taken or was it related to my having finally learned the secret to healing? A communication I received from Inner Shaman a year prior to this experience clearly addresses this issue:

*Healing is an individual affair. What is good for one is not necessarily good for another. It is important to experiment with all types of things until one finds the key. There is often at least one key that apparently leads to the healing, and there may be more than one key. The role of the key is that it appears as if this is the one thing that will do the magic. Although magic is not involved, if your unconscious thinks it is magical then it will work.*

*The main idea is that we heal not by external mechanisms or techniques or chemicals or treatments alone. We heal by changing our inner self from a place of disharmony to one of harmony, and this occurs at the spiritual level. Once this is accomplished, then the right key, the one that the person has the most faith in, will do the trick. The internal shift, in other words, is what makes it possible for the key to open the door. Whatever key helps is not important. Just recognize the fact that keys are helpers in the process at the physical, mental or emotional level, but they are not what ultimately does the healing, as this must take place at the spiritual level, the place where all healing originates. The healing, as I have said, occurs when the person has made the internal shift that involves the reconnection to Self and Spirit that is the essence of healing. The healing takes place at the spiritual level and then, through the help of the key or keys becomes manifest at the other levels. It is okay to think in terms of external helpers or keys, but they are not what really matter. They are just all part of an illusion that we all live under. Keys alone may effect a cure, but they will never bring about true healing. Keys, along with the internal shift at the spiritual level, will.*

Healing, then, according to Inner Shaman, originates on the spiritual level. Working at this level is essential, but not enough. The other levels of being must be addressed as well. If we limit ourselves to working at the spiritual level only, we may find spiritual healing, but not physical, mental and emotional healing. Spiritual healing, in other words, precedes true healing at any other level. A shift in consciousness at the mental level, likewise, precedes making a shift at the emotional level and blocked emotional energy causes pain or illness at the physical level. If we work at only the physical level we may find a cure, but not true healing.

When viewing the healing process in light of the four levels of being, it becomes clear that healing results from a multi-dimensional, simultaneous interchange between them. What occurs on one level affects what happens at all the others, and in order for true healing to take place, there needs to be a shift that occurs at all four levels. The "key" is whatever is needed to affect a change at the physical, mental and emotional levels, but it will not constitute healing unless it is accompanied by an internal shift in consciousness at the spiritual level. This is what "holistic healing" is really about—a synergistic integration of body, mind, heart and spirit. The shifts at each of the four levels together translate into healing.

At the spiritual level, once we surrender—letting go of our will and surrendering to the higher will—the door is opened and we enter into the Light of Spirit, thus opening to its grace, guidance and love, trusting that all is well. It is in the spiritual realm where we experience deep communion with Spirit, where our inner peace, harmony and power are restored to us, and where we find healing of our spirit. In my case, the internal shift at the spiritual level took place that evening in Sedona during a moment of communion with Spirit in which I learned about the necessity of transcending pain, fear and anger. It was an awakening, an "Ah Ha!" experience, as if I

285

had "seen the light." As I opened to Spirit's gifts—guidance, grace and love—I opened to its power, letting it "empower" me to bring healing to my situation.

At the mental level, a shift in consciousness or awareness is needed. This may be a shift in attitude, values or beliefs, or a letting go of limiting beliefs that prevent opening to other possibilities. It involves a shift in perspective, viewing the situation in a different way. Looking at my pain in a different light that evening in Sedona and learning to dance with it was instrumental in creating a shift at the mental level. Letting go of the limiting belief that "alternative" medicine or "natural" remedies were the only way to go, in turn, enabled me to get the medical attention required to address my needs at the physical level. Being reminded by Sky Hawk that my experience provided an opportunity, a lesson meant to teach me about the process of healing, was also a shift in consciousness at this level which, in turn, facilitated a shift at the emotional level—letting go of my fear and anger.

At the emotional level, the shift involves allowing the free flow of emotional energy. It is at this level that we need to let go of the pain and anger that accompany emotional wounds and the fear which inhibits any change or movement, fear that keeps us stuck and paralyzed. As I stated earlier, there can be no surrender as long as we refuse to accept, no trust as long as we fear, and no peace as long as we fight. That evening in Sedona, with Sky Hawk's coaching, I was able to let go of my anger and fear, dance with my pain and illness and come to a place of surrender, trust and peace.

At the physical level, the eradication of symptoms or effecting a cure is impacted by such things as medication, treatment, natural remedies, surgery, nutrition, stress management, relaxation, bodywork, etc. These are the "keys" that Inner Shaman refers to that work at the physical level. In the situation I just described, they were the painkiller (in the emergency room), natural progesterone cream and the herbal, homeopathic and vitamin remedies, which I used that brought about a shift at the physical level. It appears that by addressing my situation from all four of these levels, I have found a way to heal it.

After processing this experience and all that I had learned from it, I am reminded of the vision of climbing the mountain that I described in Chapter Three. Since having the vision over two years ago, I have had a feeling that there was an important message embedded in its story, that it was a "big vision," but I was never certain exactly what it was. It has become clear to me that this vision portrays the essence of the healing process—the movement through darkness into the light. As such, it is worth a second look to explore in more depth its richness as a model or prototype for the process of healing.

> In my vision I was leisurely walking through the forest with Sky Hawk. It was a glorious day, with the sun shining brightly overhead, and it seemed that I had not a care in the world. We were following Wolf, who was doing a superb job of navigating through the thick woods. Suddenly, Wolf just stopped and sat down, at which point Sky Hawk looked at me and told me quite unequivocally to take off my clothes. I looked back at him in surprise and responded, "Excuse me, I don't want to take off my clothes." Sky Hawk, persisted, insisting that I needed to take off my clothes; I persisted in resisting the whole idea. We bickered back and forth for a while until I finally made a deal with Sky Hawk that I would take my clothes off only if he would take his off as well. He agreed and we both disrobed. I laid my clothes on the ground next to Wolf and stood looking at Sky Hawk with a "so now what?" look in my eyes. Sky Hawk said, "Now go!" I looked at him incredulously, and responded, "Go where?" He said, "Just go!" We went back and forth, once

again, with me not at all understanding why I needed to do this ridiculous thing that he was asking of me and very strongly resisting. I finally gave in and said, "But where will I go?" Sky Hawk looked at me with wisdom in his eyes and responded quite simply, "You will know when you get there."

And so I reluctantly set off on my own, naked, into the forest having no path to follow, no one to lead me, not having the faintest idea as to why I needed to go, and feeling quite fearful and very angry about having to do so. As I walked along, my internal dialogue went something like this: "Why do I need to do this? I don't understand. Who does he think he is to send me off like this, alone, with no clothes, and no guide. Where is Bear? I never go anywhere without Bear. This doesn't make any sense. He wants me to go somewhere, but doesn't tell me where or how to get there and expects me to just comply without a question. Well, this makes me furious!" The inner dialogue went on like this for a while as I struggled to find my way through the woods. Then finally, I said to myself, "Just stop fighting it and go with it. Stop judging and scaring yourself and just see what happens. Trust that Sky Hawk knows best. He has never led you astray before."

At that very moment of surrender, at the moment that I let go of my fear, anger and confusion, my need to be in control, my need to make sense out of it all, I saw before me what looked like a searchlight. It seemed to be lighting a path before me; I decided to follow it. The pillar of light led me up and around. Spiraling up and up, I slowly made my way up the side of a mountain. As I approached the top, I noticed that the pillar of light was beginning to change form; it was shifting into a spiral of light. When I reached the top, Bear was sitting there, waiting for me. I felt so comforted knowing that he was near and that I was no longer alone. Then, I noticed that the spiral of light was shifting once again. The light was swirling and swirling, appearing to be doing some kind of a dance and, as it danced, it was taking on a shape or form. I watched intently as the light finally took form. At first glance, it looked like it was an animal, a white lamb. As I looked at the lamb, I heard a voice that said, "It's not a lamb; it's a white buffalo calf." I stood there, somewhat dazed, watching as the white buffalo calf looked back at me, gazing deeply into my eyes. I felt such incredible love and wisdom emanating from those eyes which seemed to see deep into my soul.

As the white buffalo calf and I gazed at each other, I noticed that it was now beginning to shape-shift once again. Soon I saw standing before me a beautiful Indian woman dressed all in white. I knew that this was White Buffalo Calf Woman, the legendary figure who brought the sacred pipe to the Lakota peoples long, long ago, the White Buffalo Woman that Brooke Medicine Eagle writes about. I stood in amazement, feeling a rush of excitement that she would honor me with her visit. She told me to lie face down on the ground, and as I did, she began to speak to me. She told me all that I needed to know to help me to prepare for my vision quest. In so doing, she gifted me with untold peace and calmness.

When she had finished speaking, she quickly shape-shifted once again into the swirling spiral of light, which soon faded away. I followed Bear down the mountain where Sky Hawk and Wolf were waiting for me, right where I had left them. I put my clothes back on and Sky Hawk gave me a big hug and a smile that said more than any words possibly could.

This vision is rich in symbolism and presents a vibrant metaphor suggestive of not only the healing process as Inner Shaman describes it, but also of my personal healing journey over the course of the past fifteen years.

In the vision I was going along just fine. When I first began my healing journey following an external guide, [I was leisurely walking through the forest with Sky Hawk... We were following Wolf...] I felt quite safe in the company of others, not having to make decisions or do anything other than to go where I was told. This is reminiscent of my experience in the Catholic Church when I unquestionably followed its teachings. I felt safe and had no responsibility but to do what I was told, yet I was in darkness, [the thick woods] in a sleepy haze of unawareness.

Then there was a sudden shift, a calling, a challenge to do something different. [Suddenly...Sky Hawk...told me...to take off my clothes.] The call seemed to come out of nowhere, when I least expected it. I was being asked to let go of something dear to me, to take off my clothes, my mask, and bare my soul to the world. It threw me off guard, and at first I resisted. [I persisted in resisting] I resisted leaving behind the safety of the Catholic Church and the way of life that went along with it. I was being asked to leave behind something that no longer served me. I found this difficult and went through a period of turmoil. [We bickered back and forth for a while] I wasn't sure why I needed to answer the call. [not at all understanding why I needed to do this ridiculous thing that he was asking of me] I just knew deep inside that I did, and I kept hearing the words to that song echoing in my head, "Hear I am, Lord. Is it I, Lord? I have heard you calling in the night. I will go, Lord, if you lead me. I will hold your people in my heart." I finally agreed, and shed my protective covering (the protection and safety of organized religion and its attendant belief system) and set it aside. [I disrobed ... I laid my clothes on the ground] Once free of this protective layer, I could answer the call unencumbered. [Now go!] The call was to awaken so that I might begin my spiritual journey. As long as I stayed within the confines of the Church, I was not free to embark on my journey. I needed to break the chains that held me in place.

This marked an initiation, a shaman's death in which I was dying to one way of life so that I might begin a new one. I left behind the old familiar way, went off alone into an uncharted territory, not knowing where I was going or how I would get there. [I reluctantly set off on my own, naked, into the forest having no path to follow, no one to lead me.] At this point I was on my own, alone in the dark woods, with nothing but my inner voice to guide me. I was angry with the Church; I felt it had betrayed me. I was also afraid to be on my own. What if I wasn't following the right path? [feeling quite fearful and very angry] My anger and fear made things difficult, slowing the process down considerably, as they only served to keep me disconnected from Spirit. [I struggled to find my way through the woods] All along my healing journey, whenever I was faced with challenge that came my way, fear and anger was my typical response. Letting go of fear and anger, which is dependent on an attitudinal change, a shift in consciousness, [Then I finally said to myself, "Just stop fighting it and go with it."] is what I have needed to do over and over again along the way. Finally, I came to a place where I was ready to trust that I had not been led astray, that everything was happening according to a divine plan that was for my best interest. [Trust that Sky Hawk knows best.] I let go and surrendered to Spirit, not sure where it all would end, but trusting that I was being led in the right direction.

By surrendering, I opened the doors to Spirit, moving from the darkness of disconnection into the light of Oneness. [At the very moment of surrender...I let go of my fear, anger and confusion, I saw before me what looked like a searchlight...lighting a path before me] Once I trusted and surrendered, Spirit entered my life, the light appeared and lit the path that I was to follow, the path to the mountaintop. [The pillar of light led me up...the side of the mountain] It was here in this place of Oneness, where I knew that I was not alone, that I was connected, that "We Are All Related." [I felt so comforted knowing that he (Bear) was near, that I was no longer alone.] It was here that Spirit manifested itself to me, [the light finally took on a form] bringing with it love [I felt such incredible love], the "medicine" that I was in need of, [She told me all that I needed to know] and healing [peace and calmness]. Coming to this place of Oneness with Spirit has been my healing journey, my movement through the darkness into the light. It has brought me to a place of deep communion with Spirit and has opened up a whole new world of aliveness, health and possibility.

In looking back on my experience with healing over the past fifteen years, I would humbly say that I have come a long way. I have not only healed physical symptoms, but I have healed many nonphysical aspects of my life as well. One of the things I have learned along the way is that healing is an ongoing process of becoming; it is a *process, not an event.* It is not something that you do and then you're done. I believe the process never ends. There is always room for improvement, always possibility for continued growth. As long as we are alive, situations needing healing continue to present themselves—this is the nature of life. For me, healing has been like a full-time job. I have devoted a great deal of my energy to it; my intentionality is always related to healing in one way or another. It has become my general frame of reference, both personally and professionally. Perhaps this is what it means to be a healer.

I have moved ever nearer to a goal of achieving wholeness during the past fifteen years as I consciously walked the path of healing. I have begun the life-long process of moving into the light. My plan is to continue the process, to continue moving in the direction of the light. Where exactly I'm going I'm not sure, but I trust that, as Sky Hawk told me, "I will know when I get there."

The process has been both an adventure and a sacred journey. The challenges have been great, but the rewards equally as great, rich in growth, insight, learning and understanding. My journey has been an ongoing process of trial and error, experimenting and discovering, sometimes the hard way, what worked for me and what didn't. I learned that one of the most important elements of healing involves my response. I found that responding with a positive attitude, with faith and hope in my heart, works the best to propel me along the healing path. Perhaps my approach to healing can best be described as "holistic," as I view the situation as a whole, involving all four levels of being, physical, mental, emotional and spiritual. I have come to realize that each of these four levels needs to be addressed as part of the healing process. Focusing attention on only one level may get a short-term cure, but not true healing.

How does this all translate into practical, everyday behaviors? When responding to challenging situations, what approaches seemed to work best for me? When I look back at some of the numerous situations that have needed healing in my life and my response to them, a number of common elements come to mind. I have identified some of these elements, responses and approaches that I have employed along the way which have proved to be most useful in supporting my healing process, and I want to share them with you here.

## At the Physical level:

- Being open to and experimenting with different remedies, treatments and healing modalities.

- Engaging the help of a healing team—bodyworkers, massage therapist, energy healer, acupuncturist, chiropractor, psychotherapist, MD, etc.

- Being nice to myself—pampering myself and not pushing myself with "shoulds."

- Involving myself in the process as much as needed—rolling up my sleeves and doing whatever needs to be done.

- Finding a balance in treatment, utilizing both traditional and alternative methods.

- Being in tune with my inner body wisdom—honoring messages from my body about what is good for it and what is not.

- Making sacrifices—giving up certain foods, products, activities, etc. if necessary.

- Standing up for myself to the medical profession—asking for what I want and need from them.


At the emotional level:

- Reaching out to others—finding emotional support from family, friends and professionals.

- Acknowledging and honoring my feelings—allowing myself to go into the cave (of depression) when needed, to enter into the stillness and just be with the healing process.

- Riding the waves—learning to adapt to the up and down movement of hope and disappointment, without giving in to discouragement.

- Not allowing fear and "what ifs" to overwhelm me by trusting that everything happens in perfect divine order.

- Letting go of anger and blame and coming to a place of calm acceptance.

- Being patient with the process—giving myself, or the situation, the time to heal, without rushing, pushing or forcing.

- Loving myself enough to do what needs to be done.

## At the mental level:

- Viewing the situation as an opportunity to grow and to learn—an initiation rather than a disaster—and looking for the "gift" inherent in the challenge.

- Remaining determined to heal—whatever the symptoms or problems might be—and not giving up.

- Being open to looking at things from an alternative perspective—shifting consciousness by changing my beliefs and attitudes.

- Believing that a higher purpose is being served—that the symptoms/problems are all serving an important function.

- Believing in the healing process and drawing upon the power of my own inner healer.

- Using creative visualization, healing imagery and positive affirmations as a part of my healing regimen.

- Accepting the possibility that, for me, true healing may not include the eradication of symptoms, but rather an acceptance of and coming to terms with my illness.

## At the spiritual level:

- Surrendering to Spirit and trusting that there is a higher divine plan in action and that all will be well—no matter what the outcome.

- Accepting responsibility for my own healing.

- Following my inner guidance.

- Remaining connected to Spirit and involving my non-physical teachers and guides in my healing process.

- Incorporating spiritual practices in my healing regimen—meditation, drumming, etc.

- Praying for guidance, grace and healing.

- Opening to receive healing grace.

I have learned a great deal during the course of my healing journey. One of the most important things that I have learned is that healing is not just about the eradication of symptoms. It encompasses a much broader concept than that. As I said earlier, it has been for me an ongoing, never ending process of growth, expansion, becoming and evolving, of moving through darkness into the light. The darkness was the place of ignorance, of unconsciousness, of disconnection from the spirit within and without. It was characterized by dis-ease, illness, limited thinking, self-denigration, depression, anxiety and fear. The movement into the light has been a shift in consciousness. It has been an awakening, a transformation, an opening, a remembering, a reconnecting to Self and Spirit. Living in the light has enabled me to become more in tune with my "little local self" as well as my grander Self, enabling me to follow my heart by listening to, and trusting, my inner guidance.

My experience of healing has thus been a process of becoming whole, of embracing all of whom I am on all levels of being, and living my life accordingly. It is only by becoming one with Spirit that one can be whole. Brooke Medicine Eagle points out that the word "heal" comes from the same root as the words "whole" and "holiness," and states that within the Native American tradition, the concepts of wholeness and holiness are still associated with healing. "This holiness is the essence of healing, which means to manifest wholeness in spirit and bring it into our bodies, our families, our communities, our world. We heal by beginning to consciously embody the Spirit that lives as one with us and in all things."[1] My experience of what it means to heal, of embodying the Spirit within, of being whole, is summed up in the following poem:

## To Heal is to be Whole

To heal is be whole.
To heal is to be reborn into a new life.
To heal is to be one with all that I am, all that I can be.
To heal is to find inner peace, a state of calm absence of conflict.
To heal is to know that I am always connected to the Divine Source.
To heal is to love and accept myself and others without qualification.
To heal is to learn to allow myself to be loved.
To heal is to realize that happiness is my birthright, and to
    allow it into my life.
To heal is to come to a place of forgiveness of self and others.
To heal is to warmly embrace my inner child with true love
    and compassion.
To heal is to be comfortable stretching myself to take risks.
To heal is to find my power and to accept the responsibility that goes
    with it.
To heal is to let go of the need to be a victim.
To heal is to know in my depths that no matter what happens all is well.
To heal is to allow the creative energy to flow through me,
    without resistance.
To heal is to find those parts of myself that were once lost or forgotten.
To heal is to enjoy life, to celebrate life, to find happiness in the
    smallest things.
To heal is to see the world with a new set of eyes, focusing on the joys
    rather than the woes.
To heal is to be free from the chains of fear and doubt, the pain of anger
    and self-denigration.
To heal is to open to the glorious gifts that the Universe provides.
To heal is to live in harmony with Mother Earth and the entire
    natural world.
To heal is to be in touch and in tune with my physical body.

To heal is to awaken from a long slumber, renewed, refreshed, revitalized.

To heal is to release my attachment to pain, illness and discomfort at all levels of being.

To heal is to find my path and to have the strength and courage to remain on it, no matter what.

To heal is to learn to accept life's problems as challenges that help me to learn and grow.

To heal is to stop fighting life and go with its gentle flow.

To heal is to find my own rhythm and to learn to live in sync with it.

To heal is to find balance and harmony in every aspect of life, every level of being.

To heal is to finally realize that I am one with all of life.

To heal is to find my true self and in so doing to find my god-self.

To heal is to find my way back home again.

To heal is to sing my song for all to hear.

To heal is to be happy with who I am.

To heal is to walk once again in light.

To heal is to be whole.

*August 1, 1995*

# FLIGHT

As I sit on top of the world, my heart takes flight.
I soar above the clouds and below the heavens,
soaring like a bird in flight to heights unknown.
Below I see the beauty of the seen world,
above I feel the presence of the unseen.
Within I know the calling of the Master,
hidden deep within the recesses of my soul.
No more will I abandon my calling.
No more will I forget the Who that is Me.
No more will I go on believing that I am no more than a mere human,
for I know, deep within my Soul, that I can fly . . .

— M. S.

*April 23, 1995*

# EPILOGUE

ONE DAY LATE IN THE SUMMER of 1996, I went for my usual morning walk following the same path that I always take. As I walked by the pond where I first met Sky Hawk seven years before, I felt an exceptionally strong attraction to stop, as if the pond were calling out to me, beckoning me to come to it. I rarely stopped there anymore. The development has long since been built up, and there is a very large sign right next to the pond that says "Private Property— NO TRESPASSING!" so I have hesitated to spend any time there. This particular morning, however, the urge to walk over and stand by the pond was so strong that I ignored the sign. I walked over and stood very close to the same spot where I had stood the morning that I first met the Shaman. Having grown from a vacant new construction site dotted with piles of dug-up earth, to a completed townhouse development, the area around the pond was very different than it had been seven years ago, yet somehow strangely the same. The pond was now surrounded by buildings, sidewalks and green grass. Geese had since made the pond their home and were gliding across the glistening water, bobbing their heads below the surface looking for breakfast. The sun was shinning brightly, creating the same radiant effect on the water that it had so many years before, calling to me, inviting me to dance with it once again.

I closed my eyes and immediately had a vision of Sky Hawk. He was standing before me, dressed in white. Looking down at myself, I saw that I was dressed in white as well. Sky Hawk held out his arms and we melted into an embrace that expressed the love and friendship that had developed over the years as he and I have journeyed together. We have been through so much, we have walked many miles, we have come so far together. My silent tears reflected this tender connection and the love and appreciation that I felt for my special teacher, my trusted inner guide.

I knew that a ceremony of celebration in my honor was about to take place, and I noticed that Sky Hawk had gifts to present to me. He placed an exquisitely adorned silver and turquoise necklace around my neck. Its magnificence covered a great part of my chest. He then placed a headdress of white feathers on my head that cascaded down to the ground and handed me a silver bow and arrow, also adorned with turquoise. He told me that the bow and arrow symbolized that I was now ready to be a warrior—a warrior for the proliferation of the light.

I began to hear drumming and chanting in the background, and, looking around, I noticed that we were surrounded by hundreds of beings also dressed in white. They slowly began to move to the beat of the drumming and chanting, smoothly raising their arms in rhythm. As they did, I noticed that their arms were not arms at all, but the white wings of an eagle. I was suddenly surrounded by a sea of hundreds of white eagles gently, gracefully flapping their wings. Then I realized that Sky Hawk and I also had the wings of an eagle. We also flapped our wings in rhythm, as we joined in the dance, becoming one with the sea of white eagles. Soon Sky Hawk and I began to lift off the ground and soar high into the sky. We soared higher and higher, leaving the others behind, and before long we entered into complete darkness. As we moved through the darkness, I looked back and could see a trail of light that we were leaving behind us. *We* were lighting the darkness; *we* were illuminating the night. Then, Sky Hawk looked at me and told me that I must be a beacon, a beacon of light to help others to find their way through the darkness.

As he spoke those words a wave of fear moved through my body and I shuddered at the thought of such an awesome responsibility. I also knew that my fear was inspired by that old tape from my childhood, "Lord I am not worthy..." Soon I heard another voice, a stronger, clearer voice from deep within saying, "Here I am, Lord. Is it I, Lord? I have heard you calling in the night. I will go, Lord, if you lead me. I will hold your people in my heart." And then as the tears spilled, my heart was filled with peace and the words of this prayer came forth:

> I will carry your torch, oh, Great One.
> I will be a beacon for your light to shine through,
> for it is not my light, but yours that shines.
> I am your instrument, play me.
> I am your song, sing me.
> I am your dance, dance me.
> I am your tool, work me.
> I am your messenger, send me.

And then I remembered the three feathers that I had been given by Spirit so long ago—one for *Love*, one for *Light*, and one for *Illumination*. At that moment, the meaning of that gift became perfectly clear. I realized that *Love* is the way into the *Light*, and once in the Light, we are called to *Illumination*. We are called upon to radiate the Light so that others might also find their way through the Darkness into the Light.

And so my journey continues . . .

# ONE WITH THE LIGHT

Light all around,
I am transformed into a state of complete oneness.
I am one with the light,
I am the light,
the light is I.
There is nothing but light.
That is all I can see.
Nothing but
a void filled with light-and me.
Just me,
one with the light
in complete ecstasy.

— M. S.
*June 1, 1995*

# ENDNOTES

## Introduction

1. Eliade, M. *Shamanism: Archaic Techniques of Ecstasy.* (Princeton University Press, 1964).

2. Lorler, M. Shamanic *Healing Within the Medicine Wheel* (Albuquerque, NM: Brotherhood of Life, Inc., 1989)

3. Brooke Medicine Eagle. *Buffalo Woman Comes Singing.* (New York: Ballantine Books, 1991), p.9.

## Chapter One
### The Essence of Shamanism

1. Michael Harner, *The Way of the Shaman.* (San Francisco: Harper Collins Publisher, 1980, 1990), p. 40.

2. Marie Lu-Lorler, *Shamanic Healing Within the Medicine Wheel.* (Albuquerque, NM: Brotherhood of Life, Inc., 1989), p. 21.

3. D. S. Rogo, *Shamanism, ESP and the Paranormal.* In S. Nicholson, (Ed.), *Shamanism* (pp. 133-144), Wheaton, IL; Theosophical Publishing House, 1987).

4. Joan Halifax, *Shaman: The Wounded Healer,* (London: Thames and Hudson Ltd., 1982), p. 5.

5. Serge Kahili King, *Urban Shaman.* (New York: Fireside, 1990), p. 14.

6. Harner, p. 46.

7. Kenneth Meadows, *Shamanic Experience: A Practical Guide to Contemporary Shamanism.* Rockport, Massachusetts: Element, 1991), pp. 6-7.

8. Carlos Castanada, *The Teachings of Don Juan: A Yaqui Way of Knowledge.* (New York: Washington Square Press, 1968).

9. Mircea Eliade, *Shamanism: Archaic Techniques of Ecstasy,* (Princeton University Press, 1964), p. 107.

10. Ibid, p. 43.

11. Ibid, p. 64.

12. Amber Wolfe, *In the Shadow of the Shaman: Connecting with Self, Nature, and Spirit.* (St. Paul, MN: Llewellyn Publishers, 1991), p. xiii.

13. Larry Dossey, *Recovering the Soul: A Scientific and Spiritual Search.* (New York: Bantam Books, 1989), pp. 101-102.

14. Jeanne Achterberg, *Imagery in Healing: Shamanism and Modern Medicine.* (Boston: Shambhala, 1985), p. 25.

15. Jean Houston, *Jean Houston 1992 Mystery School: Eskimo Shamanism.* (Wind Over the Earth, Cassette Recording, 1992).

16. Ed McGaa, *Mother Earth Spirituality: Native American Paths to Healing Ourselves and Our World.* (San Francisco: Harper Collins Publishers, 1988), p. 21.

17. Paula Underwood Spencer, *A Native American Worldview.* In B. McNeill and C. Guion. Noetic Sciences Collection: 1980 - 1990, pp. 102-109. ( Sausalito, CA: Institute of Noetic Sciences, 1991).

18. J. B. Townsend, *Neo-Shamanism and the Modern Mystical Movement.* In G. Doore (Ed.), *Shaman's Path; Healing, Personal Growth and Empowerment.* (Boston and London: Shambhala, 1988), p. 81.

19. Achterberg, pp. 19-20.

20. Lorler, p. 152.

21. Lewis Mehl, *Modern Shamanism: Integration of Biomedicine with Traditional Worldviews.* In G. Doore (Ed.), *Shaman's Path: Healing, Personal Growth and Empowerment.* (Boston: Shambhala, pp. 127-138).

22. Lorler, p. 153.

23. Houston

24. Joe and Lena Stevens, *Secrets of Shamanism: Tapping the Spirit Power Within You.* (New York: Avon Books, 1988), p. 173.

25. Wolfe, p. 109.

26. Harner, p. xvii.

27. Larry Dossey, *Recovering the Soul: A Scientific and Spiritual Search.* (New York: Bantam Books, 1989), p. 71.

## Chapter Two
### The Journey: Entering the World of Spirit

1. Richard Matheson, *What Dreams May Come*, (New York: G.P. Putnam's Sons, 1978), pp. 295-296.

2. In 1965 Morey Bernstein published a book, The Search for Bridey Murphy (N>Y>: Doubleday), in which he reports a case study in which a subject under hypnosis recalled a former lifetime from 1798 to 1864 in Cork, Ireland as a woman by the name of Bridey Murphy. He claims that it was factually established that there was indeed a person by the name of Bridey Murphy living in Ireland at that time who later reincarnated in the United States as the subject, Ruth Mills.

3. Morris Netherton and Nancy Shiffrin, *Past Lives Therapy*, (New York: Ace Books, 1979), p. 24.

## Chapter Three
### The Acquisition of Power

1. Louise Hay, *You Can Heal Your Life*, (Santa Monica, CA: Hay House, 1984), pp. 7, 9.

2. Gary Zukav, *The Seat of the Soul*, (New York: Simon & Schuster, 1990), p. 240.

## Chapter Six
### Energy in Healing

1. Shirley MacLaine, *Out on a Limb*, (New York: Bantam, 1983).

2. Shirley MacLaine, *Going Within: A Guide for Inner Transformation*, (New York: Bantam, 1989), p. 105.

3. Anodea Judith and Selene Vega, *The Sevenfold Journey: Reclaiming Body, Mind and Spirit through the Chakras*, (Freedom, CA: The Freedom Press, 1993), p. 6.

4. Richard Gerber, MD, *Vibrational Medicine: New Choices for Healing Ourselves*, (Santa Fe, NM: Bear and Co., 1988), p. 413.

5. Judith and Vega, pp. 6-14.

6. Ibid., p. 86.

7. Judith and Vega, p. 125, 131.

8. Gerber, p. 386.

9. Ibid, p. 386-387.

10. Ibid, p. 382.

11. Ibid, pp. 399-400.

12. Anodea Judith, *Wheels of Life: A User's Guide to the Chakra System*, (St. Paul, MN: Llewellyn Publications, 1987), pp. 36-43.

13. Judith and Vega

## Chapter Seven
## The Search for Meaning

1. John A. Grim, *The Shaman: Patterns of Religious Healing Among the Ojibway Indians*, (Norman and London: University of Oklahoma Press, 1983), pp. 47-48.

## Chapter Eight
## Co-Creation

1. Joseph Murphy, *The Power of Your Subconscious Mind*, (Englewood Cliffs, NJ: Prentice-Hall, Inc., 1963), pp. 30-34.

2. Shakti Gawain, *Creative Visualization*, (New York: Bantam, 1979), pp. 5-7.

3. C. Norman Shealy and Caroline M. Myss, *The Creation of Health: The Emotional, Psychological, and Spiritual Responses that Promote Health and Healing*, (Walpole, NH: Stillpoint Publishing, 1993), p. 107.

4 Clarissa Pinkola Estes, *The Creative Fire* (Audiotape), (Boulder, CO: Sounds True Recordings, 1991).

## Chapter Nine
## Love As Healer

1. Carolyn Myss, *Anatomy of the Spirit: The Seven Stages of Power and Healing*, (New York: Random House, 1996), p. 71.

## Chapter Ten
## The Ritual of Initiation

1. Brooke Medicine Eagle, *Buffalo Woman Comes Singing,* (New York: Ballentine Books, 1991), p. 339.

2. Stephen Larsen, *The Shaman's Doorway: Opening Imagination to Power and Myth,* (New York: Station Hill Press, 1976, 1988), p. ix.

3. Joan Borysenko, *Fire in the Soul: A New Psychology of Spiritual Optimism,* (New York: Warner Books, 1993), p. 62.

## Chapter Eleven
## The Essence of Healing

1. Brooke Medicine Eagle, "The Circle of Healing," in R. Carlson and B. Shield, Eds., *Healers on Healing* (New York: G.P. Putnam's Sons, 1989), p. 60.

# SUGGESTED READING

Abelar, T. (1992) *The Sorcerers' Crossing: A Woman's Journey.* New York: Penguin Arkana.

Achterberg, J. (1985) *Imagery In Healing: Shamanism and Modern Medicine.* Boston and London: Shambhala.

———(1988) *The Wounded Healer: Transformational Journeys in Modern Medicine.* In G. Doore, (Ed.), *Shaman's Path: Healing, Personal Growth and Empowerment.* (pp. 117-125). Boston and London: Shambhala.

Anderson, S. R. and Hopkins, P. (1991) *The Feminine Face of God: The Unfolding of the Sacred in Women.* New York: Bantam Books.

Andrews, L. V. (1981) *Medicine Woman.* New York: Harper Collins Publishers.

———(1984) *Flight of the Seventh Moon.* New York: Harper Collins Publishers.

———(1985) *Jaquar Woman.* New York: Harper Collins Publishers.

Arien, A. (1993) *The Four-Fold Way: Walking the Paths of the Warrior, Teacher, Healer, and Visionary.* Harper San Francisco.

Atwood, M. D. (1991) *Spirit Healing: Native American Magic and Healing.* New York: Sterling Publishing Co.

Barasch, M. I. (1993) *The Healing Path: A Soul Approach to Illness.* New York: Penguin Arkana.

Black Elk, W. and Lyon, W. (1990) *Black Elk: The Sacred Ways of a Lakota.* New York: Harper Collins.

Borysenko, J. (1993) *Fire in the Soul: A New Psychology of Spiritual Optimism.* New York: Warner Books.

Boyd, D. (1974) *Rolling Thunder.* New York: Dell Publishing.

Brown, J. E. (1991) *The Spiritual Legacy of the American Indian.* New York: Crossroad.

_____(1953) *The Sacred Pipe: Black Elk's Account of the Seven Rites of the Oglala Sioux.* Norman, OK: University of Oklahoma Press.

Carey, K. (1988) *Return of the Bird Tribes.* New York: Harper Collins Publishers.

_____ (1982) *The Starseed Transmissions.* Harper San Francisco.

_____ (1991) *The Third Millennium: Living in the Posthistoric World.* Harper San Francisco.

Carlson, R. and Shield, B. (Eds.) (1989) *Healers On Healing.* New York: Putnam Books.

Castanada, C. (1968) *The Teachings of Don Juan: A Yaqui Way of Knowledge.* New York: Washington Square Press.

_____(1971) *A Separate Reality: Further Conversations with Don Juan.* New York: Washington Square Press.

_____(1972) *Journey To Ixtlan: The Lessons of Don Juan.* New York: Washington Square Press.

_____(1974) *Tales of Power.* New York: Washington Square Press.

_____(1977) *The Second Ring of Power.* New York: Washington Square Press.

Chester, L. (1987) *Lupus Novice: Toward Self-Healing.* New York: Station Hill Press.

Conway, D. J. (1995) *By Oak, Ash, & Thorn: Modern Celtic Shamanism.* St. Paul, MN: Llewellyn Publications.

Dolfyn (1990) *Shamanic Wisdom: Nature, Spirituality, Sacred Power and Earth Ecstasy.* Oakland, CA: Earthspirit, Inc.

Dolfyn and Swimming Wolf (1994) *Shamanic Wisdom II: The Way of the Animal Spirits.* Oakland, CA: Earthspirit, Inc.

Dossey, L. (1989) *Recovering the Soul.* New York: Bantam Books.

Drury, N. (1989) *The Elements of Shamanism.* Rockport, Massachusetts: Element.

Eaton, V. (1978) *I Send A Voice.* Wheaton, IL: The Theosophical Publishing House.

_____(1982) *The Shaman and the Medicine Wheel.* Wheaton, IL: The Theosophical Publishing House.

Eliade, M. (1964) *Shamanism: Archaic Techniques of Ecstasy.* Princeton University Press.

Erdoes. R and Ortiz, A., Eds. (1984) *American Indian Myths and Legends.* New York: Pantheon Books.

Estes, C. P. (1991) *The Creative Fire* Audiotape, Boulder, CO: Sounds True Recordings.

Feinstein, D. (1987) *The Shaman Within.* In S. Nicholson (Ed.), Shamanism (pp. 267-279). Wheaton, IL.: The Theosophical Publishing House.

Foster, S. with Little, M. (1992) *The Book of the Vision Quest: Personal Transformation in the Wilderness.* New York: Simon and Schuster.

Gawain, S. (1993) *The Path of Transformation: How Healing Ourselves Can Change the World.* Mill Valley, CA: Nataraj.

_____(1989) *Return to the Garden: A Journey of Discovery.* Mill Valley, CA: Nataraj Publishing.

_____(1979) *Creative Visualization,* New York: Bantam.

Gerber, R. (1988) V*ibrational Medicine: New Choices for Healing Ourselves,* Santa Fe, NM: Bear and Co.

Gillett, R. (1992) *Change Your Mind, Change Your World.* New York: Fireside.

Grim. J. (1983) *The Shaman: Patterns of Religious Healing Among the Ojibway Indians.* Norman, OK: University of Oklahoma Press.

Halifax, J. (1982) *Shaman: The Wounded Healer*, London: Thames and Hudson Ltd.

Harner, M. (1980, 1990) *The Way of the Shaman.* San Francisco: Harper Collins Publishers.

_____(1988) *What Is A Shaman?* In G. Doore (Ed.), *Shaman's Path: Healing, Personal Growth and Empowerment.* (pp. 7-15), Boston and London: Shambhala.

Harner, M. and Doore, G. (1987) *The Ancient Wisdom of Shamanic Cultures* in S. Nicholson, (Ed.), *Shamanism.* Wheaton, IL: The Theosophical Publishing House.

Hay, L. (1984) *You Can Heal Your Life.* Santa Monica, CA: Hay House.

Hoffman, E. (1976, 1981) *Huna: A Beginner's Guide.* Westchester, PA: Whitford Press.

Houston, J. (1992) *Jean Houston 1992 Mystery School: Eskimo Shamanism.* [Cassette Recording]

Hughes-Calero, H. (1994) T*he Shamanic Journey of Living As Soul.* Sedona, AZ: Higher Consciousness Books.

Ingerman, S. (1991) *Soul Retrieval: Mending the Fragmented Self.* San Francisco: Harper Collins Publishers.

_____(1993) *Welcome Home: Life After Healing, Following Your Soul's Journey Home.* San Francisco: Harper Collins Publishers.

Jamal, M. (1987) *Shape Shifters: Shaman Women in Contemporary Society.* New York: Penguin Books.

Judith, A. and Vega, S. (1993) *The Sevenfold Journey: Reclaiming Body, Mind and Spirit through the Chakras,* Freedom, CA: The Freedom Press.

Judith, A. (1987) Wheels of Life: A *User's Guide to the Chakra System,* St. Paul, MN: Llewellyn Publications.

Kalweit, H. (1988) *Dreamtime and Inner Space: The World of the Shaman.* Boston and London: Shambhala.

_____(1992) Shamans, *Healers and Medicine Men.* Boston and London: Shambhala.

Keeney, B. (1994) *Shaking Out the Spirits: A Psychotherapist's Entry into the Healing Mysteries of Global Shamanism.* New York: Station Hill Press.

King, S. K. (1990) *Urban Shaman.* New York: Fireside.

_____(1987) *The Way of the Adventurer* in S. Nicholson *Shamanism.* Wheaton, IL: The Theosophical Publishing House.

_____(1988) *Seeing Is Believing: The Four Worlds of the Shaman* in G. Doore, (Ed.), *Shaman's Path: Healing, Personal Growth and Empowerment.* Boston: Shambhala.

_____(1985) *Mastering Your Hidden Self: A Guide to the Huna Way.* Wheaton, IL: The Theosophical Publishing House.

_____(1983) *Kahuna Healing: Holistic Health and Healing Practices of Polynesia.* Wheaton, IL: The Theosophical Publishing House.

Krippner, S. and Welch, P. (1992) *Spiritual Dimensions of Healing From Native Shamanism to Contemporary Health Care.* New York: Irvington Publishers.

Krippner, S. (1988) *Shamans: The First Healers.* In G. Doore (Ed.), *Shaman's Path: Healing, Personal Growth and Empowerment.* Boston and London: Shambhala.

Lake, M.G. B. (1991) *Native Healer: The Path to an Ancient Healing Art.* New York: Harper Collins Publishers.

Larsen, S. (1976, 1988) *The Shaman's Doorway: Opening Imagination to Power and Myth.* New York: Station Hill Press.

Lorler, M. (1989) *Shamanic Healing Within the Medicine Wheel.* Albuquerque, NM: Brotherhood of Life, Inc.

Lynch, J. P. B. (1994) *Dr. Lynch's Holistic Self-Health Program.* New York: Penguin Books.

MacLaine, S. (1983) *Out on a Limb,* New York: Bantam.

_____ (1989) *Going Within: A Guide for Inner Transformation,* New York: Bantam.

Mails, T. E. (1988) *Secret Native American Pathways: A Guide to Inner Peace.* Tulsa, OK: Council Oak Books.

Marciniak, B. (1992) *Bringers of the Dawn: Teachings from the Pleiadians.* Santa Fe, NM: Bear and Company Publishing.

_____ (1995) *Earth: Pleiadian Keys to the Living Library.* Santa Fe, NM: Bear and Company Publishing.

Matheson, R. (1978) *What Dreams May Come.* New York: G.P. Putnam's Sons.

Meadows, K. (1991) *Shamanic Experience: A Practical Guide to Contemporary Shamanism.* Rockport, MA: Element.

Medicine Eagle, B. (1991) *Buffalo Woman Comes Singing.* New York: Ballantine Books.

_____(1989) "The Circle of Healing," in R. Carlson and B. Shield, Eds., *Healers on Healing,* New York: G.P. Putnam's Sons.

McGaa, E. (1990) *Mother Earth Spirituality: Native American Paths to Healing Ourselves and Our World.* San Francisco: Harper Collins Publishers.

Mehl, L. (1988) *Modern Shamanism: Integration of Biomedicine with Traditional World Views.* In G. Doore (Ed.), Shaman's Path: *Healing, Personal Growth and Empowerment.* (pp. 127-138). Boston and London: Shambhala.

Mindell, A. (1993) *The Shaman's Body: A New Shamanism for Transforming Health, Relationships and the Community.* Harper San Francisco.

Moondance, W. (1994) *Rainbow Medicine: A Visionary Guide to Native American Shamanism.* New York: Sterling Publishing Co.

Murphy, J. (1963) *The Power of Your Subconscious Mind,* Englewood Cliffs, NJ: Prentice Hall, Inc.

Nau, E. S. (1992) *Huna Self-Awareness: The Wisdom of the Ancient Hawaiians.* York Beach, Maine: Samuel Weiser, Inc.

Netherton, M. and Shiffrin, N. (1979) *Past Lives Therapy.* New York: Ace Books.

Noble, V. (1991) *Shakti Woman: Feeling Our Fire, Healing Our World - The New Female Shamanism.* New York: Harper Collins Publishers.

Rogo, D. S. (1987) *Shamanism, ESP, and the Paranormal.* In S. Nicholson, (Ed.), *Shamanism* (pp. 133-144), Wheaton, IL: Theosophical Publishing House.

Ross, A. C. (1989) *Mitakuye Oyasin: "We Are All Related"* Denver, CO: Bear Publishers.

Roth, G. (1989) *Maps to Ecstasy: Teachings of an Urban Shaman.* Mill Valley, CA: Nataraj Publishing.

Scott, G. G. (1991) *Shamanism and Personal Mastery: Using Symbols, Rituals, and Talismans to Activate the Powers Within You.* New York: Paragon House.

_____(1993) *Secrets of the Shaman.* Phoenix, AZ: New Falcon Publications.

_____(1988) *Shamanism for Everyone: A Guide to Discovering the Shaman in You.* Westchester, PA: The Whitford Press.

Shealy, N. and Myss, C. (1993) *The Creation of Health: The Emotional, Psychological and Spiritual Responses that Promote Health and Healing,* Walpole, NH: Stillpoint Publishing.

Spencer, P. U. (1991) *A Native American World View.* In B. McNeill and C. Guion. *Noetic Sciences Collection: 1980 - 1990.* (pp. 102-109). Sausalito, CA: Institute of Noetic Sciences.

Steiger, B. (1984) *Indian Medicine Power.* West Chester, PA: Schiffer Publishing, Ltd.

_____(1971) *Kahuna Magic.* Westchester, PA: The Whitford Press.

Stevens, J. and Stevens, L. (1988) *Secrets of Shamanism: Tapping the Spirit Power Within You.* New York: Avon Books.

Summer Rain, M. (1985) *Spirit Song: The Introduction of No-Eyes.* Norfolk, VA: Hampton Roads Publishing Co., Inc.

_____(1987) *Phoenix Rising: No-Eyes' Vision of the Changes to Come.* Norfolk, VA: Hampton Roads Publishing Co., Inc.

_____(1988) *Dreamwalker: The Path of Sacred Power.* Norfolk, VA: Hampton Roads Publishing Co., Inc.

Sun Bear with Wabun Wind (1992) *Black Dawn Bright Day*. New York: Simon and Schuster.

Townsend, J. B. (1988) *Neo-Shamanism and the Modern Mystical Movement*. In G. Doore (Ed.), *Shaman's Path: Healing, Personal Growth and Empowerment*. Boston and London: Shambhala.

Veary, N. (1989) *Change We Must: My Spiritual Journey*. Honolulu: Water Margin Press.

Vitebsky, P. (1995) *The Shaman: Voyages of the Soul Trance, Ecstasy, and Healing from Siberia to the Amazon*. New York: Little, Brown and Company.

Vogel, V. J. (1970) *American Indian Medicine*. Norman and London: University of Oklahoma Press.

Walsh, R. N. (1990) *The Spirit of Shamanism*. Los Angeles: Jeremy P. Tarcher, Inc.

Wesselman, H. (1995) *Spiritwalker: Messages from the Future*. New York: Bantam Books.

Whitaker, K. C. (1991) *The Reluctant Shaman: A Woman's First Encounters with the Unseen Spirits of the Earth*. New York: Harper Collins Publishers.

Wolfe, A. (1991) *In the Shadow of the Shaman: Connecting with Self, Nature, and Spirit*. St. Paul, MN: Llewellyn Publishers.

Wub-E-Ke-Niew (1995) *We Have the Right to Exist: A Translation of Aboriginal Indigenous Thought*. New York: Black Thistle Press.

Zukav, G. (1990) *The Seat of the Soul*. New York: Simon and Schuster.